DEVIANT AND CRIMINAL BEHAVIOR
IN THE WORKPLACE

PSYCHOLOGY AND CRIME

GENERAL EDITORS: Brian Bornstein, University of Nebraska, and
Monica Miller, University of Nevada, Reno

*The Perversion of Youth: Controversies in the Assessment
and Treatment of Juvenile Sex Offenders*
Frank C. DiCataldo

Jury Decision Making: The State of the Science
Dennis J. Devine

Deviant and Criminal Behavior in the Workplace
Edited by Steven M. Elias

Deviant and Criminal Behavior in the Workplace

Edited by Steven M. Elias

NEW YORK UNIVERSITY PRESS
New York and London

NEW YORK UNIVERSITY PRESS
New York and London
www.nyupress.org

References to Internet websites (URLs) were accurate at the time of writing.
Neither the author nor New York University Press is responsible for URLs that
may have expired or changed since the manuscript was prepared.

LIBRARY OF CONGRESS CATALOGING-IN-PUBLICATION DATA
Deviant and criminal behavior in the workplace / edited by Steven M. Elias.
p. cm. Includes bibliographical references and index.
ISBN 978-0-8147-2260-2 (cl : alk. paper) — ISBN 978-0-8147-2261-9 (pb : alk. paper) —
ISBN 978-0-8147-2262-6 (ebook) — ISBN 978-0-8147-2289-3 (ebook)
1. Employee crimes—Psychological aspects. 2. Problem employees—Psychology.
3. Violence in the workplace. 4. Industrial psychology. I. Elias, Steven M.
HF5549.5.E43D48 2012
364.3—dc23 2012034076

New York University Press books are printed on acid-free paper,
and their binding materials are chosen for strength and durability.
We strive to use environmentally responsible suppliers and materials
to the greatest extent possible in publishing our books.

Manufactured in the United States of America

10 9 8 7 6 5 4 3 2 1

For Emile, Alexander, and Lucas
—SME

CONTENTS

PREFACE

Several years ago, Allen K. Hess contacted me and asked if I would be interested in editing a book on deviant workplace behavior. Allen, up until his untimely death in 2010, was the Psychology & Crime Series editor for NYU Press. How important a topic is deviant workplace behavior? All one need do is turn on the evening news or read a local newspaper to be reminded of the fact that deviant and criminal behavior are common occurrences in the workplace. Indeed, most employees have either witnessed or engaged in some form of counterproductive, insidious, abhorrent, or illegal behavior while on the job. Be it a CEO who "cooks the books," an hourly wage employee who "borrows" office supplies, or a disgruntled employee who commits a heinous act of violence, inappropriate behavior at work is pandemic. As Allen once told me, "Crime in the workplace extends from the mailroom to the boardroom." I believe, as Allen did, that gaining insight into the psychological and organizational causes of deviant and criminal behavior in the workplace will make a significant contribution to a number of disciplines, as well as society in general.

An interaction between psychological and organizational factors is almost always involved when an employee engages in deviant and/or criminal behavior in the workplace. Unfortunately, given the overabundance of psychological factors linked to such behavior in these environments, it is impossible for a single book to address every topic of importance and relevance to the subject. However, a review of the academic literature and popular press will reveal several trends that are informative in terms of ensuring the topics selected for inclusion make a significant contribution.

In chapter 1 of this volume, Randy Hodson and Gary F. Jensen provide a wonderful overview of criminology and the sociology of work in relation to deviant workplace behavior. Two noteworthy points from this chapter are worth mentioning here. First, the authors convincingly point out the fact that research and attention focusing on crime in the workplace is lacking. Second, they note that injustice and abuses of power are frequently at work when deviant workplace behavior occurs. This point resonates throughout this volume.

The next several chapters address employee characteristics that are associated with deviant workplace behavior. In chapter 2, Rebecca Michalak and Neal M. Ashkanasy employ a multi-level model to speak to the role of emotions in deviant workplace behavior. Specifically, they make clear the ways in which emotions are associated with deviant workplace behavior at five levels in the workplace: within person, between persons, in interpersonal interactions, in groups, and organization wide. In chapter 3, Christine (Chris) Henle and Michael Gross address the role of employee personality in workplace deviance. They pay particular attention to the Big-Five taxonomy when discussing characteristics of offenders, as well as victims, of deviance and crime. In chapter 4, Sharon Grant focuses on the role of occupational stress in workplace crime and deviance. She begins by addressing stress as an antecedent to deviance and concludes with suggested interventions to help manage the stress-deviance relationship.

The next section of the volume focuses on the role of the organization in deviant and criminal behavior at work. In chapter 5, William L. Smith, Brandon H. Haines, and Cindy L. Seipel discuss theft and fraud from the perspective of accountants and fraud examiners. In addition to providing several cases and suggested controls to prevent fraud, they emphasize the importance of reducing the opportunities for fraud to occur in the first place. In chapter 6, Philip G. Benson, Glennis M. Hanley, and Wesley A. Scroggins address the role of human resource management in deviance and crime in the workplace. Particular attention is paid to the selection, training, and evaluation of employees, as well as the legal and ethical issues associated with these processes.

As already mentioned, issues related to justice (and injustice) and abuses of power can be found throughout this volume. The next section of the volume pays particular attention to these two variables. In chapter 7, Russell Cropanzano and Carolina Moliner focus on the relationship between perceived workplace fairness and deviant workplace behavior. In a unique approach to the topic, Cropanzano and Moliner ask the question, "Where does all this injustice come from?" The authors provide several potential answers to the question while pointing out that being overly concerned with justice may actually contribute to the strength of the relationship between justice and deviance. In chapter 8, Steven M. Elias, Lindsey A. Gibson, and Chet E. Barney address the ways in which social power, and the abuse of such power, can be antecedents to deviance and crime in the workplace. Particular attention is paid to the relationships between power and sexual harassment and job discrimination.

The last set of chapters focuses on what is perhaps the most extreme form of deviant and criminal behavior in the workplace: violence. In chapter 9, Ricky W. Griffin and Yvette P. Lopez examine the role an organization's culture plays in the prevalence of workplace violence. While this chapter covers a number of key aspects involving the relationship between culture and violence, perhaps the most important aspect is the proposed interaction that occurs between an employee's predispositions for deviance and the organization's propensity to elicit deviant behavior. The focus of chapter 10, written by Allen K. Hess and Clara E. Hess, is on the prevention of violence, as well as how to cope in the aftermath of a violent occurrence. This chapter will be of particular interest to practitioners as it offers a wealth of actionable suggestions and recommendations.

As pointed out by Hodson and Jensen in chapter 1, our understanding of deviance and crime in the workplace is lacking. The contributions to this volume move us in the right direction, and will be of great interest to students, scholars, and practitioners. However, there is much to be learned, and it is my hope that this volume will spur people into action to try to develop answers and solutions to some of the more pressing questions and issues encompassing deviance and crime at work.

In closing, I would like to thank Allen Hess for inviting me to edit this volume. I first met Allen in 1995, and all the while I knew him, he was a consummate scholar. When Allen passed away, the scientific community lost a role model. I would like to thank Jennifer Hammer of NYU Press for her patience and guidance as this volume was completed. Last, but certainly not least, I would like to thank all of the contributors to this volume who worked extremely hard at making their chapters "must-read" material in the area of deviant and criminal behavior in the workplace. I am indebted to each of them as this volume would not have been possible without their contributions.

Steven M. Elias

PART I

Introduction

1

Conceptual Foundations

Insights from Criminology and the Sociology of Work

RANDY HODSON AND GARY F. JENSEN

> *In 1996, the average monthly sewer bill for a family of four in Birmingham*
> *was only $14.71—but that was before the county decided to build an elabo-*
> *rate new sewer system with the help of out-of-state financial wizards with*
> *names like Bear Stearns, Lehman Brothers, Goldman Sachs and JP Morgan*
> *Chase. . . . [The banks used] a blizzard of incomprehensible swaps and refi-*
> *nance schemes—schemes that only served to postpone the repayment date*
> *a year or two while sinking the county deeper into debt. . . . The original*
> *cost estimates for the new sewer system were as low as $250 million. But*
> *in a wondrous demonstration of the possibilities of small-town graft and*
> *contract-padding, the price tag quickly swelled to more than $3 billion. . . .*
> *Every time the county refinanced its sewer debt, JP Morgan made millions of*
> *dollars in fees. . . . In the mortgage business, this process is known as churn-*
> *ing: You keep coming back over and over to refinance, and they keep "churn-*
> *ing" you for more and more fees. . . . Birmingham became the poster child*
> *for a new kind of giant-scale financial fraud, one that would threaten the*
> *financial stability not only of cities and counties all across America, but even*
> *those of entire countries like Greece. . . . You can see a trail that leads directly*
> *from a billion-dollar predatory swap deal cooked up at the highest levels of*
> *America's biggest banks, across a vast fruited plane of bribes and felonies—*
> *"the price of doing business," as one JP Morgan banker says on tape. . . . In*
> *Birmingham, lots of people have gone to jail for the crime: More than 20*
> *local officials and businessmen have been convicted of corruption in federal*
> *court. . . . But those who greenlighted the bribes and profited most from the*
> *scam remain largely untouched. "It never gets back to JP Morgan."*
>
> —Taibbi, 2010

In a review of literature on crime and the workplace in 1999, we noted that
"Neither crime at the workplace nor crime generated by workplace experiences has received much attention in criminology" (Jensen & Hodson, 1999).
Assessments since that time have yielded similar conclusions. Based on a
citation analysis, David Shichor (2009, 175) reports an "absence of scholars

who study white-collar crime and corporate crime in criminology and criminal justice journals and textbooks."

To some degree this neglect reflects the opinion of prominent criminologists who have argued that (1) the public is most concerned with street crime (see Wilson & Herrnstein, 1985) or that (2) the causes of crime rest with characteristics of offenders established at an early age (see Gottfredson & Hirschi, 1990). Although not strongly represented in mainstream criminology and criminal justice journals and textbooks, issues involving workplace crime, white-collar crime, and occupational crime are growing in prominence in new journals and journals dealing with business, business ethics, personnel psychology, occupational health, leadership, and management, among others. An inspection of references for the chapters in this book reveals the sizeable range of outlets for research on workplace crime and related issues.

This expansion of interests and outlets has been quite eclectic and specialized, with little attention devoted to developing a general framework to encompass such a wide range of specific issues. In this chapter we propose that (1) further development of widely shared concepts in the chapters in this volume promises to move the study of white-collar crime toward a vision shared with much of sociology—the study of injustice and the abuse of power—and (2) general theories of crime can provide general frameworks for organizing the study of crime and the workplace.

White-Collar Crime and the Sociology of Work

Since some version of the concept of injustice, and explicitly or implicitly the abuse of power, is found in all but one chapter in this volume, we suggest that these concepts have promise as linking themes between specialists in the study of workplace and the study of organizational crime. Jensen (2011) notes that the concept of justice is intimately tied to conceptions of rights and that "rights refer to that set of normative standards defining the just allocation of positive and negative experiences among people (justice norms)." Injustice refers to the violation of justice norms or rights. Power is what allows the rights of some to be violated by others.

The concepts of injustice and the abuse of power can apply at all levels of analysis from societal to institutional to individual relations. Legal systems and organizational characteristics can be judged in terms of justice. The content of courses on contemporary social problems, as well as the specific sociological specialties dealing with issues such as inequality and racism, are based on conceptions of rights and their violation. It would be safe to propose that the concepts of justice and the abuse of power are widely enough used to be considered basic building blocks of the social sciences across their specific disciplines.

In research on sources of crime or deviance in the workplace, the most common use is "perceived" injustice, which can generate worker anger and potentially underwrite workplace deviance. However, the concepts of injustice and the abuse of power can be applied at the corporate or organizational level, as well as at the individual level. At the corporate level the focus is less on crime as a response to injustice than on unconstrained power as a source of immoral and even criminal corporate behavior. Historically, the thirty years since the ascension of Reagan's and Thatcher's conservative revolution with its attendant neo-liberal ideology and its commitment to deregulation have brought into full fruition an era of rampant corporate malfeasance and criminality. The history of corporate scandals of the 2000s has expanded in number and size at an exponential rate. Enron's "creative accounting" practices were quickly eclipsed by those of WorldCom. For those who thought these were isolated cases with isolated consequences, the worldwide "great recession" starting in 2008 brought about by a systematic pattern of fraudulent banking practices involving the largest banks in the world has clarified the fact that when the largest corporations bilk customers, competitors, and the government out of billions of dollars, the consequences are anything but localized. The rewriting of regulations for offshore oil-drilling practices under the Bush-Cheney presidency that allowed the massive Gulf of Mexico oil spill by British Petroleum in 2010 highlights the fact that the consequences of unconstrained corporate power leading to malfeasance and illegality influence every aspect of our lives from our jobs and pensions to the environment in which we work and live.

It is essential at this moment that students of white-collar and corporate crime step forward and make themselves heard regarding the nature, causes, and consequences of the current era of unrestrained corruption, pillage, and criminality emanating from the largest private-sector institutions. Societies that do not confront rampant white-collar crime are likely to end up in the backwaters as "previous great powers." Less industrialized nations that do not confront corporate criminality will stay poor and underdeveloped. Capitalism has tremendous potential for spurring economic activity and development, but not when capitalists are allowed unrestrained access to pillage, profiteering, corruption, externalization of the costs of production (such as through environmental pollution), and other easier—though nonsustainable—routes to profits. It is part of the historic mandate of students of white-collar and corporate crime to provide the intellectual tools to forge appropriate controls and constraints on large corporations so that they are forced down the laborious road of creative innovation in order to make profits rather than the quicker and easier road of profiteering. In this task, those who study white-collar crime are not without allies. Increasing education and information access make citizens of many countries aware of white-collar and corporate crime and deeply concerned about the consequences for their lives. Witness, for example, the emergence and rapid spread of the "Occupy Wall Street" movement of 2011 (wearethe99percent.tumblr.com).

The world of white-collar and corporate crime is different today than it was fifty years ago because of advances in electronic technology and the growth of large transnational corporations with expansive operations across both developed and less developed nations (Dodge & Geis, 2009; Rothe, 2010). It is thus a significant ongoing intellectual challenge to develop the concepts and theories needed to adequately depict new forms of white-collar and corporate crime and identify effective remedies to constrain them. In this important way, white-collar and corporate crimes are significantly different, and increasingly different, from street crime. Although the prevalence and causes of street crimes may change somewhat with time, many of the causes remain in play across time and across different settings, and change is significantly slower—murder, rape, and burglary are not dramatically different in nature or causes today than in the past. This pattern of rapid historic change in the nature of white-collar and corporate crime poses special challenges to its study.

The sociology of work is an area that similarly faces the challenge of constant change in the nature of its object of study (Hodson & Sullivan, 2011). In response, it has developed a large arsenal of both broad and mid-range concepts that are useful for organizing our understanding of the rapidly changing world of corporate behavior, including malfeasance and illegality. Most central among these concepts is that of social power—the ability to bend resources and people to one's objectives. Large corporations, and more broadly those in privileged positions, have the power to ensure the reproduction of their privileges and to garner an ever larger share of resources. To understand how power is deployed toward the preservation and enlargement of privilege, it is essential to understand white-collar and corporate crime at three distinct levels: (1) the macro-level of government policy and political economy, (2) the meso-level of organizational behavior, and (3) the micro-level of individual and small group actions.

Macro-Level Concepts about Political Economy. One of the most serious issues confronting the study of white-collar and corporate crime is the prevailing, socially constructed definition of legality itself. Through campaign contributions and hired lobbyists, corporations and powerful actors in society play a decisive role in writing the legislation that defines what is legal and illegal. The capture of regulatory agencies by those they are intended to regulate has received renewed interest with the coming to fruition of the neo-liberal era of deregulation in which admissions such as "the oil industry writes the government's energy regulatory rules" have become commonplace (Lipton & Broder, 2010). The resulting laws are extremely generous in allowing harmful behavior under the guise of encouraging economic development. And if nothing else, lobbyists at least succeed in making sure the regulations are sufficiently vague so that prosecution can be avoided or tied up indefinitely in the courts. It is thus important that students of white-collar and corporate crime not accept too quickly the bright red line of the existing laws as the definition of corporate criminality and instead look to the more theoretically defensible concepts of justice or of "harm to others" (Friedrichs, 2009). Indeed, the latter concept—harm to others—is closer to the definition more typically used in definitions of street crime. And where the criminals write the laws, as is often the case in white-collar crime, it is essential that this more realistic marker of "harm to others" be used. The greatest part of corporate criminality occurs in this opaque regulatory terrain between what the law specifically disallows and what is actually harmful to others. Much confusion can be avoided if we start with the commonsense definition of criminality as harm to others rather than limit consideration to the specifics of politically brokered (dis)regulations.

Corporate crime thus typically involves some collusion between governments and corporations (Braithwaite, 2008). Only the tip of the iceberg in such cases is ever detected and prosecuted. Indeed, the bulk of the behavior is so commonplace and accepted that its most typical manifestations are considered routine practice. Only extraordinary cases that threaten to unmask the widespread nature of corporate criminality are brought to light and prosecuted. And, interestingly, it is almost always only the politicians who are brought to law. The corporation is seen as only trying to pursue its self-interest, and we have come to accept that the buying of government officials is a failing of the officials, but not of those who attempt to buy them.

An important potential area of rich theoretical insight about the political economy of white-collar and corporate crime lies in international comparative work. Many less developed nations have extraordinarily lax laws and enforcement against white-collar and corporate crime. In these situations, graft and corruption are commonplace and are required for securing many services in society. Many analysts believe that the U.S. war in Afghanistan against Islamic extremists is being prolonged and may be lost because of pervasive corruption in the pro-Western government there that has brought economic development virtually to a standstill. Make no mistake, national development, world events, and world history itself frequently hinge on white-collar and corporate crime. Similar examples of the retarding effects of white-collar and corporate crime from Asia, Africa, and Latin America indicate that such corruption is one of the chief impediments to economic development and prosperity for the poorer people of the world (Evans & Rauch, 1999). Many lessons are to be learned from comparative work, including the potential for corruption to pervade society at every level of economic transaction.

Meso-Level Concepts about Organizational Behavior. The most serious corporate malfeasance arises not from rogue employees, but from repeated systematic actions that have acquired the status of "normal operating procedures." The payment of outrageous salaries in the hundreds of millions of dollars to CEOs is among the most obvious of these practices. Corporate boards that set top salaries are staffed by other CEOs and their willingness to pay exorbitant salaries to fellow CEOs rests on undisguised self-interest. The absence of a connection between these salaries and economic performance is evidenced by the steep rise in CEO salaries in the last fifteen years during a time of faltering growth and declining performance. The criminal nature of these salaries is further evidenced by the discrepancy between American CEO salaries and those of their competitors in Europe and Asia—whose companies often perform better.

The injustice and indefensibility of CEO salaries is, however, only the most obvious corporate criminality (meaning "harm to others"). A more profound contemporary example is the pattern established by banks of fraudulently misrepresenting risky derivatives while simultaneously betting against the success of their own financial instruments by aggressively buying insurance against their predestined decline in value (Partnoy, 2003). Similarly, the classic situations of stockbrokers churning their customers' accounts for sales commissions or selling poor quality financial instruments because of kickbacks are prime examples of criminality among professionals. Note that these practices, except in extreme cases, are not typically illegal and even extreme cases are difficult to prove. Myriad retirement accounts, however, have mysteriously dwindled through such practices. The amount of money involved in such white-collar criminality far exceeds the combined total for all types of street crime (Coleman, 1994).

For much corporate and white-collar criminality, the prevalence of bureaucratic rules governing the organizational context in which these activities occur provides an effective façade to hide the activities. People believe that there must be rules preventing such practices and that, surely, such practices could not occur within large organizations. The problem is that the bureaucratic rules are written by people who benefit from such criminality. The result is rules that either allow such practices or are so intentionally vague that the practices are allowed by omission.

Professionals working in large organizations are often complicit in such corporate criminality. For example, in the Enron scandal, the accounting firm Arthur Andersen was found to be criminally culpable for fraudulently over-representing the value of Enron assets. Similarly, doctors who receive salaries many times the average for American workers are unlikely to report overcharges and unnecessary procedures since they get fees based on these procedures, as well as kickbacks from drug companies for prescribing their most popular drugs.

Why are such practices not prohibited by regulators? There are two main reasons. First, as already mentioned, regulatory bodies are often captured by the industry they are intended to regulate. Second, the complexity and rapidly changing nature of many work practices means that there would need to be many regulators for adequate enforcement, which would be economically unfeasible. Regulatory bodies are thus chronically understaffed.

The solution to organizational criminality, both corporate and professional, instead lies in empowering all the stakeholders involved to negotiate, bargain, and make transparent ongoing practices. Thus, employees, the community, and customers all need to have a say at the corporate table if corporate criminality is to be effectively curtailed (Braithwaite, 2008). This solution may seem unlikely in the American context of corporate secrecy and the purity of neo-liberal ideologies arguing that the only path to economic efficiency is the unregulated and unconstrained pursuit of profit. However, many European nations have longstanding Works Councils and other avenues of involvement by employees, unions, and communities. The long-term consequences of involving these additional stakeholders have not been a decline in profits. Rather it has been a decline in criminal approaches to achieving profits and the highlighting of creative innovation as a necessary strategy for corporate survival (Streeck & Thelen, 2005). The criminology literature, in fact, already utilizes a similar concept acknowledging the pivotal role of stakeholder involvement in deterring street crime—in the routine activities model of criminal behavior the concept is known as a "responsible guardian" who preempts criminality. Similar responsible guardians are needed throughout corporations as empowered stakeholders if corporate malfeasance and criminality are to be checked. Regrettably, the reliance on "whistle-blowers" for internal checks on organizational practices testifies to the paucity of more routinized stakeholder involvement in organizational settings.

Micro-Level Concepts about Work Group Behavior. As with macro- and meso-level changes in the nature of work, so too are more micro-level changes in the workplace influencing white-collar and corporate criminality. One of the most profound changes is the intrusion of microchip technology into all aspects of human life. Instantaneous information flow has created new opportunities for criminal behavior not only in such obvious areas as financial theft and identity theft, but also in such areas as child pornography and child predatory activity facilitated though social network sites. Thus, computers are allowing individuals to prey on organizations and on each other in new ways. But computers also create new ways for organizations to prey on individuals as well. For example, the possibilities for government surveillance have been greatly increased by opportunities for electronic eavesdropping. In addition, corporations are able to monitor their employees on the job in ways that many feel violate basic human rights of privacy (Marx, 1990).

Some micro-level white-collar criminal behavior is isolated and secretive in nature. Padding of expense accounts or working on personal projects on company time are good examples of what are typically individual-level criminal workplace behaviors. Many seemingly individual criminal actions, however, rely on a supportive work group, or at least a work group that allows the behavior to go unchecked. Work groups are often complicit in practices such as pilferage, for example (Mars, 1982). Work group norms are also involved in allowing patterns of bullying and sexual harassment to become ingrained and taken for granted (Chamberlain et al., 2008; Roscigno, Lopez & Hodson, 2009; see also Elias, Gibson, and Barney in the current volume).

Individual and group malfeasance and criminality in the workplace are heavily dependent on the prevailing meanings that employees give to the situation and to their actions. Issues of equity and justice are particularly important in this regard. Where individuals feel aggrieved and dishonored, retribution through various forms of resistance and deviance is much more likely—perhaps even inevitable (Foucault, 1988; Hodson, 2001). These individual-level meanings are often heavily influenced by practices emanating from the macro- and meso-levels of societal and organizational behavior, again suggesting the intertwined nature of behavior across organizational levels and the necessity of understanding action at any one level as embedded in meanings and power relations involving other levels of organization and action.

Categorizing Theories of Crime

Based on numerous theoretical developments in the study of criminal behavior, psychology (see Hess and Hess in this volume) and management scholars (see Bennett & Robinson, 2000) have developed specific typologies pertaining to workplace deviance. Integrating contemporary theory and research in the sociology of crime with concepts from workplace and organizational analysis also depends on a systematic application of concepts from the sociology of crime. Some categorization of distinct theories of crime (or, more generally, deviance) is an essential step in this integration. Most of the research on crimes involving the workplace, occupations, and corporations focuses on one theory or one specific research issue, involving one theory at a time. In contrast, there is an enduring emphasis in criminological theories on testing competing theories. Jensen (Jensen & Rojek, 2009, 196) has attempted to simplify the location of specific instances of theory testing in terms of answers to basic questions:

> Does the theory incorporate or require some form of imbalance, strain, stress, or frustrated pursuit of conventional or widely shared goals? If so, it is classified as falling within the strain/frustration tradition. Many such extensions are classified as "integrated" theories because they incorporate ideas and concepts from other perspectives. But, the fact that they introduce specific forms of motivational pressure generated by some form of imbalance or discrepancy in the achievement of widely shared goals distinguishes them as strain/frustration theories.
>
> Does the theory focus on normal learning processes, including socially structured schedules of reward and punishment, variable values, norms, and beliefs, and associations with people who both encourage and discourage crime and delinquency? If so, the theory fits better with the cultural deviance/differential association/social learning category than the other two systems of ideas.
>
> Does the theory assume that it is the absence of constraints or limits on opportunity for crime that are key to the explanation of crime and delinquency? If "motivation" refers to characteristics of humans considered to be quite natural when social, cultural, or opportunity constraints are absent (such that no special pressure is required), then it falls in the social disorganization-social control tradition.

A recent work sets the stage for a more theoretically organized approach to crime and workplace topics. Encompassing much of the research under the general rubric of "white-collar crime," Benson and Simpson (2009) focus on anomie theory (which falls under the first theme stated here), differential association-social learning theory (which falls under the second theme) and "social control" theory (which falls under the third theme). They also distinguish "rational choice" theory, a theory that Jensen classifies as a subtype of social learning theory because it focuses on normal learning processes.

Several chapters in this book can be identified as falling in a specific criminological theory. For example, the focus on "occupational stress" as a motivational force leading to workplace violence locates the chapter by Grant in the strain-anomie tradition. She proposes that

> occupational stress may lead to counterproductive behavior in the form of workplace deviance: voluntary *behavior* that is in conflict with the interests of the organization and its members. For example, employees may engage in deviant or criminal behavior to compensate for feelings or anger or frustration associated with stress.

Strain theories are motivational theories with some form of deviance or crime explained as a response to stress or strain of some form. In some instances such theories assume that the behavior functions to alleviate the stress. On the other hand, the behavior may be a response to stress without necessarily alleviating the problem.

Griffin and Lopez argue that "organizational culture" is a key to understanding workplace crime:

> Organizational culture is the set of values, norms, assumptions, and beliefs that exists among organizational members which influence employee attitudes, thoughts, feelings, and behaviors. An organization's culture can control the way employees interpret or perceive situations and how they respond to situations. Several studies have examined the value system of organizations which helps create an organization's culture to determine influences on employee deviant behavior.

This type of perspective would seem to fall in the cultural deviance/differential association/social learning category of criminological theories for two reasons. Griffin and Lopez discuss reward systems and normal social learning processes. If the behavior stems from normal learning processes and requires no special pressure, the theory fits best in the social learning category. When they state that "given the influence of group norms on individual behavior, it is presumed that social cues that communicate tolerance for deviant behavior are more likely to create an organizational culture with a high propensity to elicit employee deviant behavior," their argument falls in the cultural deviance/differential association category. If cultural or group norms encourage deviance, the theory is best categorized as a cultural deviance/differential association argument.

Griffin and Lopez also discuss ways in which group norms and organizational culture can inhibit workplace deviance. It is important to note that such a feature of organizational culture would fit with the third type of theory, social control theory. Social control theory focuses on variables that inhibit deviance. In its original form as expressed by Hirschi (1969), the sole emphasis was on why people do not break laws or rules and theories requiring special problems or criminogenic norms were rejected. Cultural deviance/differential association theorists argue that it is the balance of crime-facilitating and crime-inhibiting forces that is key to the explanation of crime. There is no "differential" in social control theory.

Several chapters in this volume include dimensions of personality among the variables thought to explain workplace crime. In mainstream criminology one specific psychological trait has come to dominate the research literature—self-control. Self-control was introduced as the key to explaining crime by Gottfredson and Hirschi in 1990 in their award winning book, *A General Theory of Crime*. Their basic thesis is that the absence of self-control explains individual crime and, because it is established at an early age, it explains continuity in crime over the life-course. In addition, age-graded opportunities explained the type of crime that low self-control generated. They proposed that "people who lack self-control will tend to be impulsive, insensitive, physical risk-taking, short-sighted and non-verbal" (1990, 90). Self-control and opportunity are presented as key to understanding all forms of crime, including white-collar, occupational, and workplace crime.

Gottfredson and Hirschi (1990) argue that their theory predicts that white-collar crime is less common than other forms of crime because people low in self-control are not likely to reach positions where there is opportunity to commit such crimes. Moreover, they propose that among those who do have such an opportunity, the same personality trait explains variation in white-collar crime.

The theory has generated considerable debate and has drawn criticism for presumptions about white-collar crime. Numerous scholars argue that there is little evidence that white-collar, occupational, and/or workplace crime is less common than other types of crime (see Benson & Simpson, 2009 for a summary). Moreover, when the concept is defined, only some characteristics would seem to inhibit entry into such occupations (nonverbal and short-sighted). Risk-taking and insensitivity might be considered as assets for movement into some types of professional and managerial positions. In addition, the view of self-control as invariant after being set at an early age is controversial as well, and no one has actually shown that it helps explain white-collar crime.

Although the terminology used differs from criminological theory, theories of unethical behavior in organizations can be classified in terms of answers to the basic questions previously outlined. Consider, for example, the theory of unethical behavior proposed by Kulic, O'Fallon, and Salimath (2008) in the *Journal of Business Ethics*. Among other arguments, they propose that the reward and punishment system characterizing corporations such as Enron encourage unethical behavior by exerting unusual pressure to perform. The corporate "stacking practice," where average performance as determined by supervisors means termination, encouraged unethical behavior. When a theory introduces unusual pressure to perform, coupled with a guarantee that a certain proportion of employees will be fired, it embodies the logic of strain theories. The central argument in strain theory is that pressure to achieve coupled with structural guarantees of failure generates a high rate of crime in the streets. The same logic can apply to behavior within organizations.

Some scholars studying unethical behavior are drawing on classic criminological theories. In *Business Ethics and Moral Motivation: A Criminological Perspective*, Joseph Heath (2008) applies Sykes and Matza's "techniques of neutralization" theory to unethical behavior. He argues that it is specific excuses for unethical behavior learned in interaction within organizations that are crucial for understanding such behavior rather than flaws in basic moral character. Henle and Gross state in this volume that "employees low in conscientiousness, agreeableness, and emotional stability are more likely to commit workplace deviance." Gottfredson and Hirschi would include these dimensions of personality under the rubric of "self-control." They argue that "the dimensions of self-control are, in our view, factors affecting calculation of the consequences of one's acts. The impulsive or shortsighted person fails to consider the negative or painful consequences of his acts; the insensitive person has fewer negative consequences to consider; the less intelligent person also has fewer negative consequences to consider" (1990, 95). Their "General Theory of Crime" has been applied to a wide range of "deviant" activities and has generated a sizeable body of research in criminology. Because it focuses on a trait that inhibits deviance, it falls under the social control-social disorganization tradition in criminology.

As noted previously, the most common shared concept used in the chapters of this volume is some version of injustice or related concepts such as fairness or the violation of justice norms or perceived rights. Injustice is a type of imbalance or discrepancy between shared definitions of "rights" and organizational realities. It is introduced as a source of occupational stress by Grant and as a feature of organizational climate relevant to workplace deviance by Griffin and Lopez. Griffin and Lopez note that "research indicates that regardless of the form of injustice, when employees are treated in an unjust manner they are more likely to engage in deviant behavior." Some version of this proposition can be found in nearly every chapter in this volume, ranging from the individual to the organizational level.

Among the major criminological theories, the shared focus on injustice fits best with contemporary versions of strain theory, especially Agnew's (1985, 1992, 2005) "generalized strain theory." Strain theories assume that some form of disparity between expectations and perceived reality provides motivation for crime or deviance. Such perspectives fit well with the focus on emotion in several of the chapters in this volume in that injustice is presumed to generate anger or frustration which can result in forms of crime involving some form of emotion.

In sum, whether it be the field of management, psychology, or sociology, there are numerous possible bridges between criminological theories and the study of crime and the workplace. Most (if not all) of the variables introduced in the study of crime in the workplace have precedents in the sociology of crime and in the study of the workplace, but those connections are rarely acknowledged or developed for their potential broadening insights. Our hope is that greater attention to criminological theories, and to the linking concepts of injustice and power from the sociology of work, will build stronger bridges between criminology and the study of organizational life.

REFERENCES

Agnew, R. (1985). A revised strain theory of delinquency. *Social Forces, 64*, 151–67.

Agnew, R. (1992). Foundation for a general strain theory of crime and delinquency. *Criminology, 30*, 47–87.

Agnew, R. (2005). *Pressured into crime: An overview of general strain theory*. Los Angeles: Roxbury.

Bennett, R. J., & Robinson, S. L. (2000). Development of a measure of workplace deviance. *Journal of Applied Psychology, 85*, 349–360.

Benson, M. L., & Simpson, S. S. (2009). *White-collar crime: An opportunity perspective*. New York: Routledge.

Braithwaite, J. (2008). *Regulatory capitalism*. Cheltenham, UK: Edward Elgar.

Chamberlain, L. J., Crowley, M., Tope, D., & Hodson, R. (2008). Sexual harassment in context: Organizational and occupational foundations of abuse. *Work and Occupations, 35*, 262–95.

Coleman, J. S. (1994). *The criminal elite*. New York: St. Martin's.

DiPrete, T. A., Eirich, G. M., & Pittinsky, M. (2010). Compensation benchmarking, leap-frogs, and the surge in executive pay. *American Journal of Sociology, 115*, 1671–1712.

Dodge, Mary, & Geis, Gilbert. (2009). Social and political transformations in white-collar and crime scholarship. *Crime, Law and Social Change, 51*, 1–3.

Evans, P., & Rauch, J. E. (1999). Bureaucracy and growth: A cross-national analysis of the effects of "Weberian" state structures on economic growth. *American Sociological Review, 64*, 748–765.

Foucault, M. (1988). *Politics, philosophy, culture: Interviews and other writings*. New York: Routledge.

Friedrichs, D. O. (2009). Exorbitant CEO compensation: Just reward or grand theft. *Crime, Law and Social Change, 51*, 45–72.

Gottfredson, M. R., & Hirschi, T. (1990). *A general theory of crime*. Stanford: Stanford University Press.

Heath, J. (2008). Business ethics and moral motivation: A criminological perspective. *Journal of Business Ethics, 83*, 595–614.

Hirschi, T. (1969). *Causes of delinquency*. Berkeley: University of California Press.

Hodson, R. (2001). *Dignity at work*. New York: Cambridge University Press.

Hodson, R., & Sullivan, T. A. (2011). *The social organization of work* (5th ed.). Belmont, CA: Cengage.

Jensen, G. F. (2011). Deviance and social control. In Clifton D. Bryant (Ed.), *The Routledge handbook of deviant behavior* (chapter 1). London: Routledge.

Jensen, G. F., & Hodson, R. (1999). Synergies in the study of crime and the workplace: An editorial introduction. *Work and Occupations, 26*, 6–21.

Jensen, G. F., & Rojek, D. G. (2009). *Delinquency and youth crime* (4th ed.). Long Grove, IL: Waveland.

Lipton, E., & Broder, J. M. (2010). Regulator deferred to oil industry on rig safety. *New York Times*, May 7, www.nytimes.com/2010/05/18/us/08agency.html.

Kulic, B., O'Fallon, M., & Salimath, M. (2008). Do competitive environments lead to the rise and spread of unethical behavior? Parallels from Enron. *Journal of Business Ethics, 83*, 703–723.

Mars, G. (1982). *Cheats at work*. London: Unwin.

Marx, G. T. (1990). The case of the omniscient organization. *Harvard Business Review, 68*, 12–31.

Partnoy, F. (2003). *Infectious greed: How deceit and risk corrupted the financial markets*. New York: Holt.

Prechel, H., & Morris, T. (2010). The effects of organizational and political embeddedness on financial malfeasance in the largest U.S. corporations: Dependence, incentives, and opportunities. *American Sociological Review, 75*, 331–354.

Roscigno, V. J., Lopez, S. H., & Hodson, R. (2009). Supervisory bullying, status inequalities and organizational context. *Social Forces, 87*, 1561–1589.

Rothe, D. L. (2010). Facilitating corruption and human rights violations: The role of international financial institutions. *Crime, Law and Social Change, 53*, 457–476.

Shichor, D. (2009). Scholarly influence and white–collar crime scholarship. *Crime, Law and Social Change, 51*, 175–187.

Streeck, W., & Thelen, K. (2005). *Beyond continuity: Institutional change in advanced political economies*. New York: Oxford.

Sykes, G. M., & Matza, D. (1957). Techniques of neutralization: A theory of delinquency. *American Sociological Review, 22*, 664–670.

Taibbi, Matt. (2010). Looting Main Street: How the nation's biggest banks are ripping off American cities with the same predatory deals that brought down Greece. *Rolling Stone* (March 31). http://www.rollingstone.com/politics/news/looting-main-street-20100331.

Wilson, J. Q., & Herrnstein, R. J. (1985). *Crime and human nature*. New York: Simon and Schuster.

PART II

Employee Characteristics Associated
with Deviant Workplace Behavior

2

Emotions and Deviance

REBECCA MICHALAK AND NEAL M. ASHKANASY

> *A woman who is suing computer giant IBM for $1.1 million says she was told by her senior manager to "get her breasts out" to get sales. Susan Spiteri, who worked in Melbourne as a senior sales executive, has filed a claim in the Federal Court over alleged workplace bullying and sexual harassment. In her claim she says that a senior manager systematically harassed and bullied her, including inappropriate touching, remarks, threats, intimidation and unreasonable demands. She alleges that in one incident the manager said Ms Spiteri should "get her breasts out" to get sales and he also referred to her as "f——ing Spiteri" and called her repeatedly out of hours.*
>
> *Ms. Spiteri also alleges that when she reported the bullying to IBM's human resources department it turned a blind eye. She worked for the company for about 10 years and has not worked since November 2009. "I'm mentally and physically sick from the experience. I'm drained. It's cost me a lot of money too," she said in a statement issued by her lawyers today. "I'm out of pocket every week for doctors, specialists and medication." She said she was taking the legal action to seek compensation for what she has gone through and for loss of income. "The bullying affects everything, including my relationships with my family and friend," she said. "I still feel like a failure because that's how they made me feel. It just shouldn't be that way."*
>
> *Maurice Blackburn employment special counsel Siobhan Keating, who is representing Ms. Spiteri, said in the statement that while IBM had a detailed policy that committed it to a workplace free from harassment, it failed to act in this instance. "It's not enough for companies like IBM to have the right policies in place if they're not enforced," she said. An IBM spokeswoman said the company did not tolerate any type of harassment and it would vigorously defend itself in court. She said Ms Spiteri continued to receive compensation and support from IBM. "The person against whom the harassment allegations were made left IBM two years ago," she said.*
>
> —*Sydney Morning Herald,* 2011

In this chapter, we discuss the nexus of emotion and workplace deviance. Consistent with Robinson and Bennett (1995), we define workplace deviance as a form of behavior that violates organizational norms and that consequently negatively impacts the well-being of the organization and its members. In fact, the term has been in the literature for several decades now, including early work by Cloward (1959), Cohen (1966), and Kemper (1966). Kemper, for example, characterized deviance in terms of employees who "steal, come late, procrastinate, 'goof off,' fail to give proper service to customers and clients, forget to report details to supervisors and otherwise subvert the goals for the organization or deprive it of its rights" (288).

For the purposes of this chapter, however, we take a broad perspective on workplace deviance, and include counterproductive workplace behavior (Fox & Spector, 1999) and organizational misbehavior (Vardi & Weiner, 1996). In this respect, we note that there is ongoing controversy about whether workplace deviance should be seen to encompass all these constructs (for up-to-date reviews on the interpersonal deviance front specifically, see Hershcovis, 2011, and Tepper & Henle, 2011). Nonetheless, and to avoid being distracted by a debate on terminology, we simply refer in this chapter to all these constructs under the rubric of workplace deviance, albeit using Robinson and Bennett's (1995) differentiation between interpersonal deviance (bullying, sexual harassment, incivility) and organizational deviance (sabotage, theft, unauthorized sick days).

Our primary purpose in this chapter, therefore, is to review the literature with a view to determine the role emotions play as antecedents or consequences of deviant behavior at work. To define emotion, we refer to Fischer, Shaver, and Carnochan (1990), who state that emotion is a "discrete, innate, functional, biosocial action and expression system" (84). We also look to Affective Events Theory (AET: Weiss & Cropanzano, 1996), which holds that emotions arising from organizational events shape member's behaviors and attitudes, as an appropriate underpinning for our discussion.

This chapter is organized into seven sections. In the first, based on Ashkanasy's (2003a) Five-Level Model of Emotions in the workplace (FLME), we provide a broad overview of the role of emotions across five levels of organizational analysis. In the following five sections, we examine in more depth the emotions-deviance nexus at each of the five levels (including the related role of other organizational behavior constructs such as job satisfaction and commitment). This discussion includes, but is not limited to, topics such as (1) within-person processes, beginning with emotions that lead to deviant behavior, and including a discussion on affective events theory and injustice perceptions; (2) affect and emotion-based personality traits such as aggressiveness, as well as emotional responses by victims of deviance; (3) how deviant social exchanges (such as abusive supervision) result in emotions, and how emotional labor may also be a cause of deviance, (4) how deviance in the form of abusive supervision may lead to emotional contagion and impact upon group affective climate, and (5) how unethical climates and cultures of emotion-driven silence or voice may relate to affective climates that either foster or deter deviant behavior, and how a deviance spiral that is driven by emotions can infect an entire organization, leading ultimately to a toxic organizational culture. To conclude, we offer brief comments on implications for practice, make suggestions for future research in this field, and present a version of the FLME as it relates to deviance.

The Five-Level Model of Emotions

We earlier defined emotion as a "discrete, innate, functional, biosocial action and expression system" (Fischer, Shaver, and Carnochan, 1990, 84). More specifically, emotions are focused, intense, and short in duration, and tend to have an object or cause to which they are attached (Frijda, 1994). In particular, emotions constitute objective phenomena in that they stem from physiological changes in the body and the release of certain neurotransmitters (such as a rise in skin temperature, increase in respiration and heart rate, and the release of catecholamines). Damasio (1994) differentiates emotions from *feelings*, which are best described as the subjective meaning that an individual attaches to these internal changes, such as "I feel angry." *Mood*, on the other hand, is longer lasting than emotion, yet still relatively short-term and largely unstable (Tellegen, 1985). In contrast to emotion, a mood state may not have a clearly identifiable antecedent. It may disrupt an activity, even though the activity might not have had anything to do with the mood; this again is different than an emotion, which would be directly linked to the activity (Lazarus, 1991). Finally, trait affect is the most stable and long lasting of emotion-related constructs. Trait affect is dispositional, and commonly described as per Watson, Clark, and Tellegen (1988) as a person's general affective orientation to the world, either positive or negative (see also Lazarus, 1991).

In setting out the FLME, Ashkanasy (2003a) recognized that emotions in organizational settings can be described in terms of five levels of analysis: (1) within person, (2) between persons (individual differences), (3) interpersonal interactions, (4) group, and (5) organization-wide. At level 1, emotions are ephemeral, varying moment-by-moment within each organizational member. According to Weiss and Cropanzano (1996), organizational members experience emotions at work in response to hassles and uplifts. These emotions, in turn determine two types of behavior: immediate "affect driven" behaviors, and longer-term "judgment-driven" behaviors that derive from attitudes. At level 2, emotions are held to be between-person individual differences; for example, emotional intelligence (Mayer & Salovey, 1997), organizational commitment (Meyer & Allen, 1997), trait affectivity (Watson & Tellegen, 1985), and job satisfaction in the form of a stable attitude towards work (Fisher, 2000).

The next three levels in the model deal with interpersonal relationships (level 3), groups (level 4), and the organization as a whole (level 5). Thus, level 3 encompasses all aspects of recognizing and communicating emotion (Elfenbein, 2007), including emotional labor (Hochschild, 1983) and facial recognition of emotion (Ekman, 1999). Level 4 deals with multiple interactions as found in groups and teams, including team leadership. Key concepts here include group affective tone (George, 1990) and emotional contagion (Barsade, 2002; Hatfield, Cacioppo, & Rapson, 1994; Kelly & Barsade, 2001). Finally, level 5 refers to emotion at the whole-of-organization level, encapsulated in de Rivera's (1992) depiction of emotional climate as "an objective group phenomenon that can be palpably sensed—as when one enters a party or a city and feels an attitude of gaiety or depression, openness or fear" (197).

Emotions and Deviance at Level 1: Within-Person

As previously noted, emotions at level 1 can be understood in terms of Affective Events Theory (AET: Weiss & Cropanzano, 1996). Weiss and Beal (2005) emphasize in particular that the distinction between judgment-driven and affect-driven behavior is a critical one: affect-driven behavior tends to be temporally consistent with an affective state, whereas judgment-driven behavior results from enduring attitudes about one's job or organization. Another key contribution of the theory was to focus attention on within-person fluctuations in emotional states. AET researchers have subsequently found, among other things, that affect and job satisfaction are related but not equivalent constructs, and that positive affective experiences lead to affective commitment and helping behavior, with intention to quit predicted by attitudes rather than affective reactions (see Fisher, 2002; Weiss & Beal, 2005). Other findings suggest that specific emotions following affective events such as organizational uncertainty and task completion (namely guilt, determination, and chaos) are related to commitment via an affective process (Li, Ahlstrom, & Ashkanasy, 2010).

The relevance of AET to deviant behavior is twofold. First, AET provides a robust theoretical framework linking workplace environments, events, and emotions to individual members' propensity for, and engagement in, workplace deviance. For example, Salin (2003) noted that frustration and dissatisfaction arising from triggering circumstances such as restructuring may be an antecedent to bullying behavior. More recently, Rosen, Harris, and Kacmar (2009) found in a field study that frustration stemming from perceived politics led to lowered job satisfaction, resulting in turn in lowered performance levels and increased organizational withdrawal. In a similar vein, Bayram, Gursakal, and Bilgel (2009) found that employees' perceptions of their work environment resulted in negative affective responses such as frustration that then led to counterproductive workplace behaviors, including personal and organizational aggression.

Second, AET holds that affect-driven behavior is impulsive, and therefore has potential to be deviant (Weiss & Beal, 2005). In this case, we note that both the emotions circumplex (Larsen & Diener, 1992) and the structure of emotions proposed by Morgan & Heiss (1988) classify emotions in terms of their arousal or activation potential, with more activating emotions such as anger or fear likely to result in impulsive behavior. For example, Lerner and Keltner (2001) found that anger (an activating, negative emotion) led to risk-seeking choices, which often manifest as behaviors that lie outside accepted norms (that is, deviant behavior). In support of this idea, O'Neill, Vandenberg, Dejoy, and Wilson (2009) found that anger results in deviant behaviors including dangerous risk-taking and alcohol consumption; and Gabriel (1998) outlined how insults lead to negative feelings of shame, guilt, and anger, which in turn results in retaliation.

In line with the notion of affect-driven behavior, research on counterproductive workplace behavior (CWB) has suggested that this behavior is rooted in human aggression (Berkowitz, 1998). In this respect, hostile aggression is associated with negative emotions, is often imprudent, and has a primary aim of harming the target. For example, in dissecting the relationship between different forms of CWB and emotions, Spector, Fox, Penney, Bruursema, Goh, and Kessler (2006) reported that upsetting emotions, including anger and fury, were related to abuse against other employees (interpersonal deviance) and the organization itself (production deviance). This suggests that these two forms of CWB may share similar underlying motives, with the former being a direct form of aggression against others, and the latter being a form of displaced aggression. While the Spector et al. study was cross-sectional, and thus the presence of a process such as AET can only be inferred, the authors also found that engaging in abuse was related to other AET variables including stressors (such as organizational constraints and interpersonal conflicts), emotions, justice, and job satisfaction.

In a similar vein, Yang and Diedendorff (2009), who used AET as a basis for a twenty-five-day longitudinal study on the causes of CWB, found that negative emotions (1) partially mediated the relationship between daily stressors (perceived ambiguity) and daily CWB directed at organizational targets (CWB-O); and (2) fully mediated the relationship between customer interpersonal justice and CWB-O.

Having demonstrated that AET is relevant to the study of emotions and deviance, we now move our discussion on to related theories and subtopics, commencing with a closer look at the type of events that may trigger affective responses in the workplace; specifically, notions of injustice.

Injustice

Over recent years, we have seen the emergence of several theories and models that explore the link between emotions and injustice. Some place emotions as an antecedent to justice perceptions, others suggest they co-occur, and yet still others suggest that justice perceptions precede emotions. For example, according to Barsky, Kaplan, and Beal's (2011) model, a justice event triggers both discrete emotional reactions and perceptions of fairness concurrently. These authors outline how the intertwined nature of the two suggests that an individual may *feel* an initial appraisal of unfairness via the same physiological arousal (activation of areas of the brain, for example, which are related to the experience of emotions) as they would with any other emotionally laden experience. According to Barsky and his colleagues, individuals then go on to form more evaluative-type judgments regarding overall fairness. This multistage approach is largely consistent with Folger and Cropanzano's (2001) fairness theory, in which anger and outrage are considered automatic and adaptive reactions to mistreatment; and that serve, in turn, as catalysts for the formation of injustice perceptions.

On the other hand, Gibson and Callister (2010) suggest that the experience of a work event includes both fairness and justice perceptions that then lead to emotion: anger. This approach is more consistent with equity theory, where individuals experience negative emotions when they perceive they have been treated unjustly or unfairly. Similarly, Tzafrir and Hareli (2009) argue from an attribution theory perspective that perceptions of justice following promotion decisions lead to discrete emotional states. In line with AET, where perceptions of injustice are seen to trigger affective events, Weiss, Sucklow, and Cropanzano (1999) argue that emotion is the "central mechanism through which a sense of fairness is translated into work behavior" (786).

Greifeneder, Bless, and Pham (2011) employ the affect-as-information hypothesis (Clore, Gasper & Garvin, 2001), which is based on distinguishing affective, bodily, and cognitive feelings, to explain the role that affective feelings play in judgments. With respect to this hypothesis, Clore et al. note specifically "(a) that judgments can be genuinely feeling based, (b) that feelings influence judgment directly, and (c) that the reliance on feelings in judgment is inferential rather than purely automatic" (109).

Without any intent to minimize the importance or contribution of differing views on the order in which emotions and justice occur (this would warrant a lengthy piece on its own), we place a clear boundary around the issue in order to progress our discussion on deviance. Hence, for the purposes of parsimony, we argue that for a perception of injustice to be formed, emotions must have also occurred; either just before, concurrently, or just after the formation of the perception. It is on this basis that we treat injustice perceptions as a type of emotional reaction to an affective event.

Several scholars have theorized that injustice is related to deviance, using a plethora of robust theories to argue their case. This includes, but is definitely not limited to, AET and social exchange theory (Emerson, 1976). While social exchange relates more to other levels of the Five-Level model (levels 3, 4, and 5), we include brief mention of such studies here because the social exchange event is the cause of within-person changes in emotional state and perceptions.

For example, theft, a non-violent form of property deviance, has been conceptualized as a means to deal with distributive injustice (Greenberg & Scott, 1996). Moreover, Kelloway, Francis, Prosser, and Cameron (2010) posit that injustice is a key precursor to CWB. Folger and Skarlicki (2005) propose similarly that retaliation for injustice can take the form of deviance. Sims (2010) goes on to cite the 2006 boardroom spying scandal at Hewlett-Packard, where perceptions of power abuse led to feelings of frustration and injustice in other board members, who then retaliated against their chairman by publicly blowing the whistle on the scandal with the aim (and result) of ousting her from her position.

Empirical studies have also found relationships between injustice and deviant behavior (El Akremi, Vandenberghe & Camerman, 2010). Lim (2002) found that all three types of perceptions of injustice are related to cyber-loafing by employees, with normative conflict mediating the link between procedural injustice and retaliatory cyber-loafing (Zoghbi-Manrique-de-Lara, 2009). In a similar vein, Ambrose, Seabright, and Schminke (2002) reported that injustice is the most common cause of sabotage, and Jones (2009) found that interpersonal and informational justice (dimensions of interactional justice) accounted for the most unique variance between CWB directed at supervisors; and that procedural justice did the same for CWB directed at the organization.

Having shown how within-person changes in perceptions (of justice), within-person changes in emotions and deviance are related, we now look briefly at one particular type of event that can cause injustice perceptions—namely violation of the psychological contract, and how this can lead to deviance.

The Psychological Contract

Rousseau (1989, 123) defined a psychological contract as an "individual's beliefs regarding the terms and conditions of a reciprocal exchange agreement between that focal person and another party." As the word "belief" belies, it is a *psychological* construct, rather than a written agreement so that, in contrast to a written contract, these beliefs are not necessarily shared by the other party. Psychological contracts can range from transactional (largely *quid pro quo* based) through to highly relational (with the latter being more a socio-emotional contract underpinned by trust (see Rousseau & McLean Parks, 1993).

With emotions and injustice already in the equation, we can now add deviance. Combining agency, trait, and justice theories, Kidder (2005) proposed that violation leads to both minor and major acts of deviance. In support of this idea, Bordia, Restubog, and Tang (2008) found in a field study that experiences of violation (affective responses) led to revenge seeking manifesting as workplace deviance. Consistent with this idea, Jensen, Opland & Ryan (2010) found that deviant acts such as production deviance, withdrawal, and abuse against others were predictable in terms of relational violations, and both relational and transactional violations respectively.

Summary of Level 1

In this section, we have shown that the within-person level of the FLME, which includes AET, injustice, and psychological contract violation, is related to deviant behaviors of varying kinds through a variety of multistage processes. In doing so we have provided evidence that emotions can cause deviance, especially in the form of affect driven, impulsive behaviors. Moreover, we also provided evidence that deviance causes emotions; for example, insults (which lead to negative emotions) are not only an affective event, *they are also a form of interpersonal deviance.* We now continue our review, keeping this overarching debate in mind as we move on to the next level of the FLME, individual differences.

Emotions and Deviance at Level 2: Individual Differences

In this section, we focus on the role of specific emotion based personality traits of both perpetrators and (individual) victims of deviance, followed by a very brief section on the emotional responses and coping of individual victims of deviance. A discussion on the emotional intelligence of victims and perpetrators, including the potential for emotional intelligence to have a dark side if misused by perpetrators would have been fitting; however, we were unable to include this given the chapter length constraints, and make mention of it here only to recognize that it is an important emerging sub-topic within the emotions and deviance literature.

Emotion-Based Personality Traits

There are a number of personality traits that are emotion based. We limit our discussion here to four of them: Trait affect, anger, aggressiveness, and emotional stability (neuroticism). In the analysis that follows, we deal first with the enactors (perpetrators) of deviant behavior, and then discuss victims of deviant behavior.

Perpetrators. Typically working from a person-environment interactionism approach to organizational behavior, researchers have attempted to profile perpetrators of deviance, with many finding direct or moderating or mediating effects of the aforementioned traits on deviance. The results have not been entirely consistent, however. For example, Restubog, Garcia, Wang, and Cheng (2010) found that trait anger was directly related to deviance. This finding is consistent with a meta-analysis by Hershcovis et al. (2007), who reported finding that trait anger was related to both interpersonal and organizational aggression. In addition to direct effects, trait anger also mediates the relationship between narcissism and CWB (Penney & Spector, 2002), with trait aggressiveness moderating the relationship between interactional injustice and deviance (Aquino, Galperin & Bennett, 2004).

Hershcovis et al. (2007) also found that negative affectivity was not related to either form of aggression. However, Reio and Ghosh (2009) found that high negative affect did in fact predict incivility behavior. In terms of moderation effects, Skarlicki, Folger, and Tesluk (1999) found that negative affectivity moderated the relationship between fairness perceptions and retaliatory deviant behavior. Finally, we note that Yang and Diefendorff (2009) recently found that trait negative affectivity strengthened the within-person relationship between daily supervisor interactional justice and daily negative emotions, with negative emotions mediating between daily stressors (ambiguity) and CWB directed at the organization.

Turning now to neuroticism, we see that Berry, Ones, and Sackett (2007) reported that this personality variable correlates with deviant behavior. Chang and Smithikrai (2010) also found that CWB was predicted by neuroticism, but that the effect was moderated by distributive and interactional justice, and organizational citizenship behavior. In contrast, Ferris, Brown, and Heller (2009) were unable to find a relationship between emotional stability and organizational deviance, and Bodankin and Tziner (2009) also found that neuroticism was unrelated to destructive deviance. In terms of the moderating effects of neuroticism, Jensen, Opland, and Ryan (2010) found a moderation effect on the relationship between psychological contract breach and CWB. Colbert, Mount, Harter, Witt, and Barrick (2004) found further that neuroticism moderated the relationship between perceptions of the developmental environment and withholding effort (a form of production deviance). More recently, Rodell and Judge (2009) reported that neuroticism moderated the relationship between anger and CWB.

In summary, we conclude that the evidence of trait effects on perpetrator deviance is mixed. We suspect this may be because different measures of each construct were employed across studies. For example, deviant outcomes were operationalized using Bennett and Robinson's (2000) scale or Spector, Fox, et al.'s (2006) CWB checklist, and trait neuroticism was measured using the Wonderlic Productivity Index (WPI; Barrick, Mount & Waldschmidt, 2003) or the NEO-FFI-S (Costa & McCrae, 1992). Despite this uncertainty, however, there seems to be a strong case from meta-analysis results for the idea that trait anger and neuroticism are likely predictors of perpetrator deviant behavior, with negative affectivity a possible moderator rather than having direct effect.

Further, much like the argument for exploring discrete emotions rather than general affect (Gooty, Gavin & Ashkanasy, 2009), O'Neill and Hastings (2011) dutifully point out that using the broad domains of personality traits rather than their facets may be masking the real effects. Their findings in regard to traits such as trait manipulativeness also suggest that we should expand our horizons in terms of what traits we investigate. For example, based on O'Neill and Hastings (2011), we feel manipulativeness may potentially be related to the misuse of emotional intelligence in organizations.

Victims. As can be seen in the foregoing discussion, attempting to profile perpetrators to learn more about emotionally relevant characteristics and engaging in deviance is not easy. This is even more so the case for profiling victims, in part because this can be seen as a form of victim blaming. Nevertheless, as Zapf (1999) contends, deviant acts such as bullying involve a target, a perpetrator, and an environment; so that to exclude an analysis of potential victim correlates for the sake of being seen as "politically correct" risks omitting a potentially important part of the puzzle. Consequently, in this section we address this issue.

First, and as was the case in respect to perpetrator research, we note that results from victim research have been inconsistent (see Aquino & Thau, 2009 for a summary). Despite apparently soundly theorized relationships between victims' self-esteem, anxiety, depression, and negative affect (almost all related to neuroticism, see Zapf, 1999), links between victim emotional stability and deviance appear to vary depending on the type of interpersonal deviance studied. For example Milam, Spitzmueller, and Penney (2009) found that neuroticism was related to experiencing incivility, whereas Coyne, Seigne, and Randall (2000) reported no differences in the emotional stability of victims versus non-victims of bullying.

Target negative affect seems to have the most consistent relationship with various forms of interpersonal deviance; although it is not clear whether negative affect is (1) a causal precursor; or (2) possibly developed over time in response to being targeted (an emotion based outcome); or (3) simply a reflection of victims selectively recalling negative events more than those low in negative affect (Aquino & Thau, 2009), which presents a problematic "victim-emotion-trait first" or "victim-emotion-trait consequence" issue.

In an interesting article that suggests emotion may come first, Matthiesen and Einarsen (2007) found that, in addition to multiple prior victimization experiences, low self-esteem and high social anxiety, victims of bullying also had high levels of trait aggressiveness; a set of characteristics they referred to collectively as indicative of a "provocative victim." We agree with these authors' suggestion that multiple victimization experiences may be an indication that the targets themselves in some way provoke the behavior, and that this may be related to trait aggressiveness; but then the critical question becomes: Does the so-called victim create a perpetrator, or does the perpetrator create a victim?

We answer this by reference to *intentionality*. In other words, we believe a so-called provocative victim does not necessarily deliberately engage in behavior to elicit an act of mistreatment from a perpetrator. In reference to the trait aggressiveness aspect of the provocative victim profile, Anderson, Buckley, and Carnagey (2008) use a violence escalation model to explain how an individual with high trait aggressiveness might inadvertently escalate a potential conflict situation (accidentally bumped in a busy room) into a hostile situation by interpreting the action as deliberate. The individual is likely then to "respond" in such a way as to provoke an aggressive and deliberate response from the other person, whose initial behavior was not intentional. Therefore the person doing the bumping, while not originally a perpetrator, then becomes the aggressor. The provocative victim is likely to respond again, leading to a tit-for-tat spiral effect much like that proposed by Andersson and Pearson (1999). Individuals with lower trait aggressiveness on the other hand, tend not to let the initial ostensibly accidental situation become blown out of proportion by not responding aggressively, if at all, so acts of interpersonal deviance may never eventuate.

Our overall view on victims in terms of emotion based traits and "causes of deviance" is therefore that a great deal more needs to be done before any definitive conclusions can be drawn on this front. Clearly, there is a challenge ahead for researchers in this domain to explore. In the meantime, we move on next to a short (and much safer) discussion of emotional responses and coping by victims.

Emotional Responses and Coping

Based on AET, general stressor strain theory, and the stress, appraisal and coping models, we conclude that experiencing interpersonal deviance may represent a stressful event that results in negative emotions in victims. As Lazarus and Folkman (1984) outline, experiencing a stressor triggers a process whereby emotions and cognitive processes evaluate the stressor to determine if it is harmful. The more (potentially or actually) harmful an event is appraised to be, the more likely it is that the individual will develop a state of distress. Appraisal then affects coping (behavioral and/or cognitive responses). Thus, if an individual appraises the situation overall to be highly stressful, he or she is more likely to deploy emotion-focused coping. On the other hand, if an appraiser of an event finds it to be less stressful, this can lead to an evaluation of the situation being within an individual's control and hence the use of problem-focused coping, aimed at resolving the issue (Lazarus, 2006).

It was somewhat surprising therefore that we found very little in the literature on the topic of emotional appraisals and coping by victims of interpersonal deviance. A notable exception, however, is a study of the antecedents to coping by Scheck and Kinicki (2000), who based their research on Lazarus and Folkman's (1984) cognitive-phenomenological model. Scheck and Kinicki explored the role of negative emotion arising out of primary appraisals of a situation (but not a deviance experience) as being potentially harmful or threatening, and found that negative emotions were inversely related to the use of problem-focused coping, suggesting that negative emotions drive the use of emotion-focused coping. Choosing avoidance coping strategies such as focusing on, and venting of, emotions has also been found to be associated with emotional stability (Bishop et al., 2001), which implies a link between this trait, emotional responses, and coping following a stressful experience. Other studies have looked at coping in the erroneous absence of emotional appraisal, but have not relied on emotion-versus problem-focused categories (see Djurkovic, McCormack & Casimir, 2005; Niedl, 1996; Wasti & Cortina, 2002; and Zapf & Gross, 2001).

In the only study we found that was directly related to our two literature review topics, Cortina and Magley (2009) used stress and coping theory to formulate hypotheses as to how victims of incivility appraise their experiences in terms of negative emotions, and how these appraisals affect coping choices. They found that emotional appraisal, duration of experience, and position and power of both the victim and the perpetrator affected coping strategies, with perpetration by powerful people resulting in higher levels of negative emotions.

Summary of Level 2

By examining emotionally relevant characteristics of both the perpetrator and victim as potential causes of deviance, we have provided food for thought on the emotions causing deviance side of the debate, balanced only partially by the minimal research on the emotional responses of victims on the other side of the debate (deviance causing emotions). It seems the jury is still out on this question.

Emotions and Deviance at Level 3: Interpersonal

In this section, we summarize literature on specific interpersonal exchanges (dyadic) that relate to deviance and emotions. We focus on three topics: (1) abusive supervision and employee responses; (2) emotion regulation/displays; and (3) bystander effects.

Abusive. Abusive supervision refers to behavior enacted by individuals in managerial, leadership or supervisory roles that can be described as tyrannical (Ashforth, 1994), bullying (Hoel, Rayner & Cooper, 1999), undermining (Duffy, Ganster & Pagon, 2002), and aggressive (Mitchell & Ambrose, 2007), among other things. While abusive supervision has been defined in many

ways, we classify it as a form of deviance, and adopt Tepper's (2000) definition, that the term refers to "subordinates' perceptions of the extent to which
their supervisors engage in the sustained display of hostile verbal and non-
verbal behaviors, excluding physical contact" (178).

Evidence suggests that, in addition to affecting multisource ratings of job
performance (Harris, Kacmar & Zivnuska, 2007), as well as job satisfaction
and commitment (Lim & Teo, 2009), abusive supervision leads to emotional
responses in subordinates in terms of both actual emotions and affect, and/
or in the form of injustice perceptions. For example, Kim and Shapiro (2008)
found that supervisor rudeness during an explanation of organizational
decisions leads to negative emotions.

Experiencing abusive supervision has been directly related to supervisor-
directed, organizational, and interpersonal deviance by victims, moderated
by a negative reciprocity norm (Mitchell & Ambrose, 2007). Thau, Bennett,
Mitchell, and Marrs (2009) subsequently reported that the same direct relationship seems to be moderated by management style, with Tepper and associates (2009) finding that it was also moderated by intention to quit.

Abusive supervision can also lead to deviant behavior in subordinates following an AET path. For example, Judge, Scott, and Illies (2006) found that
interactional justice acts by supervisors that resemble abuse were indirectly
related to deviance through the mediator of job satisfaction. This is consistent with the findings of Barclay, Skarlicki, and Pugh (2005)—that laid off
employees felt both outward- and inward-focused negative emotions, differentially affected by perceptions of both procedural and supervisory interactional injustice perceptions. Moreover, Barclay and her colleagues found
that supervisory interactional justice interacted with outcome favorability
to predict retaliatory behavior, mediated by outward-focused emotions of
anger and hostility. More recently, Lim and Teo (2009) found that "supervisory cyber incivility" (419) was related to job satisfaction and organizationally deviant behavior.

Also consistent with the tenets of AET, Tepper (2000) found that abusive
supervision is related to lower job satisfaction, lower normative and affective commitment, higher continuance commitment, and psychological distress (as measured using items indicating depression and burnout), and that
injustice mainly plays a mediating role. In a more recent study, Tepper, Lambert, Henle, Giacalone, and Duffy (2008) reported that abusive supervision
led to organization deviance, and that this effect was mediated by affective
commitment. Likewise, Kim and Shapiro (2008) found that negative emotion partially mediated the relationship between abusive supervision and
retaliation.

In addition to AET, Thau and Mitchell (2010) found that deviant responses to abusive supervision can be explained in terms of the self-regulation impairment theory, whereby distributive justice strengthens the relationship between the experience and deviance owing to a drain on the resources required to maintain appropriate behavior.

Emotional Displays and Regulation. Given we know that certain events lead to affective responses, it is important that we look also at how individuals deal with emotion arising from events. The Thau and Mitchell (2010) study on maintenance of appropriate behavior is a convenient lead-in to this section on emotional labor. Emotional labor, or "the effort, planning, and control needed to express organizationally desired emotion during interpersonal transactions," (Morris & Feldman, 1996, 987) may occur during encounters with supervisors, subordinates, and coworkers, as well as with customers. Emotional labor invokes the need for emotion regulation, which can be achieved by modifying feelings (deep acting) or modifying emotional display (surface acting), both of which are influenced by individual factors such as emotional intelligence, emotional expressivity, and dispositional affect. Emotional regulation then affects stress and well-being (Grandey, 2003).

Very few studies have explored surface and deep acting as job demands or events that can lead to deviant workplace behavior, whether it is affect or attitudinally driven. An exception is the study by Bechtoldt, Welk, Hartig, and Zapf (2007), who found that surface acting was related to organizational deviance, even after controlling for self-control and injustice perceptions. This is consistent with the view that it is the emotional dissonance component of emotion regulation that occurs with surface acting but not with deep acting that is stressful (Zapf & Holz, 2006). Similarly, Seery and Corrigal (2009) found that surface acting is also related to negative work outcomes including decreased job satisfaction and affective commitment, and increased intention to quit.

Bystander Effects. Not only does the individual involved in a dyadic interaction (whether it is an emotional labor event or an interpersonal deviance event such as abusive supervision) have an emotional response, but also the bystanders that witness it. For example, bystanders in a mobbing situation can have a negative emotional response (Mulder, Pouwelse, Lodewijkx & Bolman, 2008), and coworkers' levels of emotional labor also increase when they witness injustice (mediated by discrete emotions and fairness) even if they themselves are being treated fairly (Spencer & Rupp, 2009). The performance of observers of anger displays can also be affected through both emotional and cognitive routes (Miron-Spektor & Rafaeli, 2009). Third parties may experience an automatic, emotional response to seeing someone else mistreated that can lead to retribution behavior (such as status leveling or punishment) against the perpetrator of an unjust behavior by third parties (Skarlicki & Rupp, 2010). Not only is this consistent with justice and fairness perspectives (Skarlicki & Tulik, 2005) and, to an extent, with the dual threshold model of anger (Geddes & Callister, 2007), it also relates to the notion of emotional contagion (see level 4 discussion below).

Summary of Level 3

In our discussion of emotions and deviant behavior at level 3, we have provided evidence that dyadic interactions such as abusive supervision and emotional regulation events, as well as witnessing these interactions, may lead to emotions, deviance, or both emotions and deviance. In particular, our review demonstrates the existence of affect- and judgment-driven deviance as a result of being a victim of deviance, suggesting that, rather than emotions being a cause or consequence of deviance, there may be an "emotion spiral" (Hareli & Rafaeli, 2008, 35).

Emotions and Deviance at Level 4: Groups and Teams

At this level, we identify three topics of relevance to emotions and deviance: (1) leadership (including leader-member exchange—LMX); (2) group affective climate; and (3) emotional contagion.

Leadership. As argued by Dasborough and Ashkanasy (2002), leadership is both inherently an emotional process and a process of social interaction (best explained by attribution theory). According to these authors, members make attributions about their leader's intentions that impact how the leader's style is interpreted as true or pseudo transformational leadership. Consistent with AET, Dasborough and Ashkanasy posit that members' reactions to their leader's influence attempts are determined by the member's emotional reaction to the attempt (that is, the influence attempt becomes an "affective event"). In this respect, Dasborough (2006), in a qualitative study underpinned by AET and the asymmetry effect theory of emotion, found leaders do invoke emotions in followers, and that followers recall negative emotional incidents more intensely and in more detail than positive events. Further, negative mood showed stronger convergence than positive, with follower moods more likely to converge with that of the leader, rather than the other way round, emphasizing the role of leader emotion and emotional displays in determining affect in dual dyads (Spoor & Kelly, 2009).

Using leader-member exchange theory, Pizer and Härtel (2005) take the relationship between leader and follower emotions a step further, linking specifically the currency of exchange quality (good enough, for instance, versus absent) to employee emotions (positive versus negative). Overall, they found that the affective evaluations and discrete emotions experienced by followers vary according to the currency and its quality. High quality LMX also leads to friendship, which then leads to better team-member exchange, especially when group affective climate is strong (Dasborough, Ashkanasy, Tee & Tse, 2009), which brings us now to our next topic at level 4: group affective climate.

Group Affective Climate. Group affect is thought to come about via self-reinforcing mechanisms driven by affective sharing and affective-similarity-attraction between members, otherwise referred to as a positive group affect spiral, which may in turn be impacted by contextual factors such as subgroup cynicism, and group and organizational norms (Walter & Bruch, 2008). Spoor and Kelly (2004) maintain further that group affect provides a coordination function, a mechanism through which emotions and social exchange result in ties to a group (Lawler, 2001).

Emotional Contagion. In this respect, Johnson (2008) and Sy, Côté, and Saavedra (2005) demonstrated that leader positive and negative affect translates to follower positive affect via emotional contagion. Moreover, Dasborough et al. (2009) maintain that emotional contagion can occur between leaders and followers, and at a meso-level among team members, with negative emotions spreading through the group and impacting group affective and trust climate. Both positive and negative emotions are similarly contagious, with positive emotional contagion leading to increased cooperation, perceived task performance, and decreased conflict (Barsade, 2002; Kelly & Barsade, 2001). Härtel, Gough, and Härtel (2008) argue further for the importance of individual-level emotion characteristics to the climate of work groups, with individual team member's affect being related to the other team member's affect over time (Ilies, Wagner & Morgeson, 2007). Finally, we note that during emotionally turbulent times such as organizational change, it is important that leaders are skilled in the art of what Sanchez-Burks and Huy (2009) term "emotional aperture," or the ability to recognize group-level emotions, rather than individual level emotions.

Summary of Level 4

We first relate the aforementioned topics back to evidence presented in the previous section that demonstrated a relationship between abusive supervision and emotional responses, some of which lead to deviance. The evidence on group affect and emotional contagion suggests that negative emotional displays by supervisors, such as anger, may result not only in victim negative emotion, but also group level negative affect.

Citing research by Aryee, Chen, Sun & Debrah (2007) and Zellars, Tepper, and Duffy (2002), Tepper noted that abusive supervision reflected in employee's perceptions of injustice in performance appraisal situations comes to be reflected in subsequent performance decrements. Tepper also noted that, to date, these findings have not been replicated in group settings and added that "abusive supervision may have indirect influences on unit performance through its effect on citizenship behavior" (277). In partial explanation for this, Sparr and Sonnentag (2008) found in a field study that perceptions of feedback fairness were positively related to job satisfaction and negatively related to depression and turnover intentions, and that these relationships were mediated by the quality of the employees' relationships with their supervisors (LMX). More recently, Erdogan and Bauer (2010) looked more specifically at supervisors' LMX differentiation and the tendency of supervisors to discriminate among their subordinates, and the effect this has on employees' perception of injustice. They found that LMX differentiation was related to more negative work attitudes and coworker relations, but only in the absence of what they termed "justice climate." It appears reasonable to conclude, therefore, that since team climate impacts behavior norms within a team, if one person is deviant, the whole barrel can go bad (Dunlop & Lee, 2004).

Emotions and Deviance at Level 5: The Organization

At level 5, we are referring to the organization as a whole, and notions of organizational culture and climate come to the fore. With reference to deviance, however, we are not referring to the kind of healthy positive organizational climate that Härtel and Ashkanasy (2010) describe. A deviant climate is characterized more in terms of negative idioms such as the "climate of fear" (Ashkanasy & Nicholson, 2003), where deviant behaviors, and especially supervisor abuse, become the norm rather than the exception—the sort of organization that is "toxic" (Frost, 2003).

The deviant organization will be characterized by a climate of fear, injustice (see Li & Cropanzano, 2009), and unethical behavior (Victor & Cullen, 1988), where employees fear to speak up, resulting in a "climate of silence" (Morrison & Milliken, 2000). In particular, Zoghbi-Manrique-de-Lara and Verano-Tacoronte (2007) demonstrated that such organizations develop "conflict norms" (715) where employee perceptions of procedural injustice lead to deviant behavior. Greenberg (1993) similarly found that perceptions of injustice (pay inequity) resulted in employee deviant behavior (stealing). Latham (2001) found further that management's attempts to reduce employee deviance (in this case theft) by increasing surveillance resulted in more, rather than less, theft. It was only when management engendered a culture of trust that the thieving stopped.

The effects of level 5 ultimately filter down to all the levels of emotions. Thus, an organizational environment of distrust and aggressive behavior (such as employee surveillance) generates negative affective events (level 1), encourages people with a Machiavellian personality (who manipulate emotions at level 2; see Austin, Farrelly, Black & Moore, 2007), and leads to interpersonal distrust among employees (level 3) and negative group climates (level 4). Barsky and Kaplan (2007) show in particular how individual employee experiences of procedural unfairness result in negative emotional perceptions. As Dasborough and her colleagues (2009) put it, this sets up an emotional spiral of negativity that permeates though every level of the organization. Ashkanasy (2003b) notes in this respect that emotions are hardwired human responses linking across the five levels of analysis in the Ashkanasy (2003a) model.

Another potential generator of a toxic emotional climate can take the form of organizational norms regarding emotional display. Diefendorff and Greguras (2009), for example, describe how organizationally mandated emotional display rules impose sometimes debilitating emotional strain on employees, leading to burnout and deviance. In this respect, Ashkanasy and Daus (2002) describe a situation where an employee who is under stress, but is still required to engage in positive emotional displays, might also engage in deviance (sabotage in this instance).

Finally, at the organizational level, we agree with Fineman's (2004) assessment that organizations need to take care lest an overly prescriptive focus on emotion becomes an objective in itself. Antonakis, Ashkanasy, and Dasborough (2009) refer to this as "the curse of emotions" (250), where supervisors might engage in emotional manipulation as a means to control employees, resulting in retaliatory and potentially deviant behavior.

Discussion

Having now covered each of the five levels in Ashkanasy's (2003a) multi-level model, let us summarize what we found. This is perhaps best done visually, and thus we present a version of the five-level model that includes not only the topics included in our review on emotions and deviance, but also other topics that would have been relevant but that we did not have room and/or sufficient literature to include (see figure 2.1). We put these forward as our ideas for areas desperate for researchers to explore in more detail. For example, following suggestions of Kilduff, Chiaburu, and Menges (2010), it would be more than interesting to see if the "dark side of EI" may mean it is used by perpetrators of interpersonal deviance to not only suppress their negative emotions and display appropriate positive emotions in front of important others, but also to identify victims in which negative emotions such as fear and depression can be easily evoked, resulting in a near immediate ability to exploit emotions as pure power, and engage in ongoing mistreatment of a victim who is unlikely to speak up. In our view, this is where our academic approach can be dovetailed with the more populist work of management and human resource professionals such as Clarke (2005) to generate key insights into the undeniably complex nature of deviant workplace behavior.

In terms of future research, we trust that our review has highlighted that there is a need to adopt a multi-theory approach to cover the complexities of this domain. The intersection between AET and social exchange seems a particular useful combination. As outlined by Lawler and Thye (1999), exchange theorists tend to be reason orientated, individualistic, instrumental, and emotionally vacuous, whereas emotion theorists are socially orientated, expressive, emotionally deep and complex, and passionate. We agree with these authors that a closer, intertwined marriage between the two is likely to be a fruitful one in terms of insightful research on emotions and deviance. We also have outlined that research on emotions and deviance needs to move on from what is still largely a "perpetrator, victim, or between two people" style focus, and adopt a more multi-level approach as well, inclusive of greater efforts to both theoretically and empirically explore the topics that fall within levels 4 and 5 (which we acknowledge to be difficult levels to address); for example, how leader emotional intelligence and group emotional intelligence may foster or prevent deviant behavior.

It would be unfitting in this chapter not to include at least some brief comments on what this all means in practice and why research in this domain is so vital. In particular, we emphasize that all forms of deviance can have significant and negative consequences for both individuals and organizations. The effect on individuals in particular has the potential to have a damaging impact on a wider social and community basis, with some victims of interpersonal deviance suffering ill effects from trying to cope by hiding the impact of their emotional experiences (Gross & Levenson, 1997; Hochschild, 1983), others driven to drink (Bacharach, Bamberger & Sonnenstuhl, 2002)

Fig. 2.1. A multi-level model of emotions as related to deviance

Level 5: Organization
  Cultures of fear, silence, and/or toxicity
  Emotional Spirals
  Unethical Climates
Level 4: Group
  Abusive supervision
  Group affective climate
  Emotional contagion
  Leader & group emotional intelligence
Level 3: Interpersonal (Dyadic)
  Social Exchange Theory
  Abusive supervision
  Emotional display, regulation, & labor
Level 2: Between Person (Individual Differences)
  Perpetrator/victim trait affect (negative), anger, aggressiveness, &
    emotional stability (neuroticism)
  Victim emotional response, appraisal, & emotional coping
  Perpetrator/victim emotional intelligence ('dark side' of EI)
Level 1: Within-Person
  Affective Events Theory
  Affect driven, impulsive behavior
  Injustice perceptions
  Psychological contracts

or, even worse, some developing stress related mental health disorders that require clinical treatment (Brousse et al., 2008).

The cost of such behavior is also an issue for organizations; theft, sabotage, stress claims, work withdrawal, damage to employer reputation, low job satisfaction, high turnover and retaliatory behavior (to name but a few issues) also emphasize the need to foster an environment that is not propitious of deviance—prevention is better than the cure. As we have shown, one deviant event may turn into a deviance spiral driven by emotions that in turn infects an entire organization, and leads to severely reduced profitability and sustainability. Likewise, as we learn more about emotions and deviance, we have an obligation to ensure that what we know is communicated to human resource professionals and managers in such a way as to enable them to apply our findings in the business setting.

Finally, we consolidate our literature review findings and conclude this chapter with a return to the original debate that we set out to answer, which was "Do emotions cause deviance, or does deviance cause emotions?" In the beginning of our discussion of the within-person level, it generally appeared that emotions (affective responses) seem to cause deviant behavior, whether it is affect driven or arises out of attitudes (evaluative judgments) influenced by emotions. It quickly becomes clear that in terms of events, however, it is often the *experience* of deviant behavior (especially of an interpersonal nature) that leads to emotions. Our discussion then also includes reasonable evidence that as opposed to emotions being solely a cause *or* outcome of deviance, they may be part of an emotional spiral in which deviance can both cause, and arise from, emotions. We would like to confess here that in focusing on emotions as causes or outcomes of deviance, one perspective we did not include in our review, but that may be valid nonetheless, is that some perpetrators of deviance may have no reason at all to be deviant, as found by Bunk, Karabin, and Lear (2011).

So, in conclusion, can we resolve the key question we posed in this chapter: Do emotions cause deviance, or does deviance cause emotions? Our answer to the debate is perhaps best described in the words of Aristotle: *"If there has been a first man he must have been born without father or mother—which is repugnant to nature. For there could not have been a first egg to give a beginning to birds, or there should have been a first bird which gave a beginning to eggs; for a bird comes from an egg"* (Fénelon, 1825, 202). This means, inter alia, that rather than it being a case of "chicken or the egg," emotions and deviance must have always co-existed.

REFERENCES

Ambrose, M. L., Seabright, M. A., & Schminke, M. (2002). Sabotage in the workplace: The role of organizational injustice. *Organizational Behavior and Human Decision Processes, 89,* 947–965.

Anderson, C., Buckley, K., & Carnagey, N. (2008). Creating your own hostile environment: A laboratory examination of trait aggressiveness and the violence escalation cycle. *Personality and Social Psychology Bulletin, 34,* 462.

Andersson, L. M., & Pearson, C. M. (1999). Tit for Tat? The spiraling effect of incivility in the workplace. *Academy of Management Review, 24,* 452–471.

Antonakis, J., Ashkanasy, N. M., & Dasborough, M. T. (2009). Does leadership need emotional intelligence? *Leadership Quarterly, 20,* 247–261.

Aquino, K., Galperin, B. L., & Bennett, R. J. (2004). Social status and aggressiveness as moderators of the relationship between interactional justice and workplace deviance. *Journal of Applied Social Psychology, 34,* 1001–1029.

Aquino, K., & Thau, S. (2009). Workplace victimization: Aggression from the target's perspective. *Annual Review of Psychology, 60,* 717–741.

Aryee, S., Chen, Z. X., Sun, L., Debrah, Y. A. (2007). Antecedents and outcomes of abusive supervision: Test of a trickle-down model. *Journal of Applied Psychology, 92,* 191–201.

Ashforth, B. E. (1994). Petty tyranny in organizations. *Human Relations, 47,* 755–778.

Ashkanasy, N. M. (2003a). Emotions in organizations: A multilevel perspective. In F. Dansereau & F. J. Yammarino (Eds.), *Research in multi-level issues* (Vol. 2: pp. 9–54). Oxford, UK: Elsevier/JAI.

Ashkanasy, N. M. (2003b). Emotions at multiple levels: An integration. In F. Dansereau and F. J. Yammarino (Eds.), *Research in multi-level issues* (Vol. 2: pp. 71–81). Oxford, UK: Elsevier/JAI.

Ashkanasy, N. M., & Daus, C. S. (2002). Emotion in the workplace: The new challenge for managers. *Academy of Management Executive, 16*(1), 76–86.

Ashkanasy, N. M., & Nicholson. (2003). Climate of fear in organisational settings: Construct definition, measurement and a test of theory. *Australian Journal of Psychology, 55,* 24–29.

Austin, E. J., Farrelly, D., Black, C., & Moore, H. (2007). Emotional intelligence, Machiavellianism and emotional manipulation: Does EI have a dark side? *Personality and Individual Differences, 43,* 179–189.

Bacharach, S. B., Bamberger, P., & Sonnenstuhl, W. J. (2002). Driven to drink: managerial control, work related risk factors and employee drinking behaviour. *Academy of Management Journal, 45,* 637–658.

Barclay, L., Skarlicki, D. P., & Pugh, D. (2005). Exploring the role of emotions in injustice perceptions and retaliation. *Journal of Applied Psychology, 90,* 629–643.

Barrick, M. R., Mount, M. K., & Waldschmidt, D. M. (2003). *Administering, interpreting, and making decisions with the Wonderlic Productivity Index TM.* Libertyville, IL: Wonderlic.

Barsade, S. G. (2002). The ripple effect: Emotional contagion and its influence on group behavior. *Administrative Science Quarterly, 47,* 644–675.

Barsky, A., & Kaplan, S. A. (2007). If you feel bad, it's unfair: A quantitative synthesis of affect and organizational justice perceptions. *Journal of Applied Psychology, 92,* 286–295.

Barsky, A., Kaplan, S. A., & Beal, D. J. (2011). Just feelings? The role of affect in the formation of organizational fairness judgments *Journal of Management, 37,* 248–279.

Bayram, N., Gursakal, N., & Bilgel, N. (2009). Counterproductive work behaviour among white-collar employees: A study from Turkey. *International Journal of Selection and Assessment, 17,* 180–188.

Bechtoldt, M. N., Welk, C., Hartig, J., & Zapf, D. (2007). Main and moderating effects of self-control, organizational justice, and emotional labour on counterproductive behaviour at work. *European Journal of Work and Organizational Psychology, 16,* 479–500.

Bennett, R. J., & Robinson, S. L. (2000). Development of a measure of workplace deviance. *Journal of Applied Psychology, 85,* 349–360.

Berkowitz, L. (1998). Affective aggression: The role of stress, pain, and negative affect. In R. G. Geen & E. Donnerstein (Eds.), *Human aggression: Theories, research and implications for social policy* (pp. 49–72). San Diego: Academic.

Berry, C. M., Ones, D. S., & Sackett, P. R. (2007). Interpersonal deviance, organizational deviance, and their common correlates: A review and meta-analysis. *Journal of Applied Psychology, 92,* 410–424.

Bishop, G. D., Tong, E. M. W., Diong, S. M., Enkelmann, H. C., Why, Y. P., Khader, M., & Ang, J. C. H. (2001). The relationship between coping and personality among police officers in Singapore. *Journal of Research in Personality, 35,* 353–374.

Bodankin, M., & Tziner, A. (2009). Constructive deviance, destructive deviance and personality: How do they interrelate? *Amfiteatru Economic, 11,* 549–564.

Bordia, P., Restubog, S. L. D., & Tang, R. L. (2008). When employees strike back: Investigating mediating mechanisms between psychological contract breach and workplace deviance. *Journal of Applied Psychology, 93,* 1104–1117.

Brousse, G., Fontana, L., Ouchchane, L., Boisson, C., Gerbaud, L., Bourguet, D., Perrier, A., Schmitt, A., Llorca, P. M., & Chamoux, A. (2008). Psychopathological features of a patient population of targets of workplace bullying. *Occupational Medicine, 58,* 122–128.

Bunk, J. A., Karabin, J., & Lear, T. (2011). Understanding why workers engage in rude behaviors: A social interactionist perspective. *Current Psychology, 30,* 74–80.

Chang, K., & Smithikrai, C. (2010). Counterproductive behaviour at work: An investigation into reduction strategies. *International Journal of Human Resource Management, 21,* 1272–1288.

Clarke, J. (2005). *Working with monsters: How to identify and protect yourself from workplace psychopaths.* Sydney: Random House.

Clore, G. L., Gasper, K., & Garvin, E. (2001). Affect as information. In J. P. Forgas (Ed.), *Handbook of affect and social cognition* (pp. 121–144). Mahwah, NJ: Erlbaum.

Cloward, R. A. (1959). Illegitimate means, anomie and deviant behaviour. *American Sociological Review, 24,* 164–176.

Cohen, A. K. (1966). *Deviance and control.* Englewood Cliffs, NJ: Prentice Hall.

Colbert, A. E., Mount, M. K., Harter, J. K., Witt, L. A., & Barrick, M. R. (2004). Interactive effects of personality and perceptions of the work situation on workplace deviance. *Journal of Applied Psychology, 89,* 599–609.

Cortina, L. M., & Magley, V. J. (2009). Patterns and profiles of response to incivility in the workplace. *Journal of Occupational Health Psychology, 14,* 272–288.

Costa, P. T. Jr., & McCrae, R. R. (1992). *NEO PI-R professional manual.* Odessa, FL: Psychological Assessment Resources.

Coyne, I., Seigne, E., & Randall, P. (2000). Predicting workplace victim status from personality. *European Journal of Work & Organizational Psychology, 9,* 335–349.

Damasio, A. R. (1994). *Descartes' error: Emotion, reason, and the human brain*: New York: Putnam.

Dasborough, M. T., & Ashkanasy, N. M. (2002). Emotion and attribution of intentionality in leader-member relationships. *Leadership Quarterly, 13,* 615–634.

Dasborough, M. T., Ashkanasy, N. M., Tee, E. Y. J., & Tse, H. H. M. (2009). What goes around comes around: How meso-level negative emotional contagion can ultimately determine organizational attitudes toward leaders. *Leadership Quarterly, 20,* 571–585.

de Rivera, J. H. (1992). Emotional climate: Social structure and emotional dynamics. In K. T. Strongman (Ed.), *International Review of Studies on Emotion.* New York: John Wiley.

Diefendorff, J. M., & Greguras, G. J. (2009). Contextualizing emotional display rules: Examining the roles of targets and discrete emotions in shaping display rule perceptions *Journal of Management, 35,* 880–898.

Djurkovic, N., McCormack, D., & Casimir, G. (2005). The behavioral reactions of victims to different types of workplace bullying. *International Journal of Organization Theory and Behavior, 8,* 439–460.

Duffy, M. K., Ganster, D. C., & Pagon, M. (2002). Social undermining in the workplace. *Academy of Management Review, 45,* 331–351.

Dunlop, P. D., & Lee, K. (2004). Workplace deviance, organizational citizenship behavior, and business unit performance: The bad apples do spoil the whole barrel. *Journal of Organizational Behavior, 25,* 67–80.

Ekman, P. (1999). Basic Emotions. In T. Dalgleish & M. Power (Eds.), *Handbook of Cognition and Emotion.* Sussex, UK: Wiley.

El Akremi, A., Vandenberghe, C., & Camerman, J. (2010). The role of justice and social exchange relationships in workplace deviance: Test of a mediated model. *Human Relations, 63,* 1687–1717.

Elfenbein, H. A. (2007). Emotion in organizations: A review and theoretical integration. *Academy of Management Annals, 1,* 371–457.

Emerson, R. (1976). Social Exchange Theory. In A. Inkeles, J. Colemen, & N. Smelser (Eds.), *Annual Review of Sociology.* Palo Alto, CA: Annual Reviews.

Erdogan, B., & Bauer, T. N. (2010). Differentiated leader-member exchanges (LMX): The buffering role of justice climate. *Journal of Applied Psychology, 95,* 1104–1120.

Fénelon, F. (1825). *Lives of the ancient philosophers.* London.

Ferris, D. L., Brown, D. J., & Heller, D. (2009). Organizational supports and organizational deviance: The mediating role of organization-based self-esteem. *Organizational Behavior and Human Decision Processes, 108,* 279–286.

Fineman, S. (2004). Getting the measure of emotion—and the cautionary tale of emotional intelligence. *Human Relations, 57,* 719–740.

Fischer, K. W., Shaver, P. R., & Carnochan, P. (1990). How emotions develop and how they organize development. *Cognition and Emotion, 4,* 81–127.

Fisher, C. D. (2000). Mood and emotions while working: Missing pieces of job satisfaction *Journal of Organizational Behaviour, 21,* 185–202.

Fisher, C. D. (2002). Antecedents and consequences of real-time affective reactions at work. *Motivation and Emotion, 26,* 3–30.

Folger, R., & Cropanzano, R. (2001). Fairness theory: Justice as accountability. In J. Greenberg, & R. Cropanzano (Eds.), *Advances in organizational justice* (pp. 1–55). Stanford: Stanford University Press.

Folger, R., & Skarlicki, D. P. (2005). Beyond counterproductive work behavior: Moral emotions and deontic retaliation vs. reconciliation. In S. Fox & P. E. Spector (Eds.), *Counterproductive work behavior: Investigations of actors and targets* (pp. 83–105). Washington, DC: APA Press.

Fox, S., & Spector, P. E. (1999). A model of work frustration-aggression. *Journal of Organizational Behavior, 20,* 915–931.

Frijda, N. H. (1994). Varieties of affect: Emotions and episodes, moods, and sentiments. In P. Ekman & J. Davidson (Eds.), *The nature of emotion: Fundamental questions* (pp. 59–67). Oxford: Oxford University Press.

Frost, P. J. (2003). *Toxic emotions at work: How compassionate managers handle pain and conflict.* Cambridge: Harvard Business School Press.

Gabriel, Y. (1998). An introduction to the social psychology of insults in organizations. *Human Relations, 51,* 1329–1354.

Geddes, D., & Callister, R. R. (2007). Crossing the line(s): A dual threshold model of anger in organizations. *Academy of Management Review, 32,* 721–746.

George, J. M. (1990). Personality, affect, and behavior in groups. *Journal of Applied Psychology, 75,* 107–116.

Gibson, D. E., & Callister, R. R. (2010). Anger in organizations: Review and integration. *Journal of Management, 36,* 66–93.

Gooty, J., Gavin, M., & Ashkanasy, N. M. (2009). Emotions research in OB: The challenges that lie ahead. *Journal of Organizational Behavior, 30,* 833–838.

Grandey, A. A. (2003). When "the show must go on": Surface acting and deep acting as determinants of emotional exhaustion and peer rated service delivery. *Academy of Management Journal, 46,* 86–96.

Greenberg, J. (1993). Stealing in the name of justice: Informational and interpersonal moderators of theft reactions to underpayment inequity. *Organizational Behavior and Human Decision Processes, 54,* 81–103.

Greenberg, J., & Scott, K. S. (1996). Why do workers bite the hands that feed them? Employee theft as a social exchange process, *Research in Organizational Behavior, 18,* 111–156.

Greifeneder, R., Bless, H., & Pham, M. T. (2011). When do people rely on affective and cognitive feelings in judgment? A review. *Personality and Social Psychology Review, 15,* 107–141.

Gross, J. J., & Levenson, R. W. (1997). Hiding feelings: The acute effects of inhibiting negative and positive emotion. *Journal of Abnormal Psychology, 106,* 95–103.

Hareli, S., & Rafaeli, A. (2008). Emotion cycles: On the social influence of emotion in organizations. In B. M. Staw & A. P. Brief (Eds.), *Research in organizational behavior* (Vol. 28: pp. 35–59). Oxford, UK: Elsevier.

Harris, K. J., Kacmar, K. M., & Zivnuska, S. (2007). An investigation of abusive supervision as a predictor of performance and the meaning of work as a moderator of the relationship. *Leadership Quarterly, 18,* 252–263.

Härtel, C. E. J., & Ashkanasy, N. M. (2010). Healthy human cultures as positive work environments. In N. M. Ashkanasy, C. E. P. Wilderom, & M. F. Peterson (Eds.), *The handbook of culture and climate* (2nd ed.: pp. 85–100). Thousand Oaks, CA: Sage.

Hartel, C. E. J., Gough, H., & Hartel, G. F. (2008). Work-group emotional climate, emotion management skills, and service attitudes and performance. *Asia Pacific Journal of Human Resources, 46,* 21–37.

Hatfield, E., Cacioppo, J., & Rapson, R. (1994). *Emotional contagion.* New York: Cambridge University Press.

Hershcovis, M. S. (2011). Incivility, social undermining, bullying . . . oh my! A call to reconcile constructs within workplace aggression research. *Journal of Organizational Behavior, 32,* 499–519.

Hershcovis, M. S., Turner, N., Barling, J., Arnold, K. A., Dupre, K. E., Inness, M., LeBlanc, M. M., & Sivanathan, N. (2007). Predicting workplace aggression: A meta-analysis. *Journal of Applied Psychology, 92,* 228–238.

Hochschild, A. R. (1983). *The managed heart: Commercialization of human feeling.* Berkeley: University of California Press.

Hoel, H., Rayner, C., & Cooper, C. L. (1999). Workplace bullying. *International Review of Industrial and Organisational Psychology, 14,* 189–230.

Ilies, R., Wagner, D. T., & Morgeson, F. P. (2007). Explaining affective linkages in teams: Individual differences in susceptibility to contagion and individualism-collectivism. *Journal of Applied Psychology, 92,* 1140–1148.

Jensen, J. M., Opland, R. A., & Ryan, A. M. (2010). Psychological contracts and counterproductive work behaviors: Employee responses to transactional and relational breach. *Journal of Business and Psychology, 25,* 555–568.

Johnson, S. K. (2008). I second that emotion: Effects of emotional contagion and affect at work on leader and follower outcomes. *Leadership Quarterly, 19,* 1–19.

Jones, D. A. (2009). Getting even with one's supervisor and one's organization: Relationships among types of injustice, desires for revenge, and counterproductive work behaviors. *Journal of Organizational Behavior, 30,* 525–542.

Judge, T. A., Scott, B. A., & Illies, R. (2006). Hostility, job attitudes, and workplace deviance: Test of a multilevel model. *Journal of Applied Psychology, 91,* 126–138.

Kelloway, E. K., Francis, L., Prosser, M., & Cameron, J. E. (2010). Counterproductive work behavior as protest. *Human Resource Management Review, 20,* 18–25.

Kelly, J. R., & Barsade, S. G. (2001). Mood and emotions in small groups and work teams. *Organizational Behavior and Human Decision Processes, 86,* 99–130.

Kemper, T. D. (1966). Representative roles and the legitimation of deviance. *Social Problems, 13,* 288–298.

Kidder, D. L. (2005). Is it 'who I am,' 'what I can get away with,' or 'what you've done to me'? A multi-theory examination of employee misconduct. *Journal of Business Ethics, 57,* 389–398.

Kilduff, M., Chiaburu, D. S., & Menges, J. I. (2010). Strategic use of emotional intelligence in organizational settings: Exploring the dark side. *Research in Organizational Behavior: An Annual Series of Analytical Essays and Critical Reviews* (Vol. 30: pp. 129–152). UK: Elsevier.

Kim, T. Y., & Shapiro, D. L. (2008). Retaliation against supervisory mistreatment: Negative emotion, group membership, and cross-cultural difference. *International Journal of Conflict Management, 19,* 339–358.

Larsen, R. J., & Diener, E. (1992). Promises and problems with the circumplex model of emotion. In M. S. Clark (Ed.), *Review of personality and social psychology: Emotion* (Vol. 13: pp. 25–59). Newbury Park, CA: Sage.

Latham, G. P. (2001). The importance of understanding and changing employee outcome expectancies for gaining commitment to an organizational goal. *Personnel Psychology, 54,* 707–716.

Lawler, E. J. (2001). An affect theory of social exchange. *American Journal of Sociology, 107,* 321–352.

Lawler, E. J., & Thye, S. R. (1999). Bringing emotions into social exchange theory. *Annual Review of Sociology, 25,* 217–244.

Lazarus, R. (1991). *Emotion and adaptation.* New York: Oxford University Press.

Lazarus, R. (2006). Emotions and interpersonal relationships: Towards a person-centred conceptualization of emotions and coping. *Journal of Personality, 74,* 9–46.

Lazarus, R., & Folkman, S. (1984). *Stress, appraisal and coping.* New York: Springer.

Lerner, J. S., & Keltner, D. (2001). Fear, anger, and risk. *Journal of Personality and Social Psychology, 81,* 146–159.

Li, A., & Cropanzano, R. (2009). Fairness at the group level: Interunit and intraunit justice climate. *Journal of Management, 35,* 564–599.

Li, Y., Ahlstrom, D., & Ashkanasy, N. M. (2010). A multilevel model of affect and organizational commitment. *Asia Pacific Journal of Management, 27,* 193–213.

Lim, V. K. G. (2002). The IT way of loafing on the job: Cyberloafing, neutralizing and organizational justice. *Journal of Organizational Behavior, 23,* 675–694.

Lim, V. K. G., & Teo, T. S. H. (2009). Mind your E-manners: Impact of cyber incivility on employees' work attitude and behavior. *Information & Management, 46,* 419–425.

Matthiesen, S. P., & Einarsen, S. P. (2007). Perpetrators and Targets of Bullying at Work: Role Stress and Individual Differences. *Violence and Victims, 22,* 735.

Mayer, J. D., & Salovey, P. (1997). What is emotional intelligence? In P. Salovey & D. J. Sluyter (Eds.), *Emotional development and emotional intelligence.* New York: Basic Books.

Meyer, J. P., & Allen, N. J. (1997). *Commitment in the workplace: Theory, research, and application.* Thousand Oaks, CA: Sage.

Milam, A. C., Spitzmueller, C., & Penney, L. M. (2009). Investigating individual differences among targets of workplace incivility. *Journal of Occupational Health Psychology, 14,* 58–69.

Miron-Spektor, E., & Rafaeli, A. (2009). The effects of anger in the workplace: When, where and why observing anger enhances or hinders performance. *Research in Personnel and Human Resource Management, 28,* 153–178.

Mitchell, M. S., & Ambrose, M. L. (2007). Abusive supervision and workplace deviance and the moderating effects of negative reciprocity beliefs. *Journal of Applied Psychology, 92,* 1159–1168.

Morgan, R., & Heiss, D. R. (1988). Structure of emotions. *Social Psychology Quarterly, 51,* 19–31.

Morris, A. J., & Feldman, D. C. (1996). The dimensions antecedents and consequences of emotional labour. *Academy of Management Review, 21,* 986–1010.

Morrison, E. W., & Milliken, F. J. (2000). Organizational silence: A barrier to change and development in a pluralistic world. *Academy of Management Review, 25,* 706–725.

Mulder, R., Pouwelse, M., Lodewijkx, H., & Bolman, C. (2008). Emotional and helping responses among bystanders of victims of mobbing: The role of perceived responsibility and threat of contagion. *Gedrag & Organisatie, 21,* 19–34.

Niedl, K. (1996). Mobbing and well-being: economic and personnel development implications. *European Journal of Work and organizational psychology, 5,* 239–249.

O'Neill, O. A., Vandenberg, R. J., Dejoy, D. M., & Wilson, M. G. (2009). Exploring relationships among anger, perceived organizational support, and workplace outcomes. *Journal of Occupational Health Psychology, 14,* 318–333.

O'Neill, T. A., & Hastings, S. E. (2011). Explaining workplace deviance behavior with more than just the "Big Five." *Personality and Individual Differences, 50,* 268–273.

Penney, L. M., & Spector, P. E. (2002). Narcissism and counterproductive work behavior: Do bigger egos mean bigger problems? *International Journal of Selection and Assessment, 10,* 126–134.

Pizer, K., & Härtel, C. (2005). The quality of the LMX relationship, the currency of exchange, and emotions at work. Paper presented at the Proceedings of the 40th Australian Psychological Society Annual Conference, Melbourne.

Reio. T. G., Jr., & Ghosh, R. (2009). Antecedents and outcomes of workplace incivility: Implications for human resource development research and practice. *Human Resource Development Quarterly, 20,* 237–264.

Restubog, S. L. D., Garcia, P., Wang, L., & Cheng, D. (2010). It's all about control: The role of self-control in buffering the effects of negative reciprocity beliefs and trait anger on workplace deviance. *Journal of Research in Personality, 44,* 655–660.

Robinson, S. L., & Bennett, R. J. (1995). A typology of deviant workplace behaviors: A multidimensional scaling study. *Academy of Management Journal, 38,* 555–572.

Rodell, J. B., & Judge, T. A. (2009). Can "good" stressors spark "bad" behaviors? The mediating role of emotions in links of challenge and hindrance stressors with citizenship and counterproductive behaviors. *Journal of Applied Psychology, 94,* 1438–1451.

Rosen, C. C., Harris, K. J., & Kacmar, K. M. (2009). The emotional implications of organizational politics: A process model. *Human Relations, 62,* 27–57.

Rousseau, D. M. (1989). Psychological and implied contracts in organizations. *Employee Rights and Responsibilities Journal, 2,* 121–139.

Rousseau, D. M., & McLean Parks, J. (1993). The contracts of individuals in organizations. In L. L. Cummings, & B. M. Staw (Eds.), *Research in organizational behavior* (Vol. 15: pp. 1–43). Greenwich, CT: JAI.

Salin, D. (2003). Ways of explaining workplace bullying: A review of enabling, motivating and precipitating structures and processes in the work environment. *Human Relations, 56,* 1213–1232.

Sanchez-Burks, J., & Huy, Q. N. (2009). Emotional aperture and strategic change: The accurate recognition of collective emotions. *Organization Science, 20,* 22–34.

Scheck, C., & Kinicki, A. J. (2000). Identifying the antecedents of coping with an organizational acquisition: A structural assessment *Journal of Organizational Behavior, 21,* 627–648.

Seery, B. L., & Corrigall, E. A. (2009). Emotional labor: Links to work attitudes and emotional exhaustion. *Journal of Managerial Psychology, 24,* 797–813.

Sims, R. L. (2010). A study of deviance as a retaliatory response to organizational power. *Journal of Business Ethics, 92,* 553–563.

Skarlicki, D. P., Folger, R., & Tesluk, P. (1999). Personality as a moderator in the relationship between fairness and retaliation. *Academy of Management Journal, 42,* 100–108.

Skarlicki, D. P., & Kulik, C. T. (2005). Third-party reactions to employee (mis)treatment: A justice perspective, *Research in Organizational Behavior: An Annual Series of Analytical Essays and Critical Reviews* (Vol. 26: pp. 183–229). UK: Elsevier.

Skarlicki, D. P., & Rupp, D. E. (2010). Dual processing and organizational justice: The role of rational versus experiential processing in third-party reactions to workplace mistreatment. *Journal of Applied Psychology, 95,* 944–952.

Sparr, J. L., & Sonnentag, S. (2008). Fairness perceptions of supervisor feedback, LMX, and employee well-being at work. *European Journal of Work and Organizational Psychology, 17,* 198–225.

Spector, P. E., Fox, S., Penney, L. M., Bruursema, K., Goh, A., & Kessler, S. (2006). The dimensionality of counterproductivity: Are all counterproductive behaviors created equal? *Journal of Vocational Behavior, 68,* 446–460.

Spencer, S., & Rupp, D. E. (2009). Angry, guilty, and conflicted: Injustice toward coworkers heightens emotional labor through cognitive and emotional mechanisms. *Journal of Applied Psychology, 94,* 429–444.

Spoor, J. R., & Kelly, J. R. (2004). The evolutionary significance of affect in groups: Communication and group bonding. *Group Processes & Intergroup Relations, 7,* 398–412.

Spoor, J. R., & Kelly, J. R. (2009). Mood convergence in dyads: Effects of valence and leadership. *Social Influence, 4,* 282–297.

Sy, T., Côté, S., & Saavedra, R. (2005). The contagious leader: the impact of the leader's mood on the mood of group members, group affective tone, and group processes. *Journal of Applied Psychology, 90,* 295–305.

Sydney Morning Herald. (2011). "Get your breasts out": IBM employee sues. http://www.smh.com.au/victoria/get-your-breasts-out-ibm-employee-sues-20111020-1m8ut.html, October 20, 2011.

Tellegen, A. (1985). Structures of mood and personality and their relevance to assessing anxiety, with an emphasis on self-report. In H. A. Tuma & J. D. Maser (Eds.), *Anxiety and the anxiety disorders* (pp. 681–706). Hillsdale, NJ: Erlbaum.

Tepper, B. J. (2000). Consequences of abusive supervision. *Academy of Management Journal, 43,* 187–190.

Tepper, B. J. (2007). Abusive supervision in work organizations: Review, synthesis, and research agenda. *Journal of Management, 33,* 261–289.

Tepper, B. J., Carr, J. C., Breaux, D. M., Geider, S., Hu, C. Y., & Hua, W. (2009). Abusive supervision, intentions to quit, and employees' workplace deviance: A power/dependence analysis. *Organizational Behavior and Human Decision Processes, 109,* 156–167.

Tepper, B. J., & Henle, C. A. (2011). A case for recognizing distinctions among constructs that capture interpersonal mistreatment in work organizations. *Journal of Organizational Behavior, 32,* 487–498.

Tepper, B. J., Lambert, L. S., Henle, C. A., Giacalone, R. A., & Duffy, M. K. (2008). Abusive supervision and subordinates' organization deviance. *Journal of Applied Psychology, 93,* 721–732.

Thau, S., Bennett, R. J., Mitchell, M. S., & Marrs, M. B. (2009). How management style moderates the relationship between abusive supervision and workplace deviance: An uncertainty management theory perspective. *Organizational Behavior and Human Decision Processes, 108,* 79–92.

Thau, S., & Mitchell, M. S. (2010). Self-gain or self-regulation impairment? Tests of competing explanations of the supervisor abuse and employee deviance relationship through perceptions of distributive justice. *Journal of Applied Psychology, 95,* 1009–1031.

Tzafrir, S. S., & Hareli, S. (2009). Employees' emotional reactions to promotion decisions: The role of causal attributions and perceptions of justice. *Career Development International, 14,* 351–371.

Vardi, Y., & Wiener, Y. (1996). Misbehavior in organizations: A motivational framework. *Organization Science, 7,* 151–165.

Victor, B., & Cullen, J. B. (1988). The organizational bases of ethical work climates. *Administrative Science Quarterly, 33,* 101–125.

Walter, F., & Bruch, H. (2008). The positive group affect spiral: A dynamic model of the emergence of positive affective similarity in work groups. *Journal of Organizational Behavior, 29,* 239–261.

Wasti, S. A., & Cortina, L. (2002). Coping in context: Sociocultural determinants of responses to sexual harassment. *Journal of Personality and Social Psychology, 83,* 394.

Watson, D., Clark, L. A., & Tellegen, A. (1988). Development and validation of brief measures of positive and negative affect: The PANAS scales. *Journal of Personality and Social Psychology, 54,* 1063–1070.

Watson, D., & Tellegen, A. (1985). Toward a consensual structure of mood. *Psychological Bulletin, 98,* 219–235.

Weiss, H. M., & Beal, D. J. (2005). Reflections on affective events theory. In N. M. Ashkanasy, C. Hartel, & W. Zerbe (Eds.), *Research on Emotion in Organization* (Vol. 1: pp. 1–21). Elsevier Limited.

Weiss, H. M., & Cropanzano, R. (1996). Affective events theory: A theoretical discussion of the structure, causes and consequences of affective experiences at work. *Research in Organizational Behavior, 18,* 1–74.

Weiss, H. M., Sucklow, K., & Cropanzano, R. (1999). Effects of justice conditions on discrete emotions. *Journal of Applied Psychology, 84,* 786–794.

Yang, J. X., & Diefendorff, J. M. (2009). The relations of daily counterproductive workplace behavior with emotions, situational antecedents, and personality moderators: A diary study in Hong Kong. *Personnel Psychology, 62,* 259–295.

Zapf, D. (1999). Organisational, work group related and personal causes of mobbing bullying at work. *International Journal of Manpower, 20,* 70–85.

Zapf, D., & Gross, C. (2001). Conflict escalation and coping with workplace bullying: A replication and extension. *European Journal of Work and Organizational Psychology, 10,* 497–522.

Zapf, D., & Holz, M. (2006). On the positive and negative effects of emotion work in organizations. *European Journal of Work and Organizational Psychology, 15,* 1–28.

Zellars, K. L., Tepper, B. J., & Duffy, M. K. (2002). Abusive supervision and subordinates' organizational citizenship behavior. *Journal of Applied Psychology, 86,* 1068–1076.

Zoghbi-Manrique-de-Lara, P. (2009). Inequity, conflict, and compliance dilemma as causes of cyberloafing. *International Journal of Conflict Management, 20,* 188–201.

Zoghbi-Manrique de Lara, P., & Verano-Tacoronte, D. (2007). Investigating the effects of procedural justice on workplace deviance: Do employees' perceptions of conflicting guidance call the tune? *International Journal of Manpower, 28,* 715–729.

3

Born to Be Deviant?

An Examination of the Relationship between
Workplace Deviance and Employee Personality

CHRISTINE A. HENLE AND MICHAEL A. GROSS

> *The organization has policies and procedures, but it seems that the manager in our office makes up the rules as she goes, in addition to changing rules behind closed doors without input and toward her favor. In my last review she downgraded me because I wasn't enough of a "team player" and I did not earn a raise that year even though I got my projects in on time and under budget. Afterwards, I decided if she could get away with breaking the rules, then I could too. After all, I work here too! I deserve better! I took things in the office that I felt I deserved, came and left as I desired, and blamed others for my mistakes. I stopped getting projects in on time and spent money on whatever I wanted. I went out for drinks every week with the boss after work and did whatever she asked me to do, regardless of our company's policy and procedures. Now my career is advancing and I take what's mine.*
> —Sally, an office worker in a large telecommunications company

Researchers and managers alike have sought for decades to reduce the occurrence of detrimental employee behaviors like theft, unexcused absences or tardiness, sabotage, violence, property destruction, physical assault, on-the-job alcohol or drug use, social undermining, and rudeness. Identifying the antecedents of such behaviors is important because they can impact companies' profitability and inflict psychological and physical distress on the targets of these acts. One line of research suggests that workplace deviance is driven by employee personality traits. That is, certain types of employees, such as those characterized as aggressive, impulsive, or socially inept, are more likely than others to engage in deviant work behaviors.

Based on this literature, we propose a model of workplace deviance (see figure 3.1) in which employees' personality determines whether or not they will engage in deviant work behaviors directed at the organization (organizational deviance) or other employees (interpersonal deviance). These direct relationships, however, will be moderated by additional factors. First, we adopt an interactional approach by arguing that the organizational context may encourage or trigger deviant acts by employees with a propensity toward deviance (for instance, workplace injustice) while other situations may serve as a restraint or deterrent against these behaviors (for instance, security systems). Second, we suggest that the personality traits of other employees may increase the likelihood of interpersonal deviance. Some individuals have personality traits that are perceived as inappropriate, annoying, or hostile, which may provoke deviant acts directed toward them while others may be seen as having weaknesses in their personality, which may lead to them being viewed as an easy target for deviant behavior.

Workplace Deviance: Its Definition, Prevalence, and Consequences

Although many terms have been used to describe workplace deviance, such as counterproductive work behavior, antisocial behavior, organizational retaliatory behavior, organizational misbehavior, and workplace aggression, these seemingly diverse terms have some underlying commonalities. First, these acts are voluntary or intentional. Employees engage in them because they lack the motivation to adhere to organizational norms discouraging deviance or are prompted to violate those norms (Robinson & Bennett, 1995). Second, these behaviors are intended to harm the organization and/ or its members. Even if they do not result in actual harm, they are undesirable for organizations because, at a minimum, they distract from productive work.

Early research investigating workplace deviance focused on two types of deviant behavior: production and property deviance (Hollinger & Clark, 1982). Production deviance refers to behaviors that violate the norms of acceptable production levels, which include physical withdrawal (turnover, absenteeism, lateness), psychological withdrawal (on-the-job drug use, daydreaming), and organizational sabotage (intentionally working slowly). In contrast, property deviance is the unauthorized taking or damaging of organizational property, products, or money, which includes behaviors like theft.

Robinson and Bennett (1995) expanded Hollinger and Clark's operationalization of workplace deviance by incorporating acts directed at individuals, in addition to those directed at organizations. Their typology included not only production and property deviance, but also political deviance and interpersonal aggression. Political deviance is characterized by social interactions that result in placing another at a personal or political disadvantage. Examples of political deviance include showing favoritism, gossiping about coworkers, and blaming coworkers. On the other hand, interpersonal

Fig. 3.1. Model of workplace deviance

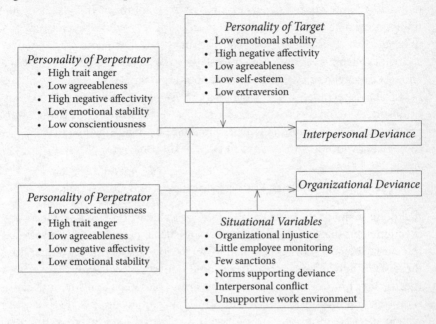

aggression refers to behaving in an aggressive or hostile way toward others, which can include threats, arguing, and physical assault.

In their later work, Bennett and Robinson (2000) developed a measure of workplace deviance and conducted confirmatory factor analyses that supported a two-factor structure consisting of interpersonal and organizational deviance. Recently, meta-analytic evidence indicates that although interpersonal and organizational deviance are highly correlated, they have differential relationships with key variables (Berry, Ones & Sackett, 2007; Hershcovis, Turner, Barling, Arnold, Dupre, Inness, LeBlanc & Sivanathan, 2007). For example, interpersonal deviance is more highly related to agreeableness, interpersonal justice, interpersonal conflict, and trait anger while organizational deviance is correlated more with conscientiousness, job dissatisfaction, situational constraints, and organizational citizenship behavior directed at the organization. Thus, researchers have concluded that interpersonal and organizational deviance are separate and distinct constructs (Berry et al., 2007) and today many differentiate workplace deviance based on whether it is aimed at the organization or its members.

Studies suggest that workplace deviance is common in organizational settings. For example, employee theft and fraud is the fastest growing type of crime in the United States (Coffin, 2003). As much as three quarters of employees steal at least once from their employer (Coffin, 2003) and 95% of all organizations experience employee theft (Case, 2000). Likewise, a recent national survey found that 2.3 million employees reported drinking before going to work, 8.9 million reported drinking during work hours, and 2.1 million reported performing their job while under the influence of alcohol (Frone, 2006). Finally, in the construction industry alone, evidence suggests that fifty-three minutes per employee is lost daily due to time theft ("How Much Can You Save," 2006).

The prevalence of these behaviors is especially disturbing when the costs to both affected organizations and individuals are considered. For instance, the financial costs associated with theft by employees in the U.S. have been estimated at $50 billion annually (Coffin, 2003) while time theft costs American companies more than $177 billion annually (McGee & Fillon, 1995). Further, employees who are targets of workplace deviance are more likely to quit, have stress-related problems, decreased productivity, low morale, lost work time (O'Leary-Kelly, Griffin & Glew, 1996), damaged self-esteem, increased fear and insecurity at work, and psychological and physical pain (Griffin, O'Leary-Kelly & Collins, 1998). Because workplace deviance is common and costly to organizations and their employees, much research has sought to identify its antecedents. Below we describe one possible determinant of workplace deviance, personality.

Personality in the Workplace

Personality refers to individuals' relatively stable and enduring predispositions to think, believe, and behave in certain ways (Ones, Viswesvaran & Dilchert, 2005). Personality consists of an overall profile or combination of traits or characteristics that can be used to differentiate between individuals. These traits result in predictable patterns of thoughts, attitudes, emotions, and behaviors over time and across contexts. Thus, personality offers a useful explanation for why individuals behave as they do both within and outside of the workplace.

The study of personality in organizational settings has had a tumultuous history with many prominent scholars arguing over the years that personality does not meaningfully predict important work outcomes (Davis-Blake & Pfeffer, 1989; Guion & Gottier, 1965; Mischel, 1968). Further, the personality literature has been thwarted by the problem of how to describe and organize the immense number of personality traits into a useful structure that can then be subjected to empirical research. To address the latter issue, researchers conducted factor analyses of studies that systematically reviewed the dictionary to identify words describing personality traits as well as work examining items from a variety of personality measures, in order to identify categories of related traits that are relatively orthogonal. This body of work (see Borgatta, 1964; Costa & McCrae, 1985; Digman & Takemoto-Chock, 1981; Fiske, 1949; Goldberg, 1990; Norman, 1963; Tupes & Christal, 1961) led to widespread acceptance of the five-factor model of personality, often called the Big Five.

The Big Five taxonomy offers a coherent way to organize, structure, and understand the vast amount of personality traits that have been identified and the relationships among them (Digman, 1990; Goldberg, 1990). This model argues that personality is hierarchically organized with five broad factors at the top: extraversion, emotional stability, agreeableness, conscientiousness, and openness to experience. Essentially all personality traits can be classified into one of these factors and this five-factor structure is thought to be universal because it has been replicated in at least fifty different cultures (McCrae, Terracciano & 78 members of the personality profiles of cultures project, 2005), is genetically based (Jang, Livesley & Vernon, 1996), and is stable across peer and self-reports of personality (McCrae, 1982) and throughout adulthood (Roberts & Delvecchio, 2000). Beneath the five broad factors are narrower, more specific and detailed personality traits called facets. For example, conscientiousness can be divided into the following facets: competence, dutifulness, order, achievement striving, self-discipline, and deliberation. Although the facets are somewhat correlated with each other and their corresponding factor, they do have some amount of unique variance (Paunonen & Ashton, 2001).

The first factor, extraversion versus introversion (also called surgency), refers to the extent that individuals are comfortable with interpersonal relationships. Extroverts tend to seek out and enjoy the company of others while introverts are more quiet, reserved, and solitary. Second, emotional stability versus neuroticism assesses the presence and outcomes of negative affect. Individuals at the high end of this factor tend to withstand stress and have a positive outlook while those at the neurotic end are likely to experience negative emotions and distress regularly and to have a pessimistic view of themselves and the world around them. Third, agreeableness evaluates individuals' tendency to be compassionate or humane towards others. Individuals rating high on this factor are often perceived as friendly and likeable. The fourth factor, conscientiousness (also referred to as conformity, dependability, or will to achieve), boils down to an assessment of one's reliability. Individuals rating high on this trait tend to demonstrate greater self-discipline and aim for high levels of achievement and competence. Finally, openness to experience (also called intellect or culture) is the propensity of individuals to relish in new experiences, thoughts, and ideas. Put another way, it represents how narrow or broad one's interests are. Table 3.1 has more details regarding these traits, including a list of the facets for each factor and descriptions of individuals rating high and low on each factor.

The study of personality in the workplace also received a major impetus from meta-analytic studies, which have the unique ability to synthesize and aggregate knowledge based on a multitude of individually conducted studies. These meta-analyses have found relationships between personality and a variety of important work outcomes and thus, demonstrate the critical role personality can play at work. For example, research shows that personality can predict training proficiency and job performance across a variety of occupations (Barrick & Mount, 1991), customer service (Ones & Viswesvaran, 2001), teamwork, organizational citizenship behavior, leadership (Ones et al., 2005), and accidents (Clarke & Roberston, 2008). Personality is even indicative of work attitudes such as job satisfaction (Judge, Heller & Mount, 2002). Further, personality explains job performance beyond that which can be attributed to general mental ability and job knowledge (Schmidt & Hunter, 1998). Thus, managers can glean meaningful insights into employee attitudes and behavior with a basic understanding of their personality.

Personality Traits of the Perpetrators of Workplace Deviance

Although organizational research has traditionally focused on the relationship between personality and prosocial work behaviors like job performance and organizational citizenship behavior, recent attention has turned to investigating whether there is a personality profile for those with a tendency to commit workplace deviance. That is, are there certain types of people who are more likely than others to engage in workplace deviance? This is an important question because if certain personality traits can be linked to workplace deviance, organizational interventions can be designed around these traits.

A growing body of research has examined the relationship between personality and workplace deviance, and in this chapter, we focus on meta-analyses investigating this relationship. Hough and colleagues conducted two meta-analyses which included deviant work behaviors and their taxonomy of personality traits, most of which can be mapped onto the Big Five. In the first study, Kamp and Hough (1986) reviewed research done between 1960 and 1984 and found that emotional stability had the strongest negative relationship with workplace deviance, followed by achievement (a facet of conscientiousness), agreeableness, extraversion, dependability (another facet

Table 3.1

A Description of the Big Five Factors (facets are from Costa and McCrae, 1995)

FACTOR	FACETS*	DESCRIPTORS OF INDIVIDUALS AT THE LOW END OF THE FACTOR	DESCRIPTORS OF INDIVIDUALS AT THE HIGH END OF THE FACTOR
Extraversion	Warmth, Gregariousness, Assertiveness, Activity Excitement seeking, Positive emotion	Reserved, solitary, somber, retiring, sober, silent, timid, cautious	Warm, outgoing, cheerful, gregarious, talkative, sociable, assertive, energetic, enthusiastic, ambitious
Emotional Stability	Anxiety Angry hostility, Depression Self-consciousness Impulsiveness Vulnerability	Sad, scared, nervous, anxious, depressed, high-strung, hypochondriacal, angry, hostile	Calm, stable, poised, composed, unworried, secure, relaxed, self-confident
Agreeableness	Trust, Straightforwardness Altruism, Compliance Modesty Tender-Mindedness	Selfish, aggressive, arrogant, hostile, indifferent to others, self-centered, spiteful, jealous, cold, irritable, suspicious, unsympathetic, uncooperative, inflexible, uncaring, intolerant	Generous, honest, modest, altruistic, nurturing, caring, emotionally supportive, good-natured, trusting, cooperative, softhearted, helpful, warm, straightforward
Conscientiousness	Competence Order Dutifulness, Achievement striving Self-discipline, Deliberation	Laidback, unambitious, weak-willed, disorganized, impulsive, careless, easily distracted, undependable	Hardworking, purposeful, disciplined, responsible, dependable, achievement oriented, persistent, well organized, competent, orderly, dutiful
Openness to Experience	Fantasy Aesthetics Feelings Actions Ideas Values	Rigid, practical, traditional, down to earth, conventional, find comfort in the familiar, simple, cautious, narrow interests	Imaginative, curious, exploratory, open to feelings and new ideas, flexibility of thought, readiness to indulgence in fantasy, creative, artistically sensitive, broad-minded, intellectual, original, polished

of conscientiousness), and openness to experience. In a later meta-analysis, Hough (1992) found that dependability, achievement, emotional stability, and openness to experience were the strongest predictors of workplace deviance while agreeableness and extraversion had very small to no relationship with the criterion. However, it is important to note that neither study corrected the observed correlations for criterion unreliability or range restriction. After making these corrections, Salgado (2002) found that the best predictors of workplace deviance were conscientiousness, agreeableness, and openness to experience.

Meta-analyses regarding integrity tests also shed light on the relationship between personality and workplace deviance. Personality-based integrity tests are compound measures of personality, which means that they evaluate more than one of the Big Five factors (Hough & Schneider, 1996). Empirical evidence indicates that these tests primarily assess conscientiousness, agreeableness, and emotional stability (Sackett & Wanek, 1996). The premise behind compound traits is that measuring multiple personality traits, especially if they are theoretically and empirically selected, should result in higher criterion related validity than using any one factor or facet. In their review of the validity of integrity tests for personnel selection, Ones, Viswesvaran, and Schmidt (1993) found that personality-based integrity tests had an operational validity of .32 for predicting workplace deviance.

Some general conclusions can be drawn from this body of work. Similar to Sackett and DeVore (2001), we believe that conscientiousness is the strongest indicator of workplace deviance. Likewise, it appears that emotional stability and agreeableness have moderate relationships with deviance and that openness to experience and extraversion seem to be the weakest predictors of these behaviors. Together, conscientiousness, emotional stability, and agreeableness may be the best determinants of workplace deviance. However, there is a growing body of work that suggests the narrower facet measures of personality offer incremental validity over the aforementioned factors in predicting workplace deviance (see Ashton, 1998; Dudley, Orvis, Lebiecki & Cortina, 2006; Mount & Barrick, 1995).

Empirical work indicates that aggregating facet measures into an overall factor can mask important relationships and lead researchers to falsely assume that a particular factor is not related to a criterion when its subcomponents may provide important insight. Hastings and O'Neill (2006) found that the appropriate level of analysis (factor versus facet) depended on the personality trait under examination. Their findings suggest that agreeableness and conscientiousness were better predictors of workplace deviance than their respective individual facets. However, for the other factors, their facets provided more useful information regarding the occurrence of deviance. First, extraversion was not a significant predictor of workplace deviance, but its facets, friendliness and excitement seeking, were negatively and positively related to deviance, respectively. Similarly, neuroticism was not related to deviance, but its facets, anger and immoderation, were positively related. Finally, openness to experience was negatively related to deviance, but three of its facets (artistic interests, emotionality, and intellect) were slightly better predictors. Thus, measuring extraversion, neuroticism, and openness to experience at the factor level would mask important facet level findings and lead to inappropriate conclusions regarding the relationship between personality and workplace deviance. This may explain why meta-analyses at the factor level did not find a significant relationship between workplace deviance and either extraversion or openness to experience. Thus, both broad and narrow personality traits are valid predictors of deviance, especially if selected a priori based on strong theoretical and empirical relationships to the type of deviance under investigation (Schneider, Hough & Dunnette, 1996; Tett, Jackson & Rothstein, 1991).

Although the aforementioned studies suggest a relationship between workplace deviance and personality, they fail to distinguish between the different types of deviance. In their meta-analysis, Berry et al. (2007) argue that combining various forms of deviance may mask important and differential relationships with personality. These researchers found that interpersonal deviance most strongly correlated with agreeableness, followed by emotional stability and conscientiousness while organizational deviance was most strongly related to conscientiousness, followed by agreeableness and emotional stability. Openness to experience and extraversion had small to no relationship with either type of deviance. Likewise, Hershcovis and colleagues (2007) found that trait anger was a stronger predictor of interpersonal deviance than it was of organizational deviance. These results support our previous conclusion that conscientiousness, emotional stability, and agreeableness are the best predictors of workplace deviance. However, the relative importance of these traits varies depending on the type of deviance under consideration.

Personality Traits of the Targets of Workplace Deviance

The personality characteristics of employees on the receiving end of workplace deviance should also be taken into consideration as they may explain why some employees, unwittingly or wittingly, become targets of interpersonal deviance. Olweus (1978), in his research on bullying among schoolchildren, identified two types of victims. First, submissive victims include individuals who are perceived by bullies as unable to defend themselves or to retaliate because they are passive, insecure, socially withdrawn, and anxious. Individuals displaying these personality traits signal to aggressors that they would be easy targets. Conversely, provocative victims are often targets of interpersonal aggression because they provoke it by exhibiting personality driven behaviors that are considered to be hostile, annoying, threatening, demanding, or interpersonally inappropriate (they are irritable, uncooperative, unsympathetic, disorganized, unreliable, or careless).

Studies investigating the personality characteristics of the targets of interpersonal deviance have mostly focused on the victims of workplace bullying. This research, conducted primarily in Europe, suggests that the strongest predictor of a person being a target of bullying is low emotional stability (Coyne, Chong, Seigne & Randall, 2003; Coyne, Seigne & Randall, 2000; Glaso, Matthiesen, Nielsen & Einarsen, 2007; Vartia, 1996). This finding is also supported by research regarding the victims of uncivil workplace behaviors such as rude or unprofessional comments, exclusion, insinuating glances, and negative gestures (Milam, Spitzmueller & Penney, 2009). Similarly, research examining the targets of workplace bullying (Zapf, 1999), abusive supervision (Tepper, Duffy, Henle & Lambert, 2006), and workplace victimization (Aquino & Bradfield, 2000; Aquino, Grover, Bradfield & Allen, 1999) found that negative affectivity, a trait similar to neuroticism, significantly differentiates between employees who are singled out as targets for interpersonal deviance and those who are not.

Although low emotional stability and high negative affectivity appear to be the best indicators of being a target of interpersonal deviance, past research demonstrates that other personality traits may play a role. For example, victims of interpersonal deviance have also been shown to be low in agreeableness (Glaso et al., 2007; Milam et al., 2009) and self-esteem (Vartia, 1996; Zapf, 1999). Extraversion and conscientiousness may contribute as well, but the findings for these traits are less than conclusive. Some research suggests that individuals low in extraversion are more likely to be targets of workplace bullying (Coyne et al., 2000; Glaso et al., 2007) while other studies failed to find a significant relationship (Coyne et al., 2003; Vartia, 1996). Likewise, there have been mixed findings regarding conscientiousness as some studies suggest that the targets of bullying were more likely to be high in conscientiousness (Coyne et al., 2000) while others found that those low in conscientiousness were more likely to be targets (Glaso et al., 2007).

In summary, the literature offers evidence that there are personality differences between employees who are targets of interpersonal deviance and those who are not. Specifically, victims of these deviant behaviors are more likely to be anxious, nervous, depressed, distressed, high-strung, easily upset, neurotic, and to experience negative emotions. Targets may also be characterized as introverted, ill-tempered, difficult, stubborn, and hampered by self-doubt. In some cases, these traits may illicit interpersonal deviance because they violate social norms while in other instances they signal to instigators a weakness to be exploited. With that said, we offer a caveat to this discussion. We are not blaming the victims of interpersonal deviance, downplaying their suffering as a result of these behaviors, or excusing the perpetrators of these acts from blame. Rather, we are suggesting that by analyzing the personality traits that differentiate the targets of interpersonal deviance from nontargets, we can identify those employees who may currently be the recipients of deviance or who are at risk for being targets in the future and intervene to minimize or prevent the negative effects of these behaviors. These interventions will be discussed in more detail in a later section.

An Interactional Approach to Workplace Deviance:
Personality by Situation Interactions

The interactional perspective recognizes that personality alone cannot explain all incidents of workplace deviance. Rather, this approach acknowledges that more variance can be accounted for in deviant work behaviors by focusing on how personality traits interact with the work environment (Hattrup & Jackson, 1996; House, Shane & Herold, 1996). According to this perspective, personality traits may predispose individuals to behave in a deviant manner, but they will only do so when the situation or work setting triggers or enables this tendency. That is, situations can influence personality in one of two ways. First, personality is contextual because it influences how individuals interpret, and thus respond, to different situations (see Mischel, 1973). For example, employees high in negative affectivity tend to perceive situations or events in a negative manner even when they objectively are not. These negative perceptions may, in turn, cause them to react with workplace deviance.

Second, the effects of personality are often moderated by the strength of the situation (Barrick & Mount, 2005). Strong situations offer clear and unambiguous signals of appropriate and inappropriate behavior and incentives to comply with these cues while weak situations have few guidelines as to what is acceptable or expected. In strong situations most individuals will behave in the same manner because personality is constrained by explicit directives or norms. However, in weak situations employees have greater discretion in how they behave, thus allowing their personality to influence their actions. For instance, employee theft is less likely in companies with a zero tolerance policy that is enforced through surveillance cameras and regular employee searches (strong situation) than in companies whose supervisors occasionally turn a blind eye to these behaviors (weak situation). In conclusion, any discussion of the relationship between personality and workplace deviance must take into account the organizational context because certain individuals may interpret and react differently depending on the situation and certain situations may encourage or suppress displays of personality.

We reviewed interactional studies of workplace deviance and found that organizational justice was a commonly examined situational variable. Taken together, these studies suggest that certain types of employees are more likely to react to workplace injustices with deviance. For instance, distributive injustice (perceived unfairness of workplace outcomes like pay or raises) was more strongly related to deviance when individuals were low in agreeableness (Flaherty & Moss, 2007). Likewise, workplace deviance was more likely to occur in response to interactional injustice (perceived unfairness of interpersonal treatment received from decision makers) when individuals were low in agreeableness (Scott & Colquitt, 2007), low in socialization, or high in impulsivity (Henle, 2005). Two studies found more complex interactions between personality and organizational justice. Skarlicki, Folger, and Tesluk (1999) demonstrated that employees were more likely to retaliate against their employer when they perceived either low distributive justice or low interactional justice, and were either high in negative affectivity or low in agreeableness. Finally, one study found that organizational deviance was more prevalent when employees perceived low distributive justice, were low in self-control, and had jobs requiring high levels of emotional regulation (Bechtoldt, Welk, Hartig & Zapf, 2007).

A second set of studies indicates that organizational controls or deterrents, like employee monitoring, sanctions for those caught behaving in a deviant fashion, and organizational norms discouraging deviance, could minimize the likelihood of workplace deviance by those with a predisposition toward these behaviors. For example, Mikulay, Neuman, and Finkelstein (2001) found that undergraduate students low in integrity were more likely to report intentions to commit workplace deviance when they perceived little likelihood of being caught and few consequences if they were caught. Similarly, Marcus and Schuler (2004) showed that employees low in internal control (that is, low self-control, low integrity) were more likely to engage in deviant work behaviors when they perceived few organizational controls. Finally, one study found a three-way interaction between integrity, organizational controls, and employee engagement (Fine, Horowitz, Weigler & Basis, 2010). Employees were more likely to perform deviant acts when they were low in integrity, perceived few organizational controls, and were not engaged at work.

Although most interactional studies of workplace deviance looked at organizational justice or controls, other work suggests that companies can also minimize deviance by certain types of employees by creating jobs and a work environment that is supportive, challenging, and encouraging (Colbert, Mount, Harter, Witt & Barrick, 2004) or by reducing organizational constraints (such as lack of resources), incivility, interpersonal conflict (Penney & Spector, 2005), and workplace exclusion (such as rejection, ostracism, silent treatment; Hitlan & Noel, 2009). Admittedly, our review of the literature is not exhaustive; however its findings do offer some interesting insights. Employees with a propensity for workplace deviance will be more likely to act in a deviant manner when their employer treats them unfairly, takes few security precautions or sanctions against deviance, does not instill norms discouraging deviance, is unsupportive, offers mundane work, or has pervasive interpersonal conflict.

Organizational Interventions for the
Perpetrators of Workplace Deviance

Although we acknowledge that there are many things companies can do in response to deviance, such as disciplining or firing perpetrators or modifying the workplace to create strong situations in which the personality traits associated with deviance are suppressed, we will focus our discussion specifically on personality-based interventions.

Integrity Tests. Empirical research demonstrates that individuals most likely to engage in workplace deviance are those who are low in conscientiousness, agreeableness, and emotional stability. Employers can prevent these individuals from becoming organizational members by screening for these personality traits during the hiring process. Integrity tests are one such measure that companies can implement because they measure all of the aforementioned personality traits. Integrity tests refer to pre-employment paper-and-pencil tests used to screen out job applicants who are likely to engage in deviant work behaviors once on the job. These tests are relatively inexpensive, valid predictors of not only deviance, but also job performance, and are legally defensible because they have little to no adverse impact.

Sackett, Burris, and Callahan (1989) distinguished between two types of integrity tests. First, overt integrity tests, also referred to as clear purpose tests, are designed to predict a particular type of deviance such as theft, violence, or on-the-job alcohol or drug use. The first section of these tests directly asks about attitudes, beliefs, and thoughts regarding a specific type of workplace deviance (most often theft) and includes items such as "Every normal person is tempted at times to steal" and "Nearly every person that has a job could figure out a way to steal something without getting caught" (Dalton, Metzger & Wimbush, 1994). The second section solicits admissions about past or current participation in theft and other deviant behaviors, such as "I have taken some things from my previous employers."

The second type of integrity test, personality-based or disguised purpose, is of more relevance for our purposes. These tests do not blatantly ask about beliefs toward or participation in workplace deviance, but rather assess personality traits that are often associated with the tendency to engage in these behaviors. The purpose of these tests is to predict a broad array of deviance versus one narrow type (such as theft). Items contained in these tests are things like "You love to take chances," "You never would talk back to a boss or a teacher," and "You work hard and steady at whatever you undertake" (Sackett et al., 1989).

As mentioned in an earlier section, Ones et al. (1993) found that personality-based integrity tests have a corrected mean validity of .32 for predicting deviant work behaviors. Further, they found that these tests are also valid predictors of job performance. Indeed, integrity tests have been singled out as the employee selection tool with the largest incremental validity in predicting job performance over cognitive ability tests (Schmidt & Hunter, 1998). Thus, organizations can effectively use these tests to determine which applicants will refrain from workplace deviance and are likely to be high performers once on the job.

However, a major concern regarding the use of integrity tests is the likelihood that individuals will be able to "fake good" on them or make themselves appear as more honest than they really are. This is a legitimate issue because individuals who distort their responses on these tests may score higher, and thus be more likely to be considered for employment (see Mueller-Hanson, Heggestad & Thornton, 2003). Research in experimental and organizational settings has found that individuals can fake good on these tests (Rothstein & Goffin, 2006), but that overt integrity tests are more susceptible to faking and coaching on how to answer test items in order to score more favorably than personality-based tests (Alliger & Dwight, 2000). Although research suggests that faking can happen, especially for overt tests, Ones et al. (1993) concluded after their extensive meta-analysis that faking does not seem to hurt the validity of these tests. That is, despite applicants' efforts to "beat" these tests, they are still valid predictors of workplace deviance and job performance.

Other concerns organizations may have when considering the use of personality-based integrity tests is how they will be perceived by job applicants and the legality of these tests. First, negative reactions to the selection process may result in perceptions of unfairness, feelings of privacy invasion, lower likelihood of accepting a job offer, and bad publicity. Fortunately, a literature review by Sackett and Wanek (1996) found that these tests are not usually perceived negatively and they fall in the middle of a wide range of employee selection devices in terms of relevance, fairness, and invasiveness. Second, there is currently no federal law prohibiting the use of integrity tests in employments settings (they are prohibited in Massachusetts, however, and their use is restricted in Rhode Island). Further, research indicates that integrity tests do not have adverse impact (Sackett et al., 1989), and thus, should not result in discrimination claims or hurt companies' diversity efforts. In summary, personality-based integrity tests are valid predictors of workplace deviance and job performance, are relatively immune to faking, are perceived favorably by applicants, and are not likely to be legally challenged.

Employment Interviews. Employment interviews are the most commonly used method for selecting new hires and they can be divided into two broad categories. First, unstructured interviews are informal conversations between an interviewer and a job applicant in which the interviewer does not follow a prepared list of questions, but rather asks any question that comes to mind. This free flowing exchange of information may not necessarily be relevant to the job vacancy. Conversely, structured interviews adhere to a predetermined list of job-related questions that are asked of every applicant. These questions ask how the applicant has handled (behavioral) or would handle (situational) job relevant situations. Meta-analyses suggest that interviews, especially structured ones, are reliable and valid predictors of job performance across many different jobs (see Conway, Jako & Goodman, 1995; Schmidt & Hunter, 1998; Schmidt & Rader, 1999). Further, interviews do not result in adverse impact against protected classes, they are relatively easy and inexpensive to conduct (Hough, Oswald & Ployhart, 2001), and applicants often perceive and react to them more favorably than other selection methods (Hausknecht, Day & Thomas, 2004).

One reason why interviews may be a useful tool for assessing personality, and thus reducing workplace deviance, is that managers already use them to evaluate applicant personality even though more specific measures, like integrity tests, exist (Huffcutt, Conway, Roth & Stone, 2001). Many interviewers believe that an important goal of interviews is to gather information about an applicant's personality (Rothstein & Jackson, 1984) and meta-analytic evidence suggests that personality, especially conscientiousness and emotional stability, is the most commonly assessed construct during interviews (Huffcutt et al., 2001). Thus, interviews are commonly used to gauge personality, but are they accurate in this regard?

Research suggests that interviewers' assessments of personality are valid predictors of job performance and converge with self and peer reports of applicant personality. For instance, a meta-analysis found that interviewer ratings of personality, especially in structured interviews, predicted job performance (Huffcutt et al., 2001). In particular, emotional stability, agreeableness, and conscientiousness, the personality traits most related to workplace deviance, had high corrected mean validities and the first two were valid predictors of performance across many different jobs. Further, Barrick, Patton, and Haugland (2000) found moderate correlations between interviewers' ratings of personality and self-reported personality. Likewise, Blackman (2002) found relatively high agreement among interviewer, peer, and self ratings of an applicant's personality, which indicates that interviewers are fairly accurate at assessing personality. It is important to note that these studies did not specifically design their interviews to assess personality. However, Van Iddekinge, Raymark, and Roth (2005) created interview questions to measure job relevant personality traits and found support for their use. They also provide preliminary evidence that structured interviews designed to assess personality may be harder to fake than traditional paper-and-pencil tests of personality.

Given this research, it is reasonable to assume that structured interviews could be a valid mechanism for evaluating applicant personality. Managers commonly use interviews to get a feel for an applicant's personality and research shows that they are accurate when compared to self and peer ratings of personality. Further, interviewers' ratings of personality are valid predictors of prosocial behaviors, like job performance, and it is hard to fake personality in an interview setting. Thus, managers should incorporate questions pertaining to conscientiousness, emotional stability, and agreeableness into structured interviews in order to screen out applicants likely to behave in a deviant manner on the job. We provide some examples of such interview questions in table 3.2.

As our review of the literature indicates, certain types of employees are more likely than others to be targets of interpersonal deviance. Specifically, individuals low in emotional stability or agreeableness or high in negative affectivity are likely to be provocative victims while those who are introverted or low in self-esteem are likely to be submissive victims. Organizations need to identify at-risk individuals before they become victims, increase their awareness of how their behavior may lead to others perceiving them as a target for interpersonal deviance, and provide them with the training and support they need to avoid or diffuse situations involving deviance. Self-awareness could be facilitated through a mentor while conflict management techniques would give potential targets the skills they need to handle these negative behaviors.

Mentoring. The first step in protecting employees from being targets of interpersonal deviance is to enhance their awareness of what personality

Table 3.2
Examples of Structured Interview Questions: Organizational Interventions for the Targets of Workplace Deviance

Personality Factor	Sample Questions
Conscientiousness	Sometimes we need to go above and beyond our normal job duties and requirements in order to deliver quality service and products. Describe a time when you took on additional roles or duties and what the outcomes were of this effort.
	Tell me about a time when a project you were working on wasn't quite up to the standards you thought it should be. That is, it was not of the quality you would have liked it to be. How did you handle this discrepancy between your standards and others and what was the outcome?
	Describe to me a time when you took the initiative in a major project. What did you specifically do and how did it turn out?
Emotional Stability	Tell me about a time when your workload was beginning to be too much and you were experiencing a lot of pressure. How did you handle this situation?
	Describe a time when you felt irritated or frustrated while dealing with a customer or coworker who was demanding beyond an acceptable level. What steps did you take to resolve this situation and what was the outcome?
	Tell me about a time when something or someone shocked or upset you at work, but you had to appear composed. How did you handle this situation?
Agreeableness	Tell me about a time that you got coworkers who disagreed with each other to work together and become a productive team.
	Describe a time when a coworker came to you for help. What was the situation? Describe what you did.
	Give an example of a time when you could not provide what a customer or coworker wanted. Explain how you handled the situation.

characteristics may provoke or enable deviance. One way that at-risk individuals can acquire this insight is through mentoring. Mentoring refers to one-on-one situations in which a more experienced employee in a position of power (mentor) provides a less experienced employee (mentee) with support, advice, and training in order to assist with his or her career goals (Kram, 1985). This relationship has been characterized as "the most intense and powerful one-on-one developmental relationship, entailing the most influence, identification, and emotional involvement" (Wanberg, Welsh & Hezlett, 2003, 41).

Mentoring has two main purposes (Kram, 1985). The first, career functions, refers to supportive actions designed to provide mentees with opportunities to develop their human capital and advance their careers (through challenging work assignments, exposure to powerful others, sponsorship for promotion, skill development, protection). Conversely, psychosocial functions offer interpersonal support through friendship, counseling, encouragement, acceptance, listening, confirmation, and role modeling. This type of support facilitates the mentee's feelings of competence and helps him or her assimilate into the organization's culture. Both mentoring functions have beneficial career outcomes for employees such as greater compensation, promotions, and career and job satisfaction (Allen, Eby, Poteet, Lentz & Lima, 2004).

The psychosocial function of mentoring is especially relevant to those with personality traits that may make them susceptible to interpersonal deviance. Mentors could provide these individuals with feedback on the appropriateness of their behaviors and how they are perceived by others in the organization. Likewise, mentors can counsel them on more appropriate and socially acceptable behaviors and serve as a role model by demonstrating the behaviors that are less likely to encourage deviance. Specifically, mentors need to highlight and encourage behaviors that are consistent with high levels of emotional stability, agreeableness, self-esteem, and extraversion and discourage behaviors associated with low levels of these traits. However, for mentoring to be successful, the matching process between mentor and mentee is crucial (Wanberg, Kammeyer-Mueller & Marchese, 2006). Selecting mentors who are also low on the aforementioned traits would be counterproductive. Thus, the personality of potential mentors must be determined to make sure that they exhibit traits that are not likely to induce deviance. In summary, mentoring may assist "at-risk" individuals with successful integration into their workgroup as well as the organization as a whole (Chao, 2009), which in turn, may reduce their likelihood of being targets of interpersonal deviance.

Conflict Management Behaviors. Mentoring can enhance potential targets' awareness of the types of behaviors that are more or less likely to induce interpersonal deviance. The next step is to acquire conflict management skills, through either mentors or formalized training programs, that can improve victims' responses to incidences of interpersonal deviance; thus, providing them with the skills necessary for effectively managing situations involving deviance. Conflict management falls into three types of behaviors: avoiding, contending, and collaborating. We argue that submissive and provocative victims tend to overuse avoiding and contending, respectively, and could benefit instead from regularly using a collaborating approach.

Submissive victims may be perceived as unlikely to defend themselves against acts of deviance because they over rely on avoidant conflict management behaviors. Avoidance or withdraw occurs when employees physically or psychologically remove themselves from a situation. This indirect and uncooperative approach includes behaviors such as denial, being indirect and evasive, changing and/or avoiding topics, employing noncommittal remarks, and making irrelevant remarks or joking as a way to avoid dealing with the issue at hand (Gross & Guerrero, 2000; Gross, Guerrero & Alberts, 2004; Sillars, 1986; Wilmot & Hocker, 2007).

Victims of interpersonal deviance need to recognize that avoiding behaviors are not appropriate in all situations, and thus they should not use this strategy as their default way of handling conflict. For instance, protecting (actively working to keep from confronting the other party), withdrawing (removing oneself from the situation to avoid further exposure to deviance), and smoothing (emphasizing commonalities with the perpetrator and completely avoiding sensitive issues; Jones & Brinkert, 2008) may be viable avoidance behaviors when a situation is of low importance, when both the situation and the work relationship is of low importance, and when attempts of collaboration and contending are not likely to be effective and may even make the situation worse. Avoidance can also be beneficial in avoiding embarrassment and for buying time to prepare for a collaborating or contending approach. Unfortunately, submissive victims often use avoidance in inappropriate situations, such as when the issue is important to them, when it is their responsibility to make a decision, when both parties are unwilling to make concessions and the issue must be resolved, and when prompt attention is needed (Rahim, 2002). Victims need to recognize that the inappropriate use of avoidance may intensify the level of deviance, further damage relationships, or signal a lack of commitment to others in the workplace.

Contending (also referred to as distributive or controlling) conflict management behaviors take a direct and uncooperative approach to situations involving conflict and try to maximize one's own interests at the expense of others' needs. These behaviors rely on the use of position power, aggression, verbal dominance, and perseverance and include things like confrontational remarks, accusations, personal criticism, rejection, hostile imperatives or threats, antagonistic jokes or teasing, aggressive questions, presumptive remarks, and denial of responsibility at the expense of the other person (Gross & Guerrero, 2000; Gross et al., 2004; Sillars, 1986; Wilmot & Hocker, 2007).

This approach is often associated with provocative victims of interpersonal deviance as their behaviors are frequently aggressive, uncooperative, and competitive. These victims need to be aware that contending behaviors may lead to their own perceived incivility in the workplace and may attract additional deviant behaviors directed at them. Further, contending is not an effective strategy in situations, like the workplace, where there are long-term relationships with regular interaction. These behaviors can harm relationships because they focus on one party's desired outcomes at the expense of the other party's needs, neglect building and maintaining relationships, and often resort to covert means to hurt the other party (Wilmot & Hocker, 2007).

Rather, provocative victims need to learn to use contending appropriately when an issue is very important to them and they want to demonstrate their commitment to it, other conflict management strategies will not work, and when others agree that contending behavior is a sign of strength and a natural response to the context and/or circumstance (Wilmot & Hocker, 2007). For example, situations where a contending style can be appropriate include when the issue is routine, when a speedy decision is needed, when an unpopular course of action is to be implemented, when it is necessary to overcome an assertive subordinate, when an unfavorable decision by the other party may be costly, when subordinates lack expertise to make technical decisions, and when an issue is of personal importance (Rahim, 2002). Conversely, contending is often inappropriate when the issue is complex, when the issue is not personally important, when both parties are equally powerful, when a decision does not have to be made quickly, and when subordinates possess a high degree of competence (Rahim, 2002).

Collaborating (also called integrating or solution-oriented) conflict management behaviors are both direct and cooperative because they overtly address the conflict through creative problem solving so that both parties can meet their needs. As shown in table 3.3, these behaviors include analytic remarks (descriptive, disclosing, qualifying, and soliciting statements) and conciliatory remarks (supportive comments, concessions, and statements showing acceptance of responsibility) designed to keep future interactions intact by opening the lines of communication and increasing information seeking and sharing (Gross & Guerrero, 2000; Gross et al., 2004; Sillars, 1986; Wilmot & Hocker, 2007).

Table 3.3
Descriptions of Collaborative Tactics (adapted from Sillars, 1986)

Analytic Remarks

1. Descriptive statements: Nonevaluative statements about observable events related to conflict.
2. Disclosing statements: Nonevaluative statements about events related to conflict that the partner cannot observe, such as thoughts, feelings, intentions, motivations, and past history.
3. Qualifying statements: Statements that explicitly qualify the nature and extent of conflict.
4. Solicitation of disclosure: Nonhostile questions about events related to conflict that cannot be observed (thoughts, feelings, intentions, motives, or past history).
5. Solicitation of criticism: Nonhostile questions soliciting criticism of oneself.

Conciliatory Remarks

1. Supportive remarks: Statements that refer to understanding, support, acceptance, positive regard for the partner, shared interests, and goals.
2. Concessions: Statements that express a willingness to change, show flexibility, make concessions, or consider mutually acceptable solutions to conflicts.
3. Acceptance of responsibility: Statements that attribute responsibility for conflict to self or to both parties.

Conclusion

Workplace deviance is a costly and prevalent phenomenon in everyday organizational life. As a result, managers need to understand the causes of deviance in order to prevent its occurrence. Our model of workplace deviance suggests that employees' personality determines whether or not they will engage in interpersonal or organizational deviance. Specifically, research indicates that employees low in conscientiousness, agreeableness, and emotional stability are more likely to commit workplace deviance. Unfortunately, the perpetrators of interpersonal deviance are more likely to target certain individuals who they perceive as deserving or easy victims. Employees are more likely to be the recipient of deviance if they are introverted or low in emotional stability, agreeableness, or self-esteem. However, employees are less likely to show deviant behavior in situations where their employer treats them fairly, monitors their behavior, cultivates norms against and imposes sanctions for deviance, is supportive, or minimizes unhealthy interpersonal conflict.

In order to mitigate the relationship between employee personality and workplace deviance, managers need to prevent individuals with a predisposition towards deviance from entering the workplace. Research suggests that employers can do this through integrity tests, which are not only valid predictors of workplace deviance, but also job performance. Hiring managers can also use structured interviews to determine whether job applicants have the personality traits commonly associated with workplace deviance. Not only are these selection tools effective, but they are also relatively inexpensive and easy to administer, they are hard to fake, they are perceived favorably by applicants, and they do not have adverse impact on protected groups. Unfortunately, no selection system is perfect and some individuals with a propensity towards deviance may be hired and act deviantly towards their coworkers. Companies need to identify employees who are at risk for becoming targets of interpersonal deviance, increase their awareness of the personality traits likely to induce deviance, and teach them behaviors that will minimize their chances of becoming a victim. Self insight could be facilitated through mentoring while conflict management skills would protect at risk individuals from deviant acts and help them successfully resolve them should they occur.

The authors would like to thank Ray Hogler for his insightful comments on an earlier version of this chapter.

REFERENCES

Allen, T. D., Eby, L. T., Poteet, M. L., Lentz, E., & Lima, L. (2004). Career benefits associated with mentoring for protégés: A meta-analysis. *Journal of Applied Psychology, 89*, 127–136.

Alliger, G. M., & Dwight, S. A. (2000). A meta-analytic investigation of the susceptibility of integrity tests to faking and coaching. *Educational and Psychological Measurement, 60*, 59–72.

Aquino, K., & Bradfield, M. (2000). Perceived victimization in the workplace: The role of situational factors and victim characteristics. *Organization Science, 11*, 525–537.

Aquino, K., Grover, S. L., Bradfield, M., & Allen, D. G. (1999). The effects of negative affectivity, hierarchical status, and self-determination on workplace victimization. *Academy of Management Journal, 42*, 260–272.

Ashton, M. C. (1998). Personality and job performance: The importance of narrow traits. *Journal of Organizational Behavior, 19*, 289–303.

Barrick, M. R., & Mount, M. K. (1991). The Big Five personality dimensions and job performance: A meta-analysis. *Personnel Psychology, 44*, 1–26.

Barrick, M. R., & Mount, M. K. (2005). Yes, personality matters: Moving on to more important matters. *Human Performance, 18,* 359–372.

Barrick, M. R., Patton, G. K., & Haugland, S. N. (2000). Accuracy of interviewer judgments of job applicant personality traits. *Personnel Psychology, 53,* 925–951.

Bechtoldt, M. N., Welk, C., Hartig, J., & Zapf, D. (2007). Main and moderating effects of self-control, organizational justice, and emotional labour on counterproductive behavior at work. *European Journal of Work and Organizational Psychology, 16,* 479–500.

Bennett, R. J., & Robinson, S. L. (2000). The development of a measure of workplace deviance. *Journal of Applied Psychology, 85,* 349–360.

Berry, C. M., Ones, D. S., & Sackett, P. R. (2007). Interpersonal deviance, organizational deviance, and their common correlates: A review and meta-analysis. *Journal of Applied Psychology, 92,* 410–424.

Blackman, M. C. (2002). Personality judgment and the utility of the unstructured employment interview. *Basic and Applied Social Psychology, 24,* 241–250.

Borgatta, E. F. (1964). The structure of personality characteristics. *Behavioral Science, 9,* 8–17.

Case, J. (2000). *Employee theft: The profit killer.* Del Mar, CA: John Case.

Chao, G. T. (2009). Formal mentoring: Lessons learned from past practice. *Professional Psychology: Research and Practice, 40,* 314–320.

Clarke, S., & Roberston, I. (2008). An examination of the role of personality in work accidents using meta-analysis. *Applied Psychology: An International Review, 57,* 94–108.

Coffin, B. (2003). Breaking the silence on white-collar crime. *Risk Management, 50,* 8.

Colbert, A. E., Mount, M. K., Harter, J. K., Witt, L. A., & Barrick, M. R. (2004). Interactive effects of personality and perceptions of the work situation on workplace deviance. *Journal of Applied Psychology, 89,* 599–609.

Conway, J. M., Jako, R. A., & Goodman, D. F. (1995). A meta-analysis of interrater and internal consistency reliability of selection interviews. *Journal of Applied Psychology, 80,* 565–579.

Costa, P. T., & McCrae, R. R. (1985). *The NEO Personality Inventory manual.* Odessa, FL: Psychological Assessment Resources.

Coyne, I., Seigne, E., & Randall, P. (2000). Predicting workplace victim status from personality. *European Journal of Work and Organizational Psychology, 9,* 335–349.

Coyne, I., Chong, P. S., Seigne, E., & Randall, P. (2003). Self and peer nominations of bullying: An analysis of incident rates, individual differences, and perceptions of the working environment. *European Journal of Work and Organizational Psychology, 12,* 209–228.

Dalton, D. R., Metzger, M. B., & Wimbush, J. C. (1994). Integrity testing for personnel selection: A review and research agenda. *Research in Personnel and Human Resources Management, 12,* 125–160.

Davis-Blake, A., & Pfeffer, J. (1989). Just a mirage—The search for dispositional effects in organizational research. *Academy of Management Review, 14,* 385–400.

Digman, J. M. (1990). Personality structure: Emergence of the five-factor model. *Annual Review of Psychology, 41,* 417–440.

Digman, J. M., & Takemoto-Chock, N. K. (1981). Factors in the natural language of personality: Re-analysis, comparison, and interpretation of six major studies. *Multivariate Behavioral Research, 16,* 149–170.

Dudley, N. M., Orvis, K. A., Lebiecki, J. E., & Cortina, J. M. (2006). A meta-analytic investigation of conscientiousness in the prediction of job performance: Examining the intercorrelations and the incremental validity of narrow traits. *Journal of Applied Psychology, 91,* 40–57.

Fine, S., Horowitz, I., Weigler, H., & Basis, L. (2010). Is good character good enough? The effects of situational variables on the relationship between integrity and counterproductive work behaviors. *Human Resource Management Review, 20,* 73–84.

Fiske, D. W. (1949). Consistency of the factorial structures of personality ratings from different sources. *Journal of Abnormal and Social Psychology, 44,* 329–344.

Flaherty, S., & Moss, S. A. (2007). The impact of personality and team context on the relationship between workplace injustice and counterproductive work behavior. *Journal of Applied Social Psychology, 37,* 2549–2575.

Frone, M. R. (2006). Prevalence and distribution of alcohol use and impairment in the workplace: A U.S. national survey. *Journal of Studies on Alcohol, 67,* 147–156.

Glaso, L., Matthiesen, S. B., Nielsen, M. B., & Einarsen, S. (2007). Do targets of workplace bullying portray a general victim personality profile? *Scandinavian Journal of Psychology, 48,* 313–319.

Goldberg, L. R. (1990). An alternative "description of personality": The big-five factor structure. *Journal of Personality and Social Psychology, 59,* 1216–1229.

Griffin, R. W., O'Leary-Kelly, A., & Collins, J. (1998). Dysfunctional work behaviors in organizations. In C. L. Cooper & D. M. Rousseau (Eds.), *Trends in organizational behavior* (Vol. 5, pp. 65–82). Chichester, UK: Wiley.

Gross, M. A., & Guerrero, L. K. (2000). Managing conflict appropriately and effectively: An application of the competence model to Rahim's organizational conflict styles. *International Journal of Conflict Management, 11,* 200–226.

Gross, M. A., Guerrero, L. K., & Alberts, J. K. (2004). Perceptions of conflict strategies and communication competence in task oriented dyads. *Journal of Applied Communication Research, 32,* 249–270.

Guion, R. M., & Gottier, R. F. (1965). Validity of personality measures in personnel selection. *Personnel Psychology, 18,* 135–164.

Hastings, S. E., & O'Neill, T. A. (2006). Predicting workplace deviance using broad versus narrow personality variables. *Personality and Individual Differences, 47,* 289–293.

Hattrup, K., & Jackson, S. E. (1996). Learning about individual differences by taking situations seriously. In K. R. Murphy (Ed.), *Individual Differences and Behavior in Organizations* (pp. 507–547). San Francisco: Jossey-Bass.

Hausknecht, J. P., Day, D. V., & Thomas, S. C. (2004). Applicant reactions to selection procedures: An updated model and meta-analysis. *Personnel Psychology, 57,* 639–683.

Henle, C. A. (2005). Predicting workplace deviance from the interaction between organizational justice and personality. *Journal of Managerial Issues, 17,* 247–263.

Hershcovis, M. S., Turner, N., Barling, J., Arnold, K. A., Dupre, K. E., Inness, M., LeBlanc, M. M., & Sivanathan, N. (2007). Predicting workplace aggression: A meta-analysis. *Journal of Applied Psychology, 92,* 228–238.

Hitlan, R. T., & Noel, J. (2009). The influence of workplace exclusion and personality on counterproductive work behaviours: An interactionist perspective. *European Journal of Work and Organizational Psychology, 18,* 477–502.

Hollinger, R. C., & Clark, J. P. (1982). Formal and informal social controls of employee deviance. *The Sociological Quarterly, 23,* 333–343.

Hough, L. M. (1992). The "Big Five" personality variables—construct confusion: Description versus prediction. *Human Performance, 5,* 139–155.

Hough, L. M., Oswald, F. L., & Ployhart, R. E. (2001). Determinants, detection, and amelioration of adverse impact in personnel selection procedures: Issues, evidence, and lessons learned. *International Journal of Selection and Assessment, 9,* 152–194.

Hough, L. M., & Schneider, R. J. (1996). Personality traits, taxonomies, and applications in organizations. In K. R. Murphy (Ed.), *Individual differences and behavior in organizations* (pp. 31–88). San Francisco: Jossey-Bass.

House, R. J., Shane, S. A., & Herold, D. M. (1996). Rumors of the death of dispositional research are vastly exaggerated. *Academy of Management Review, 21,* 203–224.

How much can you save with automated time and attendance? (2006, March). *Contractor's Business Management Report, 6,* 1, 11–14.

Huffcutt, A. I., Conway, J. M., Roth, P. L., & Stone, C. J. (2001). Identification and meta-analytic assessment of psychological constructs measured in employment interviews. *Journal of Applied Psychology, 86,* 897–913.

Jang, K. L., Livesley, W. J., & Vernon, P. A. (1996). Heritability of the Big Five personality dimensions and their facets: A twin study. *Journal of Personality, 64,* 575–591.

Jones, T. S., & Brinkert, R. (2008). *Conflict coaching: Conflict management strategies and skills for the individual.* Thousand Oaks, CA: Sage.

Judge, T. A., Heller, D., & Mount, M. K. (2002). Five-factor model of personality and job satisfaction: A meta-analysis. *Journal of Applied Psychology, 87,* 530–541.

Kamp, J. D., & Hough, L. M. (1986). Utility of personality assessment: A review and integration of the literature. In L. M. Hough (Ed.), *Utility of temperament, biodata, and interest assessment for predicting job performance: A review and integration of the literature* (ARI Research Note No. 88-02, pp. 1–90). Alexandria, VA: U.S. Army Research Institute for the Behavioral and Social Sciences.

Kram, K. E. (1985). *Mentoring at work: Developmental relationships in organizational life.* Glenview, IL: Scott Foresman.

Marcus, B., & Schuler, H. (2004). Antecedents of counterproductive behavior at work: A general perspective. *Journal of Applied Psychology, 89,* 647–660.

McCrae, R. R. (1982). Consensual validation of personality traits: Evidence from self-reports and ratings. *Journal of Personality and Social Psychology, 43,* 293–303.

McCrae, R. R., Terracciano, A., & 78 members of the Personality Profiles of Cultures Project. (2005). Universal features of personality traits from the observer's perspective: Data from 50 cultures. *Journal of Personality and Social Psychology, 88,* 547–561.

McGee, M. K., & Fillon, M. (1995, March 20). Honesty is still the best policy. *Information Week, 519,* 156.

Mikulay, S., Neuman, G., & Finkelstein, L. (2001). Counterproductive workplace behaviors. *Gender, Social, and General Psychology Monographs, 127,* 279–300.

Milam, A. C., Spitzmueller, C., & Penney, L. M. (2009). Investigating individual differences among targets of workplace incivility. *Journal of Occupational Health Psychology, 14,* 58–69.

Mischel, W. (1968). *Personality and assessment.* New York: Wiley.

Mischel, W. (1973). Toward a cognitive social learning reconceptualization of personality. *Psychological Review, 80,* 252–283.

Mount, M. K., & Barrick, M. R. (1995). The Big Five personality dimensions: Implications for research and practice in human resources management. *Research in Personnel and Human Resources Management, 13,* 153–200.

Mueller-Hanson, R., Heggestad, E. D., & Thornton, G. C. (2003). Faking and selection: Considering the use of personality from select-in and select-out perspectives. *Journal of Applied Psychology, 88,* 348–355.

Norman, W. T. (1963). Toward an adequate taxonomy of personality attributes: Replicated factor structure in peer nomination personality ratings. *Journal of Abnormal and Social Psychology, 66*, 574–583.

O'Leary-Kelly, A. M., Griffin, R. W., & Glew, D. J. (1996). Organization-motivated aggression: A research framework. *Academy of Management Review, 21*, 225–253.

Olweus, D. (1978). *Aggression in schools: Bullies and whipping boys.* Washington, DC: Hemisphere.

Ones, D. S., & Viswesvaran, C. (2001). Personality at work: Criterion-focused occupational personality scales used in personnel selection. In B. W. Roberts & R. Hogan (Eds.), *Personality psychology in the workplace* (pp. 63–92). Washington, DC: American Psychological Association.

Ones, D. S., Viswesvaran, C., & Dilchert, S. (2005). Personality at work: Raising awareness and correcting misconceptions. *Human Performance, 18*, 389–404.

Ones, D. S., Viswesvaran, C., & Schmidt, F. L. (1993). Comprehensive meta-analysis of integrity test validities: Findings and implications for personnel selection and theories of job performance. *Journal of Applied Psychology, 78*, 679–703.

Paunonen, S. V., & Ashton, M. C. (2001). Big Five factors and facets and the prediction of behavior. *Journal of Personality and Social Psychology, 81*, 524–539.

Penney, L. M., & Spector, P. E. (2005). Job stress, incivility, and counterproductive work behavior (CWB): The moderating role of negative affectivity. *Journal of Organizational Behavior, 26*, 777–796.

Rahim, M. A. (2002). Toward a theory of managing organizational conflict. *The International Journal of Conflict Management, 13*, 206–235.

Roberts, B. W., & DelVecchio, W. F. (2000). The rank-order consistency of personality traits from childhood to old age: A quantitative review of longitudinal studies. *Psychological Bulletin, 126*, 3–25.

Robinson, S. L., & Bennett, R. J. (1995). A typology of deviant workplace behaviors: A multidimensional scaling study. *Academy of Management Journal, 38*, 555–572.

Rothstein, M. G., & Goffin, R. D. (2006). The use of personality measures in personnel selection: What does current research support? *Human Resource Management Review, 16*, 155–180.

Rothstein, M. G., & Jackson, D. N. (1984). Implicit personality theory and the employment interview. In M. Cook (Ed.), *Issues in Person Perception.* London: Methuen.

Sackett, P. R., Burris, L. R., & Callahan, C. (1989). Integrity testing for personnel selection: An update. *Personnel Psychology, 42*, 491–529.

Sackett, P. R., & Devore, C. J. (2001). Counterproductive behaviors at work. In N. Anderson, D. S. Ones, H. Sinangil, & C. Viswesvaran (Eds.), *Handbook of Industrial, Work, and Organizational Psychology*, Vol. 1. London: Sage.

Sackett, P. R., & Wanek, J. E. (1996). New developments in the use of measures of honesty, integrity, conscientiousness, dependability, trustworthiness, and reliability for personnel selection. *Personnel Psychology, 49*, 787–829.

Salgado, J. F. (2002). The Big Five personality dimensions and counterproductive behaviors. *International Journal of Selection and Assessment, 10*, 117–125.

Schmidt, F. L., & Hunter, J. E. (1998). The validity and utility of selection methods in personnel psychology: Practical and theoretical implications of 85 years of research findings. *Psychological Bulletin, 124*, 262–274.

Schmidt, F. L., & Rader, M. (1999). Exploring the boundary conditions for interview valid-ity: Meta-analytic validity findings for a new interview type. *Personnel Psychology, 52,* 445–464.

Schneider, R. J., Hough, L. M., & Dunnette, M. D. (1996). Broadsided by broad traits: How to sink science in five dimensions or less. *Journal of Organizational Behavior, 17,* 639–655.

Scott, B. A., & Colquitt, J. A. (2007). Are organizational justice effects bounded by indi-vidual differences? An examination of equity sensitivity, exchange ideology, and the Big Five. *Group & Organization Management, 32,* 290–325.

Sillars, A. L. (1986). Procedures for coding interpersonal conflict (revised). Unpublished manuscript. Department of Interpersonal Communication, University of Montana.

Skarlicki, D. P., Folger, R., & Tesluk, P. (1999). Personality as a moderator in the relationship between fairness and retaliation. *Academy of Management Journal, 42,* 100–108.

Tepper, B. J., Duffy, M. K., Henle, C. A., & Lambert, L. S. (2006). Procedural injustice, vic-tim precipitation, and abusive supervision. *Personnel Psychology, 59,* 101–123.

Tett, R. P., Jackson, D. N., & Rothstein, M. (1991). Personality measures as predictors of job performance: A meta-analytic review. *Personnel Psychology, 44,* 703–742.

Tupes, E. C., & Christal, R. E. (1961). *Recurrent personality factors based on trait ratings* (Technical Report No. ASD-TR-61-97). Lackland Air Force Base, TX: U.S. Air Force.

Van Iddekinge, C. H., Raymark, P. H., & Roth, P. L. (2005). Assessing personality with a structured employment interview: Construct-related validity and susceptibility to response inflation. *Journal of Applied Psychology, 90,* 536–552.

Vartia, M. (1996). The sources of bullying—Psychological work environment and organiza-tional climate. *European Journal of Work and Organizational Psychology, 5,* 203–214.

Wanberg, C. R., Kammeyer-Mueller, J., & Marchese, M. (2006). Mentor and protégé predic-tors and outcomes of mentoring in a formal mentoring program. *Journal of Vocational Behavior, 69,* 410–423.

Wanberg, C. R., Welsh, E. T., & Hezlett, S. A. (2003). Mentoring research: A review and dynamic process model. In J. J. Martocchio & G. R. Ferris (Eds.), *Research in personnel and human resources management* (Vol. 22, pp. 39–124). Oxford, UK: Elsevier Science.

Wilmot, W. W., & Hocker, J. L. (2007). *Interpersonal Conflict* (7th ed.). New York: McGraw Hill.

Zapf, D. (1999). Organisational, work group related and personal causes of mobbing/bully-ing at work. *International Journal of Manpower, 20,* 70–85.

4

The Role of Occupational Stress in Workplace Deviance

SHARON L. GRANT

Martin is friendly and outgoing. He has worked for the same large retail chain for many years and has been a reliable and valued employee. He enjoys his job because he likes working with people. Recently, the retail chain was acquired by another company. The change of ownership brought rapid change and there has been little consultation with staff during this process. Martin feels that the new owners are profit-driven and have little regard for workers. Human Resources has been centralized and work rosters are no longer negotiated at the store level. The casual work force, which had previously supported permanent staff during peak periods, is being phased out and "full-timers" are being forced to work more hours, including nights and weekends to bridge the gap. Workers who are unable to fit in with the new hours have been forced to leave.

Staff cutbacks mean that there are fewer salespeople to attend to the customers. Martin is often the only person in his area on the selling floor and he has to attend to three times as many customers as before, as well as helping out in other areas that are understaffed. Many of the customers he deals with are angry and abusive because they have been kept waiting. Before too long, Martin starts to snap back at customers and is often rude and sarcastic. He is usually too busy to take his much-needed breaks, so when he can get away he takes longer than he is entitled and is sometimes gone for more than an hour, leaving his area unattended. He doesn't care about sales targets anymore; "Why should I?" he thinks, "The organization doesn't care about us."

Martin only gets one weekend off per month, which he uses to catch up on chores at home. He has little time to relax and unwind or socialize with friends. The long, hard hours are beginning to affect his health. He feels tired and frustrated all the time lately. He speaks to his manager, but is told that nothing can be done until staff contacts are renewed at the end of the year. Perhaps then his roster might change.

When Martin wakes up in the morning, he doesn't feel like going to work. He doesn't enjoy it anymore and the thought of going there makes him feel anxious. He decides to call in sick and immediately feels better. He thinks about taking more sick leave and perhaps using up his annual leave to look for another job.

Occupational stress is a serious issue for employees and organizations alike. At the employee level, occupational stress is associated with a range of physical and psychological health problems, including chronic illness and disease. Furthermore, there is increasing consensus that occupational stress is related to both short-term and long-term quality of life. For instance, occupational stress may have a collateral effect on health behavior (for instance, substance use), relationship quality, and self-esteem. At the organizational level, occupational stress has been linked with absenteeism, low morale, poor productivity/performance, and turnover. In addition, occupational stress may lead to counterproductive behavior in the form of workplace deviance: voluntary behavior that is in conflict with the interests of the organization and its members. For example, employees may engage in deviant or criminal behavior to compensate for feelings of anger or frustration associated with stress. The purpose of this chapter is to address the role occupational stress plays in the occurrence of workplace deviance.

Chapter Overview

Workplace deviance is a common occurrence in many organizations, ranging from relatively minor forms of counterproductive behavior such as unauthorized breaks, to antisocial and criminal forms of behavior such as aggression and physical violence (see Kidwell & Martin, 2005). Irrespective of its guise, the negative impact of workplace deviance on organizations is substantial (Lawrence & Robinson, 2007). In addition to its financial consequences (due say, to underperformance), workplace deviance may have legal implications, given that employers are mandated by law to meet occupational health and safety standards (Taylor, 2005). Workplace deviance may have a cascading effect throughout organizations, whereby employees who are targeted by deviant behavior develop their own emotional and performance-related problems (Henle, 2005). As such, workplace deviance is an important concern for organizations and workers alike.

Understanding the antecedents of workplace deviance is an essential step in its prevention and management. This chapter focuses on the role of occupational stress as a contributing factor in workplace deviance and/or crime. Discussion of stress-related workplace deviance is grounded in Lazarus and Folkman's (1984) Transactional Model of Stress and Coping, a stress process model in which cognitive appraisal and coping strategies mediate between potentially stressful conditions/events ("stressors") and the subsequent experience of distress and related psychological, physical and behavioral ("strain") outcomes.

Although the focus of this chapter is on occupational stress as an antecedent of workplace deviance, in line with the wider stress literature, the author acknowledges that certain personality characteristics may moderate the relationship between job stressors and workplace deviance in the same way that such characteristics moderate the relationship between job stressors and other forms of strain (see Code & Langan-Fox, 2001; Grant & Langan-Fox, 2006, 2007).

For the purpose of this chapter, workplace deviance is conceptualized as a dimension of overall job performance and is defined broadly as any voluntary behavior that is in violation of organizational norms and is intended to be harmful or threatening to the interests of an organization, its members or both (Bennett & Robinson, 2003; Colbert, Mount, Harter, Witt & Barrick, 2004; Dalal, 2005; Lawrence & Robinson, 2007; Miles, Bomna, Spector & Fox, 2002; Robinson & Bennett, 1995). Accordingly, the chapter is intended to apply broadly to negative workplace behavior, as opposed to specific forms or particular domains of deviant behavior. As such, the chapter does not purport to cover all forms of deviant behavior, but it is suggested that many forms of workplace deviance can be related to occupational stress. As described within other chapters in this volume, workplace deviance may vary in terms of dimensions such as its target (regarding interpersonal versus organizational; see Bennett & Robinson, 2003; Lawrence & Robinson, 2007; Mitchell & Ambrose, 2007) and severity (regarding counterproductivity versus theft; see Boye & Slora, 1993). The link between occupational stress and workplace deviance will be discussed in general terms, on the basis that different forms of employee misbehavior tend to be inter-correlated (see for example Gruys & Sackett, 2003). Research examining interpersonal and organizational workplace deviance, for example, has shown the two forms of deviance to be highly correlated (Dalal, 2005).

The Psychological Impact of Occupational Stress

Defining Stress: A Stimulus-Response Process. Psychological models of stress define the concept in terms of a stimulus-response or "stressor-strain" process (Brantley & Garrett, 1993; Cox & Ferguson, 1991; Dewe, Cox & Ferguson, 1993; Fleming, Baum & Singer, 1984; Jex, 1998). According to Lazarus and Folkman's influential (1984) Transactional Model of Stress and Coping, the prevailing psychological framework (Dewe et al., 1993; Leventhal & Tomarken, 1987; Monroe & Kelley, 1997), stress is a product of the perceptual interface between a person and his or her environment. Specifically, cognitive appraisal and coping are theorized to serve as mediators between the perception of a potentially stressful situation and the subsequent experience of stress, such that appraisal and coping influence the person's response to the situation (Tomaka, Blascovich, Kesley & Leitten, 1993). Within this framework, the term "stressor" is used to refer to a psychologically meaningful condition or event in the environment, and the term "strain" is used to describe the negative psychological, physical, or behavioral outcome(s) of the stimulus-response process (Jex, 1998; Penny & Spector, 2005; Shinn, Rosario, Mørch & Chestnut, 1984). Examples of strain outcomes include anxiety, tension, and behavioral problems. Physical strain outcomes may stem from both the physical demand of managing the stressor itself and/or the physiology of psychological distress (Spector, 2002). Behavioral strain outcomes provide a means for the individual to cope with the stressor (for instance, substance abuse; see Penny & Spector, 2005).

Cognitive appraisal consists of three phases: (1) Primary Appraisal— evaluation of the significance of a potentially stressful situation for personal well-being; (2) Secondary Appraisal—evaluation of what can be done about the situation, including the subsequent initiation of a coping response; and (3) Reappraisal—re-evaluation of the situation and whether a further coping response is necessary (Lazarus & Folkman, 1984). Coping responses are typically distinguished on the basis of function as either (1) "problem-focused coping strategies," the function of which is to alter/manage the source of stress, or (2) "emotion-focused coping strategies," the function of which is to regulate emotional distress associated with the stressor (Dewe et al., 1993; Ingledew, Hardy, Cooper & Jemal, 1996). Stress is thought to arise from (a) the appraisal of a situation as harmful, threatening, or challenging and (b) the appraisal that an adequate or appropriate coping response is unavailable (Cohen, Kamarck & Mermelstein, 1983; Cohen & Edwards, 1989). Stress is typically associated with a change in emotional state and a subsequent deviation from normal physiological and psychological functioning (Cox & Ferguson, 1991), and is thought to affect illness and disease via deregulation of the autonomic nervous system and the immune system (Brantley & Garrett, 1993; Brown, 1993; Michaels, Michaels & Peterson, 1997; Siegrist, 1995; Wiebe & Smith, 1997). In addition, stress may affect illness and disease indirectly, via coping (Brantley & Garrett, 1993); although the aim of coping is to restore normal functioning, coping strategies may be adaptive or maladaptive (Parkes, 1994). Genetic predisposition to a specific illness or disease, or psychological make-up, may also intensify the impact of stress (Endler, 1997).

In summary, according to the prevailing psychological model of stress, an individual's response to a potentially stressful situation is a function of the perceptual inter-face between person and environment, as opposed to the quality or intensity of the situation per se (Cohen et al., 1983; Fleming et al.,

1984; Monroe & Kelley, 1997). With regard to strain, the causal event is the individual's cognitively-mediated response to the situation, the product of which is related to physiological and psychological arousal and subsequent vulnerability to illness or disease (Cohen et al., 1983).

Occupational Stress. The first large scale research program on occupational stress took place at the University of Michigan's Institute for Social Research in the early 1960s, although it was not until over a decade later that occupational stress came to be regarded as an important area of scientific inquiry in its own right (Jex, 1998; Newton, 1989). A major turning point was the publication of Beehr and Newman's (1978) article on "job stress, employee health, and organizational effectiveness," the first major literature review on the topic to appear in an Industrial/Organizational psychology journal (Beehr, 1998; Jex, 1998).

A relatively "new" field of scientific inquiry, the study of occupational stress has generated considerable research interest in a relatively short time frame (Jex, 1998), a probable reflection of its potential to affect organizational performance. Occupational stress may arise from financial, social, or general working conditions and may include, for instance, interpersonal stressors (abusive supervisors, conflict with coworkers), stressors relating to the nature of the job itself (boring, repetitive, or routine work, complex or difficult tasks, heavy workload, shift work), or stressors associated with organizational context (inadequate resources, unfair pay or reward systems; Spector, 2002). In an occupational sense, strain may include health, well-being, or performance-related outcomes (Adkins, 1997).

Occupational stress is a significant workplace health issue in industrialized countries (Spector, 2002). While the primary focus of occupational health and safety used to be protection against workplace hazard (worksite safety), this emphasis is changing. Acute or episodic forms of occupational stress such as assault and trauma are on the decline, while chronic and passive forms such as bullying, organizational change, and quantitative workload are on the rise (Burrow, 2002). Although chronic stress is relatively pervasive and is often a reality of organizational life, its impact may be just as detrimental as acute stress in the long-term (Bailey & Bhagat, 1987). Accordingly, the focus has shifted to the "psychosocial" side of stress and the promotion of total employee health and well-being, as opposed to simply the absence of illness (Schreurs, Winnubust & Cooper, 1996; Siegrist, 1995).

The toll of occupational stress on employee health and well-being is on the increase and the magnitude and subsequent cost of the problem is immense (Burrow, 2002; Mäkikangas & Kinnunen, 2003). At the employee level, occupational stress has been linked with a range of physical and psychological symptoms including fatigue, headache, high blood pressure, insomnia, muscular tension, stomach upset, anxiety, irritability, job dissatisfaction, and withdrawal, as well as chronic illness and disease such as cardiovascular disease, burnout, and depression (Adler & Matthews, 1994; Beehr & Newman, 1978; Caplan, Cobb, French, Van Harrison & Pinneau, 1980; Hepburn, Loughlin & Barling, 1997; Jamal, 1999; Jex, 1998; National Institute for Occupational Safety and Health [NIOSH], 2002; Shinn et al., 1984; Theorell, 1993; Van Harrison, 1985).

Given that the development of disease is gradual, its relationship to occupational stress has been difficult to establish (NIOSH, 2002). However, longitudinal research has confirmed that occupational stress is indeed a causal factor (see for instance, Karasek & Theorell, 1990). Furthermore, there is increasing consensus that occupational stress is related to both short-term and long-term quality of life (Murphy, 1996). For example, occupational stress may have a collateral effect on health behavior (substance use, decreased relationship quality, and social isolation; Murphy, 1996).

At the organizational level, occupational stress has been linked with absenteeism, communication problems, morale, and productivity/performance issues (Beehr & Newman, 1978; Hepburn et al., 1997; Jex, 1998). Finally, occupational stress may affect the community at a micro-level, through its impact on relationship breakdown and family discord, or at a macro-level, through its impact on the prevalence of chronic illness and disease and subsequent strain on infrastructure.

In the United States, approximately one million people per day are absent from work due to occupational stress (American Institute of Stress, 2004). In Europe, occupational stress is a common grievance for up to one third of the workforce, or approximately 40 million people (Burrow, 2002). In Australia, occupational stress is the second highest cost category of workers' compensation, with an annual payout of approximately $50 million (Comcare, 2004). Moreover, when the broader context of the problem is taken into account (such as government expenditure and personal hardship), the real impact, though difficult to estimate, is undoubtedly much greater (Langan-Fox, 2002).

The problem of occupational stress is also costly for industry, both directly through sick pay, and indirectly through its impact on productivity and performance. For instance, it is estimated that up to 50% of absenteeism is due to occupational stress (Schreurs et al., 1996). Bruk-Lee and Spector (2006) noted the recent shift in the occupational stress literature to investigating aspects of strain that are related to performance, such as counterproductive behavior and other forms of employee misbehavior. The link between occupational stress and workplace deviance is the topic of the next section. The psychological underpinnings of workplace deviance are examined, focusing in particular on stress-related antecedents, situated within a transactional model of stress and coping.

The Role of Occupational Stress in Workplace Deviance and/or Crime

A number of possible antecedents of workplace deviance have been described in the literature. Broadly, these antecedents can be classified in terms of two general perspectives: person-oriented perspectives and situation-oriented perspectives. Person-oriented perspectives attribute workplace deviance to individual difference variables such as personality traits, while situation-oriented perspectives attribute workplace deviance to work environment characteristics such as job stressors (see Bordia, Restubog & Tang, 2008; Henle, 2005; Lawrence & Robinson, 2007; Spector & Fox, 2002). Others have considered the interplay between person and situation variables in the prediction of workplace deviance (Colbert et al., 2004; Fox & Spector, 2005; Robinson & Bennett, 1997). These differing perspectives are considered in turn below.

Person-Oriented Models of Workplace Deviance. Person-oriented perspectives assume that the effect of individual difference variables on workplace deviance is independent of the situation or work environment (Henle, 2005). That is, there are certain characteristics or dispositions that predispose employees to engage in workplace deviance and these variables increase the propensity for deviant behavior regardless of work environment characteristics, such as job stressors. The person-oriented perspective has focused largely on dispositional factors such as "integrity" or the personality traits of emotional stability (low neuroticism), conscientiousness and agreeableness (Colbert et al., 2004; Ones, Viswesvaran & Schmidt, 1993). Other person-oriented models have been couched in attachment theory, and have focused on individual difference variables such as organizational attachment, commitment, identification, involvement, and trust (see Becker & Bennett, 2007; Hollinger, 1986; Thau, Crossley, Bennett & Sczesny, 2007).

An alternative idea to the dispositional approach is that occupational stress has a "sleeper effect," gradually weakening (and eventually overriding) the cognitive mechanisms that ordinarily control and prevent workplace deviance (Tucker, 2006). According to this "temporal" perspective, it is important to consider *within-person* differences in addition to *between-person* differences in the management of workplace deviance.

Situation-Oriented Models of Workplace Deviance. In contrast to person-oriented models, situation-oriented models assume that workplace deviance is solely a product of the organization or work environment (Henle, 2005). That is, there are certain work environment characteristics that induce employees to engage in workplace deviance. Situational perspectives can be separated into two broad model types: (1) models that conceptualize workplace deviance as a reaction to injustice versus (2) models that conceptualize workplace deviance as an adaptive response to the work environment (Bennett & Robinson, 2003). Within the injustice model, workplace deviance has been described in terms of social exchange models (see Cropanzano & Mitchell, 2005); as a compensatory or reciprocal response to unfair, unsupportive or otherwise unfavorable work conditions (see Cohen-Charash & Mueller, 2007). For example, equity and justice-based models maintain that workplace deviance is motivated by needs for restoration (corrective function) and retribution (retributive function) respectively (Bordia et al., 2008). According to these models, workplace deviance is a cognition-based response to inequity or injustice: employees who experience negative work environment conditions reciprocate (or retaliate!) with workplace deviance.

Other authors have adopted emotion-centered models, emphasizing the mediating role of negative emotions (anger, frustration) in the work environment-workplace deviance relationship, and highlighting occupational stress as a key variable in this process (see Bruk-Lee & Spector, 2006; Fox et al., 2001; Fox et al., 2007; Penney & Spector, 2005; Spector & Fox, 2002, 2005). Consistent with the Transactional Model of Stress and Coping described earlier, stressor-emotion models of counterproductive work behavior propose that negative emotions are an immediate response to stressful work environment conditions/events and play a central role in the stressor-strain process (see figure 4.1). That is, negative emotions mediate between job stressors and counterproductive work behavior.

According to these models then, workplace deviance is an emotion-based, behavioral strain response to perceived negative work environment conditions/events ("job stressors"). Spector (2002) suggested that employees who feel they have lost control may use workplace deviance to covertly or passively strike out at the perceived source of stress and make themselves feel better. From this perspective, workplace deviance can be seen as an adaptive response—an emotion-focused coping strategy used to vent negative emotions associated with uncontrollable workplace stressors. The notion of deviant behavior as a coping strategy is not new; Arter (2008) noted the parallel between the occupational stress-workplace deviance link in adults and the life stress-delinquency link in adolescents, citing delinquency as an "effective" (albeit maladaptive) coping strategy among youths. There is evidence from the wider stress literature to suggest that coping strategies are selected

Fig. 4.1. Stressor-emotion models of counterproductive work behavior

Events in work environment are monitored and evaluated

▼

Events are perceived as a threat to well-being

▼

Anger and frustration increase in physiological arousal

▼

Counterproductive work behavior as a behavioral response to reduce negative affect/increase positive affect

on the basis of their "goodness of fit" with the situation or stressor type, in particular the *perceived* "controllability" of the stressor (Forsythe & Compas, 1987; Vitaliano, DeWolfe, Maiuro, Russo & Katon, 1990). Problem-focused coping strategies are more likely to be selected when the situation is changeable or controllable, while emotion-focused coping strategies are more likely to be used when the situation cannot be changed/controlled and must simply be accepted and endured (Lazarus, 1990).

Empirical work has provided support for several components of the stressor-emotion model. For example, several studies have shown that job stressors, such as interpersonal conflict, are associated with workplace deviance (Chen & Spector, 1992; Fox et al., 2001; Mitchell & Ambrose, 2007). Furthermore, Fox et al. (2001) found that negative emotions mediated the relationship between job stressors (organizational constraints, interpersonal conflict, perceived injustice) and strain (counterproductive work behavior). Arter (2008) found that police officers who reported a higher level of job stressors also reported a higher level of deviant behavior in response to those stressors. In support of emotion-centered models of workplace deviance, anger and frustration were identified as key negative emotions among many of those who reported a higher level of job stressors.

Spector and Fox (2002) argued that conditions/events in the work environment are appraised in such a way that they induce emotional reactions, whether positive or negative, with negative emotions leading to extra-role behavior (ERB) in the form of counterproductive work behavior and positive emotions leading to ERB in the form of organizational citizenship behavior (OCB). OCB includes behavior that is oriented towards helping specific people in the organization (such as altruism, courtesy) and the organization itself (such as conscientiousness and obedience; see Van Dyne, Cummings & McLean Parks, 1995). In line with the stress literature, Spector and Fox suggested that uncontrollable events are more likely to lead to negative emotions (and hence counterproductive behavior). Components of their stressor-emotion model of ERB were subsequently tested by Miles et al. (2002), who found support for both positive and negative emotions as mediators between work environment conditions and ERB. More recently, Fox et al. (2007) found support for the stressor-emotion model using both incumbent and co-worker reports of job stressors and counterproductive work behavior.

Moderated Effect (Person by Situation) Models. A criticism of situational models is that not all employees who are exposed to negative work environment conditions/events respond with workplace deviance. For example, Robinson and Bennett (1997) argued that there is a causal link between (perceived) negative work environment characteristics and workplace deviance, but this link is more or less "potent" for employees with certain personality traits than for others. That is, the strength and/or direction of the effect of job stressors on workplace deviance are dependent on personality traits in some way. Personality may (a) increase or exacerbate the effect of job stressors on workplace deviance (a "synergistic" effect, in which personality and job stressors both influence workplace deviance in the same direction) or, alternatively, (b) decrease or soften the effect of job stressors on workplace deviance (a "buffering" effect in which personality and job stressors influence workplace deviance the opposite direction; Cohen et al., 2003). For example, neuroticism might increase the effect of job stressors on workplace deviance, while conscientiousness might decrease the effect of job stressors on workplace deviance. Accordingly, several authors have considered the interplay between person variables and situation variables in the prediction of workplace deviance (see Colbert et al., 2004; Fox & Spector, 2005; Henle, 2005; Penney & Spector, 2005; Robinson & Bennett, 1997).

Several models in the stress literature propose a central role for personality. For example, it has been theorized that personality may influence the likelihood that an individual will enter a potentially stressful situation (stressor exposure). Once in a potentially stressful situation, personality may impact the individual's propensity to evaluate the situation as being "stressful" (cognitive appraisal), the selection of more or less adaptive coping strategies in response to stress (coping), and emotional or physiological reactivity (distress). Furthermore, personality may very well influence the etiology, vulnerability to, and progression of stress-related illness and disease (as due to concurrent or prior life stress, or underlying pathology; Mäkikangas & Kinnunen, 2003; Suls & Rittenhouse, 1990; Wiebe & Smith, 1997). In the context of stressor-emotion models of workplace deviance, the effect of personality on emotional reactivity and coping is likely to be particularly relevant.

For example, to the extent that counterproductive behavior is associated with negative emotions, people with traits that predispose them to experience negative emotions more frequently or intensely (such as neuroticism) will be more likely to engage in such behavior.

In addition, personality traits may predispose a person to cope with stress in a certain way. When confronted with a job stressor such as a shortage of resources, employees may (a) engage in forms of coping that are destructive to other employees and/or the organization (deviant behavior) or (b) engage in constructive forms of coping such as problem-focused strategies (as in finding a way to compensate for the shortage; Spector, 2002). A defining characteristic of the original formulation of the Transactional Model of Stress and Coping was its conceptualization of coping as specific to the situation or stressor at hand and/or the stage of the person-environment transaction (Suls, David & Harvey, 1996). However, it has since been recognized that coping may be "dispositional" or stylistic in nature (Carver, Scheier & Weintraub, 1989; Cox & Ferguson, 1991; Dewe et al., 1993; Newton, 1989; Newton & Keenan, 1990; Parkes, 1994; Revenson, 1990; Semmer, 1996). For example, there is some evidence to suggest that neuroticism is associated with maladaptive and ineffective forms of coping (see Deary et al., 1996; Fickova, 2001; Shewchuk, Elliott, MacNair-Semands & Harkins, 1999). At a more general level, Revenson (1990) suggested that personality may place a "boundary" around an individual's behavioral repertoire and limit the range of coping strategies available to the individual. Perhaps those who engage in workplace deviance have fewer strategies available to them. Thus, individual difference variables, such as personality traits, may moderate the effect of job stressors on workplace deviance in much the same way that they moderate the effect of job stressors on other forms of strain (see Code & Langan-Fox, 2001; Grant & Langan-Fox, 2006, 2007).

In support of a moderated effect model of stress and workplace deviance, Colbert et al. (2004) found that conscientiousness, emotional stability, and agreeableness moderated the relationship between perceived work environment characteristics (such as a developmental environment) and workplace deviance. The relationship between developmental environment and organizational deviance was stronger for employees who were low in conscientiousness and high in neuroticism, and the relationship between organizational support and interpersonal deviance was stronger for employees who were low in agreeableness. Similarly, Penney and Spector (2005) found that the relationship between job stressors and counterproductive behavior was stronger for those who scored high on negative affectivity than those who scored low on this trait.

Drawing the various previously described theoretical models together, Bordia et al. (2008) recently proposed an integrated model in which the relationship between work environment characteristics and workplace deviance is explained in terms of cognitive, affective, and motivational mediators, with dispositional moderators buffering the relationship between antecedents (such as job stressors) and behavioral consequences (deviant behavior). They identified the motivational intent for workplace deviance as revenge that is triggered by a "chain of cognitions and emotions." The authors argued that negative work environment conditions/events lead to cognitions of disparity (when the situation is lacking in what was expected) and a negative emotional response (such as anger). These cognitions and emotions in turn lead to a motivational intent to engage in deviant behavior to (a) restore the imbalance in the employee-organization exchange relationship (instrumental motivation) and/or (b) vent negative emotions to improve one's affective state (expressive motivation). The instrumental component of motivational intent in this model is consistent with equity or justice-based models of workplace deviance, while the expressive component is aligned with the emotion-centered models, in which workplace deviance is conceptualized as an adaptive response to the work environment (that is, an emotion-focused coping strategy). Spector and Fox (2002) similarly recognized the dual function of counterproductive behavior as actively and directly attacking the agent of the stressor, and passively and indirectly coping with the emotion.

These differing aspects of motivational intent may have different emotional paths. For instance, Spector and Fox (2006) noted the distinction between instrumental ("cold") aggression, in which aggression is a means to a desired end (remuneration), and affective ("hot") aggression, in which the primary goal is the physical or psychological injury of a given target. Affective aggression is associated with negative emotion, while instrumental aggression is not. Indeed, there is evidence to suggest that different forms of employee misbehavior have different emotional antecedents. For example, Spector et al. (2006) found that abuse and sabotage were most strongly related to anger and stress, and withdrawal was associated with boredom and being upset, while theft was unrelated to emotion. They concluded that "the distinct forms of counterproductive behavior may suggest distinct underlying dynamics that vary in their balance of hostile and instrumental motivational systems" (46).

Integrating the various models hitherto outlined with concepts from the wider stress literature, such as those described in Lazarus and Folkman's (1984) Transactional Model of Stress and Coping, results in the overall model of the role of occupational stress in workplace deviance shown in figure 4.2.

Despite its negative outcomes for the organization, from an "employee-perspective," workplace deviance may be an adaptive response to negative work environment conditions/events in the sense of enabling workers to protect their needs for autonomy, fairness, and self-respect (Lawrence & Robinson, 2007), and to vent negative emotions (Dalal, 2005). For example, employees may use workplace deviance to show that they are deserving of respect and have socially-valued attributes (Lawrence & Robinson, 2007).

While workplace deviance may be an adaptive response to occupational stress in the short-term, it may lead to maladaptive consequences, such as organizational or even criminal reprimands in the long-term. Furthermore, unlike problem-focused coping strategies which seek to alleviate job stressors directly, workplace deviance is essentially an avoidance coping strategy; it provides immediate relief from negative emotions, but ultimately the causal agent or source of stress is left unchanged. An early study of police officers (Violani & Marshall, 1983) found that although workplace deviance was one of the most commonly used coping strategies, it failed to reduce stress and actually introduced additional organizational pressures. In addition, workplace deviance may have a cascading effect throughout organizations, whereby employees who are targeted by the deviant behavior develop their own stress- and productivity-related problems (Henle, 2005).

Managing Stress-Related Workplace Deviance and/or Criminal Behavior: Intervention Strategies

Workplace deviance is a significant problem that has negative consequences at both the individual level and the organizational level. Based on the overall model of occupational stress and workplace deviance presented in this chapter, three types of strategies for managing stress-related workplace deviance and/or crime are recommended: preventative strategies (incorporating integrity and personality testing in employee selection systems); primary stress interventions at the organizational-level (such as job redesign), and secondary stress interventions at the employee-level (such as stress education). These are described in more detail below.

Prevention: Integrity and Personality Testing in Employee Selection Systems

Although individual difference variables such as personality traits have been identified as moderators of the job stressor-workplace deviance relationship, traits may not be responsive to intervention. The path to behavior change is difficult, traits are hard to alter, and some employees may resist intervention

Fig. 4.2. The role of occupational stress in workplace deviance

PERSONALITY
▼

Work environment conditions/events:
  Potential job stressors
  ▼

Cognitive appraisal:
  Negative perception of work environment
  e.g., unfair/unsupportive/threat to well-being
  ▼

Negative emotions:
  Stress
  ▼

Motivational intent:
  Instrumental (restore balance)
  Expressive (improve affective state)
  ▼

Behavioral strain response (coping):
  Workplace deviance

altogether (Goldberg 2005; Stevens 2005). Furthermore, a considerable amount of energy and time is needed if any behavior change that is achieved is to be permanently imbedded (Day, 2000). Accordingly, traits that increase the risk of stress-related workplace deviance are probably best managed through the implementation of preventative measures in the first instance. Such measures include using screening tools (such as integrity and personality testing) in employee selection systems to help screen out personality types who are more likely to perpetrate workplace deviance if hired, and identify the "right people," such as those who are more likely to perform organizational citizenship behavior (Boye & Slora, 1993; Detert, Trevino, Burris & Andiappan, 2007; Henle, 2005; Spector & Fox, 2002). Colbert et al. (2004) suggested that selecting employees on the basis of personality traits such as agreeableness, conscientiousness and emotional stability (low neuroticism) is likely to reduce the frequency and severity of workplace deviance.

Post-employment interventions such as monitoring systems (corporate hotlines and surveillance; Detert et al., 2007) are likely to be costly to organizations. Screening out "high risk" candidates in the first instance should prevent the need for these correction mechanisms later on, saving the organization and its employees unnecessary discomfort, energy, and time (Schneider, Goldstein & Smith, 1995; Wilk, Desmarais & Sackett, 1995). However, interventions that focus exclusively on identifying/eliminating deviant employees are likely to be inadequate, given that both person and situation variables have been identified as antecedents of workplace deviance. As Spector and Fox (2002) noted, although employee selection procedures may help to reduce workplace deviance, such systems are no substitute for good working conditions, and employees are likely to perform better in a work environment that is encouraging and fulfilling. Strategies for reducing situational antecedents of workplace deviance, namely job stressors, are described below.

Interventions

A longstanding issue in the occupational stress literature is whether reducing occupational stress is the responsibility of the organization or the worker (see Mallinger, 1986). The position adopted here is that stress interventions should be targeted at both the organizational-level (primary interventions) and employee-level (secondary interventions), with the dual aim of decreasing stress-inducing conditions/events and increasing employee control (Spector & Fox, 2002). Primary interventions focus on identifying and altering the *sources* of stress (stressors) and have the advantage of being a proactive approach to stress management in that they seek out the source/s of stress *before* they may become a problem; secondary interventions focus on altering the ways in which employees cope with job stressors (Caulfield, Chang, Dollard & Elshaug, 2004; Murphy & Sauter, 2003; Richardson & Rothstein, 2008).

Organizational Interventions: Redesigning Work Systems to Reduce Stress

At the organizational level, widely implemented stress interventions have included clarifying role expectations, decentralizing authority, enriching and/or redesigning jobs, refining performance evaluation standards, improving communication networks, and implementing innovative reward systems (Mallinger, 1986). Such measures aim to decrease ambiguity, powerlessness, and uncertainty, and increase fulfillment, involvement, and meaning. Arter (2008) found that reducing job stressors through job reassignment reduced deviant behavior among police officers. Bennett (1998) suggested that interventions should focus on enhancing employees' sense of control through initiatives such as employee empowerment.

In addition to targeting stress-related antecedents of workplace deviance directly through measures such as those hitherto listed, organizations could introduce managerial practices that promote ethically correct behavior such as codes of ethical conduct and management/supervisory styles that focus on maximizing positive behavior (ethical leadership) and minimizing negative behavior (abusive supervision; Colbert et al., 2004; Detert et al., 2007). Organizational interventions that promote ethical behavior through leading by example should assist in building an ethical organizational culture and cultivating appropriate norms at the level of individual workgroups

Employee Interventions: Stress Education

At the employee level, a popular stress intervention is stress management courses, which typically provide general stress education coupled with targeted content to assist employees in identifying their own sources of stress and developing strategies for dealing with these (Murphy, 1996; Vrugt, 1996). With regard to reducing workplace deviance as a behavioral strain response, stress management courses could focus on helping employees to adapt to stressors that might otherwise provoke misbehavior by providing training in the regulation of negative emotions and ruminations and by teaching coping strategies that enhance feelings of control in positive ways (Bordia et al., 2008). In addition, courses in general stress management skills such as assertiveness, career planning, problem solving and time management may be helpful in this regard (Mallinger, 1986). Organizations could be proactive by offering these courses in conjunction with other large-scale, corporate training programs such as employee induction.

In this chapter, workplace deviance was conceptualized as a manifestation of behavioral strain in response to job stressors. Occupational stress is a significant problem in its own right that has been an ongoing challenge in organizations for many years. Addressing occupational stress is more important than ever, given its link to the similarly costly and destructive problem of workplace deviance; the aim is to build healthy *and* productive organizations.

REFERENCES

Adkins, J. A. (1997). Base closure: A case study in occupational stress and organizational decline. In M. K. Gowing, J. D. Kraft, & J. C. Quick (Eds.), *The new organizational reality: Downsizing, restructuring and revitalization* (pp. 111–141). Washington, DC: American Psychological Association.

Adler, N., & Matthews, K. (1994). Health psychology: Why do some people get sick and some stay well? *Annual Review of Psychology, 45,* 229–259.

American Institute of Stress (2004). Job stress. In *Home page of the American Institute of Stress*. Retrieved February 13, 2005, from http://www.stress.org/job.htm.

Arter, M. L. (2008). Stress and deviance in policing. *Deviant Behavior, 29*, 43–69.

Bailey, J. M., & Bhagat, R. S. (1987). Meaning and measurement of stressors in the work environment: An evaluation. In S. V. Kasl & C. L. Cooper (Eds.), *Stress and health: Issues in research methodology* (pp. 207–229). Oxford, England: Wiley.

Becker, T. E., & Bennett, R. J. (2007). Employee attachment and deviance in organizations. In J. Langan-Fox, C. L. Cooper, and R. J. Klimoski (Eds.), *Research companion to the dysfunctional workplace: Management challenges and symptoms* (pp. 136–148). Northampton, MA: Edward Elgar.

Beehr, T. A. (1998). Research on occupational stress: An unfinished enterprise. *Personnel Psychology, 51*, 835–844.

Beehr, T. A., & Newman, J. E. (1978). Job stress, employee health and organizational effectiveness: A facet analysis, model and literature review. *Personnel Psychology, 31*, 665–699.

Bennett, R. J. (1998). Perceived powerlessness as a cause of employee deviance. In R. W. Griffin, A. O-Leary-Kelly, & J. M. Collins (Eds.), *Dysfunctional behavior in organizations: Violent and deviant behavior* (pp. 221–239). Greenwich, CT: Elsevier Science/JAI.

Bennett, R. J., & Robinson, S. L. (2003). The past, present, and future of workplace deviance research. In J. Greenberg (Ed.), *Organizational behavior: The state of science* (2nd ed.: pp. 247–281). Mahwah, NJ: Erlbaum.

Bordia, P., Restubog, S. L. D., & Tang, R. L. (2008). When employees strike back: Investigating mediating mechanisms between psychological contract breach and workplace deviance. *Journal of Applied Psychology, 93*, 1104–1117.

Boye, M. W., & Slora, K. B. (1993). The severity and prevalence of deviant employee activity within supermarkets. *Journal of Business and Psychology, 8*, 245–253.

Brantley, P. J., & Garrett, D. (1993). Psychobiological approaches to health and disease. In P. B. Sutker & H. E. Adams (Eds.), *Comprehensive handbook of psychopathology* (2nd ed.) (pp. 647–670). New York: Plenum.

Brown, D. (1993). Stress and emotion: Implications for illness development and wellness. In S. L. Albion, D. Brown, E. J. Khantzian & J. E. Mack (Eds.), *Human feelings: Explorations in affect development and meaning* (pp. 281–301). Hillside, NJ: Analytic.

Bruk-Lee, V., & Spector, P. E. (2006). The social stressors-counterproductive work behaviors link: Are conflicts with supervisors and coworkers the same? *Journal of Occupational Health Psychology, 11*, 145–156.

Burrow, S. (2002). Occupational stress: The union perspective. Paper presented at the Academy of the Social Sciences Australia (ASSA) Workshop on Occupational stress in Australia, Adelaide, Australia.

Caplan, R. D., Cobb, S., French, J. R. P., Van Harrison, R. Jr. & Pinneau, S. R. (1980). *Job demands and worker health: Main effects and occupational differences*. Washington, DC: U.S. Government Printing Office.

Carver, C. S., Scheier, M. F., & Weintraub, J. K. (1989). Assessing coping strategies: A theoretically based approach. *Journal of Personality and Social Psychology, 56*, 267–283.

Caulfield, N., Chang, D., Dollard, M. F., & Elshaug, C. (2004). A review of occupational stress interventions in Australia. *International Journal of Stress Management, 11*, 149–166.

Chen, P. Y., & Spector, P. E. (1992). Relationships of work stressors with aggression, withdrawal, theft and substance use: An exploratory study. *Journal of Occupational and Organizational Psychology, 65*, 177–184.

Code, S. L., & Langan-Fox, J. (2001). Motivation, cognitions and traits: Predicting occupational health, well-being, and performance. *Stress and Health*, 17, 159–174.

Cohen, J., Cohen, P., Aitken, L. S., & West, S. G. (2003). *Applied multiple regression: Correlation analysis for the behavioral sciences* (3rd ed.). Mahwah, NJ: Erlbaum.

Cohen, S., & Edwards, J. R. (1989). Personality characteristics as moderators of the relationship between stress and disorder. In R. W. J. Neufeld (Ed.), *Advances in the investigation of psychological stress* (pp. 235–283). New York: Wiley.

Cohen, S., Kamarck, T., & Mermelstein, R. (1983). A global measure of perceived stress. *Journal of Health and Social Behavior*, 24, 385–396.

Cohen-Charash, Y., & Mueller, J. S. (2007). Does perceived unfairness exacerbate or mitigate interpersonal counterproductive work behaviors related to envy. *Journal of Applied Psychology*, 92, 666–680.

Colbert, A. E., Mount, M. K., Harter, J. K., Witt, L. A., & Barrick, M. R. (2004). Interactive effects of personality and perceptions of the work situation on workplace deviance. *Journal of Applied Psychology*, 89, 599–609.

Comcare (2004). *Comcare Annual Report 2003–2004*. Canberra: Australian Government.

Cox, T., & Ferguson, E. (1991). Individual differences, stress and coping. In C. L. Cooper & R. Payne (Eds.), *Personality and stress: Individual differences in the stress process* (pp. 7–30). New York: Wiley.

Cropanzano, R., & Mitchell, M. S. (2005). Social exchange theory: An interdisciplinary review. *Journal of Management*, 31, 874–900.

Dalal, R. S. (2005). A meta-analysis of the relationship between organizational citizenship behavior and counterproductive work behavior. *Journal of Applied Psychology*, 90, 1241–1255.

Day, D. V. (2000). Leadership development: A review in context. *Leadership Quarterly*, 11, 581–613.

Deary, I. J., Blenkin, H., Agius, R. M., Endler, N. S., Zealley, H., & Wood, R. (1996). Models of job-related stress and achievement among consultant doctors. *British Journal of Psychology*, 87, 3–29.

Detert, J. R., Trevino, L. K., Burris, E. R., & Andiappan, M. (2007). Managerial modes of influence and counterproductivity in organizations: A longitudinal business-unit-level investigation. *Journal of Applied Psychology*, 92, 993–1005.

Dewe, P., Cox, T., & Ferguson, E. (1993). Individual strategies for coping with stress at work: A review. *Work and Stress*, 7, 5–15.

Endler, N. S. (1997). Stress, anxiety and coping: The multidimensional interaction model. *Canadian Psychology*, 38, 136–153.

Fickova, E. (2001). Personality regulators of coping behavior in adolescents. *Studia Psychologia*, 43, 321–329.

Fleming, R., Baum, A., & Singer, J. E. (1984). Toward an integrative approach to the study of stress. *Journal of Personality and Social Psychology*, 46, 939–949.

Forsythe, C. J., & Compas, B. E. (1987). Interaction of cognitive appraisals of stressful events and coping: Testing the goodness of fit hypothesis. *Cognitive Therapy and Research*, 11, 473–485.

Fox, S., & Spector, P. E. (2005). *Counterproductive work behavior: Investigations of actors and targets*. Washington, DC: American Psychological Association.

Fox, S., Spector, P. E., & Miles, D. (2001). Counterproductive work behavior (CWB) in response to job stressors and organizational justice: Some mediator and moderator tests for autonomy and emotions. *Journal of Vocational Behavior*, 59, 291–309.

Fox, S., Spector, P. E., Goh, A., & Bruursema, K. (2007). Does your coworker know what you're doing? Convergence of self- and peer-reports of counterproductive work behavior. *International Journal of Stress Management, 14*, 41–60.

Goldberg, R. A. (2005). Resistance to coaching. *Organization Development Journal, 23*, 9–16.

Grant, S. L., & Langan-Fox, J. (2006). Occupational stress, coping and strain: The combined/ interactive effect of the big five traits. *Personality and Individual Differences, 41*, 719–732.

Grant, S. L., & Langan-Fox, J. (2007). Personality and the occupational stressor-strain relationship: The role of the Big Five. *Journal of Occupational Health Psychology, 12*, 20–33.

Gruys, M. L., & Sackett, P. R. (2003). Investigating the dimensionality of counterproductive behavior. *International Journal of Selection and Assessment, 11*, 30–42.

Henle, C. A. (2005). Predicting workplace deviance from the interaction between organizational justice and personality. *Journal of Management Issues, 17*, 247–263.

Hepburn, C. G., Loughlin, C. A., & Barling, J. (1997). Coping with chronic work stress. In B. H. Gottlieb (Ed.), *Coping with chronic stress* (pp. 343–366). New York: Plenum.

Hollinger, R. C. (1986). Acts against the workplace: Social bonding and employee deviance. *Deviant Behavior, 7*, 53–75.

Ingledew, D. K., Hardy, L., Cooper, C. L., & Jemal, H. (1996). Health behaviors reported as coping strategies: A factor analytic study. *British Journal of Health Psychology, 1*, 263–281.

Jamal, M. (1999). Job stress and employee well-being: A cross-cultural empirical study. *Stress Medicine, 15*, 153–158.

Jex, S. M. (1998). *Stress and job performance: Theory, research and implications for managerial practice*. Thousand Oaks, CA: Sage.

Karasek, R. A., & Theorell, T. (1990). *Healthy work: Stress, productivity and the reconstruction of working life*. New York: Basic Books.

Kidwell, R. E. Jr., & Martin, C. L. (Eds.), (2005). *Managing organizational deviance*. Thousand Oaks, CA: Sage.

Langan-Fox, J. (2002). Communication in organizations: Speed, diversity, networks and influence on organizational effectiveness, human health and relationships. In N. Anderson, D. S. Ones, H. K. Sinangil, & C. Viswesvaren (Eds.), *Handbook of industrial, work and organizational psychology (Vol. 2)* (pp. 188–205). London: Sage.

Lawrence, T. B., & Robinson, S. L. (2007). Ain't misbehavin: Workplace deviance as organizational resistance. *Journal of Management, 33*, 378–394.

Lazarus, R. S. (1990). Stress, coping, and illness. In H. S. Friedman (Ed.), *Personality and disease*. New York: Wiley.

Lazarus, R. S., & Folkman, S. (1984). *Stress, appraisal, and coping*. New York: Springer-Verlag.

Leventhal, H., & Tomarken, A. (1987). Stress and illness: Perspectives from health psychology. In S. V. Kasl & C. L. Cooper (Eds.), *Stress and health: Issues in research methodology. Wiley series on studies in occupational stress* (pp. 27–55). Oxford: Wiley.

Mäkikangas, A., & Kinnunen, U. (2003). Psychosocial work stressors and well-being: Self-esteem and optimism as moderators in a one-year longitudinal sample. *Personality and Individual Differences, 35*, 537–557.

Mallinger, M. A. (1986). Stress management: An organizational and individual responsibility. *Training and Development Journal*, February, 16–17.

Michaels, C., Michaels, A., & Peterson, C. (1997). Motivation and health. *Advances in Motivation and Achievement, 10*, 339–374.

Miles, D. E., Bomna, W. E., Spector, P. E., & Fox, S. (2002). Building an integrative model of extra role work behaviors: A comparison of counterproductive work behavior with organizational citizenship behavior. *International Journal of Selection and Assessment, 10,* 51–57.

Mitchell, M. S., & Ambrose, M. L. (2007). Abusive supervision and workplace deviance and the moderating effects of negative reciprocity beliefs. *Journal of Applied Psychology, 92,* 1159–1168.

Monroe, S. M., & Kelley, J. M. (1997). Measurement of stress appraisal. In S. Cohen, R. C. Kessler & L. Underwood-Gordon (Eds.), *Measuring stress: A guide for health and social scientists* (pp. 122–147). New York: Oxford University Press.

Murphy, L. R. (1996). Stress management techniques: Secondary prevention of stress. In M. J. Schabracq, J. A. M. Winnubust, & C. L. Cooper (Eds.), *Handbook of work and health psychology* (pp. 427–441). New York: Wiley.

Murphy, L. R., & Sauter, S. L. (2003). The USA perspective: Current issues and trends in the management of work stress. *Australian Psychologist, 38,* 151–157.

National Institute for Occupational Safety and Health (2002). *Stress at work* (Publication No. 99-101). Washington, DC: Department of Health and Human Services.

Newton, T. J. (1989). Occupational stress and coping with stress: A critique. *Human Relations, 42,* 441–461.

Newton, T. J., & Keenan, T. (1990). The moderating effect of the Type A behavior pattern and locus of control upon the relationship between change in job demands and change in psychological strain. *Human Relations, 43,* 1229–1255.

Ones, D. S., Viswesvaran, C., & Schmidt, F. L. (1993). Comprehensive meta-analysis of integrity test validities: Findings and implications for personnel selection and theories of job performance. *Journal of Applied Psychology, 78,* 679–703.

Parkes, K. R. (1994). Personality and coping as moderators of work stress processes: Models, methods and measures. *Work and Stress, 8,* 110–129.

Penney, L. M., & Spector, P. E. (2005). Job stress, incivility, and counterproductive work behavior (CWB): The moderating role of negative affectivity. *Journal of Organizational Behavior, 26,* 777–796.

Revenson, T. A. (1990). All other things are not equal: An ecological approach to personality and disease. In H. S. Friedman (Ed.), *Personality and disease* (pp. 65–94). New York: Wiley.

Richardson, K. M., & Rothstein, H. R. (2008). Effects of occupational stress management intervention programs: A meta-analysis. *Journal of Occupational Health Psychology, 13,* 69–93.

Robinson, S. L., & Bennett, R. J. (1995). A typology of deviant workplace behaviors: A multidimensional scaling study. *Academy of Management Journal, 38,* 555–572.

Robinson, S. L. & Bennett, R. J. (1997). Workplace deviance: Its definition, its nature and its causes. In R. J. Lewicki, B. H. Sheppard, & R. J. Bies (Eds.), *Research on negotiation in organizations* (Vol. 6, pp. 3–27). Greenwich, CT: JAI.

Schneider, B., Goldstein, H. W., & Smith, D. B., (1995). The ASA framework: An update. *Personnel Psychology, 48,* 747–773.

Schreurs, P. J. G., Winnubust, J. A. M., & Cooper, C. L. (1996). Workplace health programs. In M. J. Schabracq, J. A. M. Winnubust, & C. L. Cooper (Eds.), *Handbook of work and health psychology* (pp. 463–481). New York: Wiley.

Semmer, N. (1996). Individual differences, work stress and health. In M. J. Schabracq, J. A. M. Winnubust, & C. L. Cooper (Eds.), *Handbook of work and health psychology* (pp. 51–86). New York: Wiley.

Shewchuk, R. M., Elliott, T. R., MacNair-Semands, R. R., & Harkins, S. (1999). Trait influences on stress appraisal and coping: An evaluation of alternative frameworks. *Journal of
Applied Social Psychology, 29,* 685–704.

Shinn, M., Rosario, M., Mørch, H., & Chestnut, D. E. (1984). Coping with job stress and
burnout in the human services. *Journal of Personality and Social Psychology, 46,* 864–876.

Siegrist, J. (1995). Emotions and health in occupational life: New scientific findings and
policy implications. *Patient Education and Counseling, 25,* 227–236.

Spector, P. E. (2002). Employee control and occupational stress. *Current Directions in Psychological Science, 11,* 133–136.

Spector, P. E., & Fox, S. (2002). An emotion-centered model of voluntary work behavior:
Some parallels between counterproductive work behavior and organizational citizenship
behavior. *Human Resource Management Review, 12,* 269–292.

Spector, P. E., & Fox, S. (2005). The stressor-emotion model of counterproductive work
behavior. In S. Fox & P. E. Spector (Eds.), *Counterproductive work behavior: Investigations
of actors and targets* (pp. 151–174). Washington, DC: American Psychological Association.

Spector, P. E., & Fox, S. (2006). Emotions, violence, and counterproductive work behavior.
In E. K. Kelloway, J. Barling, & J. J. Hurrell (Eds.), *Handbook of workplace violence* (pp.
29–46). Thousand Oaks, CA: Sage.

Spector, P. E., Fox, S., Penney, L. M., Bruursema, K., Goh, A., & Kessler, S. (2006). The
dimensionality of counterproductively: Are all counterproductive behaviors created
equal? *Journal of Vocational Behavior, 68,* 446–460.

Stevens, J. H. (2005). Executive coaching from the executive's perspective. *Consulting Psychology Journal: Practice and Research, 57,* 274–285.

Suls, J., David, J. P., & Harvey, J. H. (1996). Personality and coping: Three generations of
research. *Journal of Personality, 64,* 711–735.

Suls, J., & Rittenhouse, J. D. (1990). Models of linkages between personality and disease. In
H. S. Friedman (Ed.), *Personality and disease* (pp. 38–64). New York: Wiley.

Taylor, M. (2005). The relationships between workplace violence, deviant workplace
behavior, ethical climate, organizational justice, and abusive supervision. *Dissertation
Abstracts International: Section B: The Sciences and Engineering, 66 (I-B),* 605.

Thau, S., Crossley, C., Bennett, R. J., & Sczesny, S. (2007). The relationship between trust,
attachment, and antisocial work behaviors. *Human Relations, 60,* 1155–1179.

Theorell, J. (1993). Medical and physiological aspects of job interventions. In C. L. Cooper
& I. T. Robertson (Eds.), *International review of industrial and organizational psychology*
(pp. 173–192). Chichester: Wiley.

Tomaka, J., Blascovich, J., Kesley, R. M., & Leitten, C. L. (1993). Subjective, physiological
and behavioral effects of threat and challenge appraisal. *Journal of Personality and Social
Psychology, 65,* 248–260.

Tucker, J. S. (2006). The multilevel effects of occupational stress on counterproductive work
behavior: A longitudinal study in a military context. *Dissertation Abstracts International:
Section B: The Sciences and Engineering, 67 (5-B),* 2867.

Van Dyne, L., Cummings, L. L., & McLean Parks, J. (1995). Extra-role behaviors: in pursuit
of construct and definitional clarity (a bridge over muddied waters). *Research in Organizational Behavior, 17,* 215–285.

Van Harrison, R. (1985). The person-environment fit model and the study of job stress. In T.
A. Beehr & R. S. Bhagat (Eds.), *Human stress and cognition in organizations* (pp. 23–55).
New York: Wiley.

5

Accounting in Organizational Environments

Contextualizing Rules and Fraud

WILLIAM L. SMITH, BRANDON HILL HAINES, AND CINDY L. SEIPEL

In 1998, the telecommunications industry began to slow down and World-Com's stock was declining. CEO Bernard Ebbers came under increasing pressure from banks to cover margin calls on his WorldCom stock that was used to finance his other business endeavors (including timber, yachting). The company's profitability took another hit when it was forced to abandon its proposed merger with Sprint in late 2000. During 2001, Ebbers also per-suaded WorldCom's board of directors to provide him corporate loans and guarantees totaling more than $400 million. Finally, in 2002, when Ebbers was unable to cover the margin calls, he was ousted as CEO of WorldCom. The ouster of Ebbers brought to light a major fraud. Beginning in 1999 and continuing through May 2002, WorldCom, under the direction of Ebbers (CEO), Scott Sullivan (CFO), David Myers (Controller), and Buford Yates (Director of General Accounting), used shady accounting methods to mask its declining financial condition by falsely professing financial growth and profitability to increase the price of WorldCom's stock.

The main elements of the fraud took two forms. First, WorldCom's accounting department underreported "line costs" (interconnection expenses with other telecommunication companies) by capitalizing these costs on the balance sheet rather than properly expensing them on the income statement. Second, the company inflated revenues with bogus accounting entries from "corporate unallocated revenue accounts."

The first discovery of possible illegal activity was by WorldCom's own internal audit department who uncovered approximately $3.8 billion of the fraud in June 2002. The company's audit committee and Board of Direc-tors were notified of the fraud and acted swiftly: Sullivan was fired, Myers resigned, and the Securities and Exchange Commission (SEC) launched an investigation. By the end of 2003, it was estimated that the company's total assets had been inflated by around $11 billion.

WorldCom filed for bankruptcy protection on July 21, 2002. At that time, it was the largest corporate bankruptcy filing in United States history, far exceeding Enron. The company finally succumbed after admitting to the

improper accounting for $3.8 billion in operating expenses only one month
earlier (Beltran, 2002). Bernard Ebbers was found guilty of all charges and
convicted on fraud, conspiracy, and filing false documents with regulators,
and was sentenced to 25 years in prison. Scott Sullivan was convicted for his
role in the massive accounting fraud and sentenced to five years in prison.
In addition, David Myers and Buford Yates were also found guilty for their
respective part in the accounting fraud and sentenced to a year in prison
(Bayot & Farzad, 2005). The moral of the story–there are consequences for
acts of fraud.

—Jonesington, 2007

Merely say the name WorldCom or Enron and most individuals will respond
with a grimace. These once respected companies are known today as mere
commonplace names that symbolize fraud and deception. While less known
than WorldCom and Enron, numerous other cases of widely reported corporate fraud and misconduct exist, involving the names of Sunbeam, Bap-
tist Foundation of Arizona, and Tyco to name a few. In addition, there are
countless examples of companies that experienced differing levels of fraud
little known about beyond a local newspaper headline or listing in the local
police blotter. The lower level of publicity in these cases, however, does not
reduce the seriousness of the malfeasance. Regardless of the notoriety, or
lack thereof, corporate fraud is ever present in our society.

Deviant and criminal behavior in the form of employee fraud can greatly
impact the overall financial health of an organization. Whether the dollar
amount is relatively small, as in the case of an employee not properly including a ten-dollar sale, or relatively large as in the case of a top executive fraudulently misstating a company's financials in order to increase its stock price,
the overall impact is harmful. In fact, there may be a tendency to disregard
small dollar amounts of fraud as negligible and therefore not important. Perhaps the lack of attention such forms of fraud generate, or the feeling that the
amounts are so small that there is no real harm, can be misleading.

A single employee stealing from the company by padding an expense
account may not seem financially significant; however, every dollar stolen
reduces company profit. For a small company where every dollar counts,
the affect can be harmful. And for a larger company with many employees
padding expense accounts, the aggregate financial impact can also adversely
affect profitability, which in turn affects all the stakeholders. Further, reduced
profitability for a business can reduce the amount of salary and benefits the
business can pay, also harming innocent employees. When taking this into
consideration, fraudulent workplace behavior directed at the organization

may have unintended negative consequences for individuals throughout the organization.

In this chapter we will discuss employee fraud in organizations and the related checks and balances that should be in place to reduce its occurrence. The discussion is not an exhaustive discourse of accounting and auditing rules and their related applications, but should serve rather as informative for all levels of management in heightening awareness of the many forms that fraud in the workplace can take. In addition, both the necessity of an appropriate internal control environment and the respective roles of internal and external auditors will be considered. This should provide a better understanding of employee fraud and the related financial implications for the organization and its stakeholders.

Background: Types of Fraud

The key terms associated with fraud are "intent" and "deception." Two categories of fraud defined by the Association of Certified Fraud Examiners (ACFE, 2008), and adopted by the Statement on Auditing Standards (SAS) No. 99 as set forth by the American Institute of Certified Public Accountants (AICPA), are (a) misappropriation of assets and (b) fraudulent financial reporting (AICPA, 2002). Misappropriation is the theft or misuse of company assets most often by employees. It is often regarded as "fraud against the organization" because it involves stealing from the business and is consistent with what other contributors to this text refer to as "deviant workplace behavior." Although misappropriation is often associated with lower level employees, this is not always the case. According to the ACFE 2010 Report to the Nation on Occupational Fraud and Abuse (ACFE, 2010, 50), misappropriation by employees represented only 46.2% of the cases while the remaining 53.8% of the cases were committed by owners, executives, and management level individuals. This same ACFE report (ACFE, 2010, 61) highlighted that the accounting department continues to be the single greatest source of fraud cases.

The dollar amount of asset misappropriation incidences can be small where an employee fails to record a sale, large where an employee steals an expensive inventory item, or any dollar amount in between. The point is simply that such a fraud constitutes a loss to the company that adversely affects profitability. According to Ian Sherr (2009), thefts by employees of U.S. retail merchandise accounted for $15.9 billion, or 44 percent of theft losses at stores—more than shoplifting and vendor fraud combined. Further, a study by consultancy group Jack L. Hayes International found that as many as one out of every thirty employees was apprehended for theft in 2008 (Hayes, 2009). In sum, misappropriation of assets by employees is extremely costly and problematic to companies. Whether the dollar amount per episode is small or large, management must be made aware of the problem and remain ever vigilant.

A second, more publicized but less common, type of fraud is fraudulent financial reporting. This type of fraud is represented by cases such as WorldCom and Enron and is referred to as "fraud on behalf of the organization," since the objective is to make the company look better by "cooking the books." Such a fraud is most likely committed by upper management in order to obtain a needed loan, increase the stock price, benefit from good publicity for the company and/or management, or even to obtain performance bonuses based on company profit. Fraudulent financial reporting is most often associated with larger companies although it can occur in any organization. Figure 1 illustrates the difference between the two types of fraud and the manner in which they impact the organization.

Is the difference between these two types of fraud really important, and accordingly, should we even care? Both activities are detrimental to the organization; however, a single case of fraudulent financial reporting fraud can be monetarily large whereas a single case of misappropriation of assets may not. Simply consider a CFO fraudulently misstating the financial statements by several million dollars compared to an employee misstating some expense reports for several hundred or even several thousand dollars. Both employees engaged in malfeasance yet the focus is too often on the high level act of fraud. The dollar amounts may perhaps be deemed less significant and therefore not as important when asset misappropriation is involved. However, the difference is analogous to several hundred people who are injured in a commuter train accident compared to just a few people who are injured in a single car accident. The focus is on the large number injured in the single event yet the aggregate number of people injured annually due to automobile accidents far exceeds those injured in the relatively isolated occurrence of commuter train accidents.

Of course the deterrence of both types of fraud is aided by certain safeguards inherent in the requirements for publicly held companies. Publicly held companies are overseen by the SEC and are required to have an independent audit, follow certain reporting requirements, and have a system of internal controls in place which should reduce the instances of all types of fraud. This system of internal controls should include checks and balances (such as reconciliations, or multiple approvals on large purchases) to help ensure that the company runs the way it is intended. However smaller

Fig. 5.1. Fraud on behalf of and against the organization

The Organization

▼   ▲

Misappropriation of assets or "fraud against the organization" causes the removal of assets from the organization

Fraudulent financial reporting or "fraud on behalf of the organization" is done to make the organization look better than it is

nonpublic companies are much less regulated than public companies. Therefore, the importance of owner and management oversight and an appreciation for the importance of internal controls (even when not mandated) are magnified for these smaller companies.

Internal Controls and Management Responsibility

Consistent with the notion of an organization's culture (see chapter 8 of this book), management is responsible for the establishment of an effective control environment that ensures appropriate accountability and oversight of the financial reporting and the related processes that are responsible for creating value. In 1985 the Committee of Sponsoring Organizations (COSO) was created to sponsor the National Commission on Fraudulent Financial Reporting to provide guidance in assisting management with the development of internal controls. COSO's first publication, Internal Control–Integrated Framework (COSO, 1992), set forth five components of internal control: (1) the control environment, (2) risk assessment, (3) control activities, (4) information and communication and (5) monitoring.

The control environment is also referred to as the "tone at the top" of the organization; the perceived importance management places on internal control. Risk assessment is the company's assessment of their own risk areas (relating to geographic area and product types, for example). Control activities are the policies and procedures, such as segregation of duties and security of assets, which are put into place to help further the objectives of the company's management. Information and communication is the system in which different responsible parties obtain the reports and documents necessary to properly direct the business. Finally, monitoring by management is the process in which deficiencies in the internal controls are identified and modified as necessary.

The responsibility of management for the establishment of the internal control environment continues to be reinforced by the auditing standards that external auditors must follow. Statement on Auditing Standards (SAS) No. 85 (AICPA, 1997), International Standard on Auditing (ISA) 580 (IAASB, 2008) and the Sarbanes-Oxley Act of 2002 (SOX, 2002) all require that external auditors obtain certain representations from management of the company being audited regarding the control environment to ensure full compliance with the assertions made by management to the independent auditors. Auditors, as well as the SEC, recognize that the implementation and application of internal controls are the purview of management.

The AICPA further clarified the responsibility of the auditor with respect to fraud in SAS 110 (AICPA, 2006). The SAS stated that management credibility regarding the reliability of the financial reporting process is critical. Further, the credibility of management must be considered by the auditors when planning the financial audit. This is especially important, as the perceived credibility of management will now directly affect the amount of "digging" that an auditor must do in the accounting records. In the event that the auditor cannot perform the necessary audit procedures and related work to overcome this concern, it may provide cause for the auditor to consider withdrawing from the audit engagement.

The AICPA has recognized that management assertions fall into the following three key financial reporting activities: (1) the legitimacy of the actual business transaction - Did it really happen and was the entire population of actual events captured in the correct accounting period and is often referred to as a proper accounting cut off; (2) the legitimacy of the journal entries to record transactions that are posted to the general ledger and what management does to ensure that the accounting for those transactions captured in the first category is appropriate; and (3) the legitimacy of the internal control environment established by management for ensuring the propriety of the public presentation and disclosures of the financial impacts of the transactions aggregated in the financial statements (financial statement presentation).

Table 5.1 gives a summary of the specific assertions outlined by the AICPA's SAS 110 (AICPA, 2006) that management is responsible for providing as internal controls.

A review of the table indicates the human resource implications associated with the AICPA's SAS 110. Given the responsibility of management in properly implementing such internal controls, human resource managers may want to pay particular attention to which individuals are recruited for managerial positions, as well as to which employees are promoted to managerial

Table 5.1
Internal Control Assertions

Transactions:

- The activity actually took place.
- 100% of the activity was accurately captured.
- The activity was in the correct accounting period.
- The activity was properly presented in the financial disclosure.

Accounting:

- All assets and liabilities have been properly valued.
- All items reflected in the general ledger actually exist.
- All existing items have been properly captured by the accounting system.
- All legal rights and responsibilities have been captured and accounted for.

Financial Statement Presentation:

- The financial disclosures are accurate.
- The financial disclosures include all valid accounts.
- The financial disclosures are properly classified and are understandable.

---

positions. In essence, if management is responsible for the successful implementation of internal controls, human resource managers should do all they can to ensure the competence and integrity of those individuals in managerial positions.

The Roles of External vs. Internal Auditors

The role of external auditors as described by professional standards is to express an opinion about whether the financial statements prepared by management are fairly presented, in all material respects, in conformity with the generally accepted accounting principles at work in the United States. The external auditor is only required to look for fraud to the extent that it may have a material impact on the decisions made by the users of the financial statement information. External auditors, therefore, do not provide absolute assurance regarding the correctness of the financial statements, and cannot be held responsible by management—or by those outside the

organization—to guarantee that all errors and/or fraud are found and corrected during the audit. The level of responsibility associated with an external audit is "reasonable assurance" of finding material misstatements due
to errors and fraud; however, nothing in the auditing literature specifically
defines the level of materiality.

Materiality is necessarily a matter of judgment, depending both upon the
specific company involved and the particular users of the accounting information. Generally, "rules of thumb" such as 5–10% of net income or ½–1%
of total revenues are all that is available. There is no "one size fits all" dollar amount that defines a material amount. The rule-of-thumb percentages
are merely utilized to provide some threshold of financial impact relative to
the size of the organization. Therefore materiality for an auditor may be an
amount much larger than the owners or management of the company would
choose to lose.

The more comprehensive and complete the internal controls over the
financial statement numbers are, the less audit testing is necessary. In order
to prove that controls are reliable and justify the reduction of additional audit
testing, the auditor must test such controls. Therefore, the more extensive the
internal control environment is, the less extensively the audit testing needs to
be performed, as the information is more reliable. Auditors are tasked with
providing information to management and the board of directors regarding
the weakness of such controls. In the case of a strong internal control environment, the auditors can focus more on the audit rather than overcoming
weaknesses resulting from less extensive control environments.

Unlike internal controls affecting the financial statement numbers, however, environmental or process controls are often untested by the external
auditor. The extent of testing of these controls would depend on either the
contractual requirements of the auditee or whether the auditor feels that the
controls could be relied upon to reduce the overall testing requirement of
the financial records. In addition, although the external auditors, as previously stated, provide some feedback on financial statement controls, recall
that they also only have the responsibility to detect material misstatements
due to error and fraud, with the logical result that not all financial statement
controls are under their purview, but only ones that the auditors view as possibly preventing material misstatement. Outsiders, as well as those within
the company, should be aware, therefore, that there may be lapses in internal
controls during the audit that may not come to light.

While external auditors may discover fraud or even have the skill base to
assist in the investigation of corporate fraud, they are precluded from advo-
cating on behalf of their client if the situation progressed to the point of a

trial. If expected to provide expert witness testimony at a trial, the external auditor would be forfeiting independence from the client and thus no longer function as an external auditor. An external auditor is required to maintain independence from an audit client in compliance with the ethical rules set forth by the AICPA. Otherwise the CPA would not be able to state as part of the respective audit opinion that the audit was conducted in accordance with generally accepted auditing standards. The general concept of Rule 101 of the AICPA Code of Professional Conduct (AICPA, 1988) is that the auditor must not have any vested interest in the outcome of the audit and that the auditee does not have any ability to influence the auditor, in what is often referred to as independence in appearance as well as in fact. Audit clients would generally have to hire a second accounting firm to serve as an expert witness.

Internal auditors typically are not as focused on the propriety of financial statements as on the effectiveness and efficiency of an organization's activities. The act of auditing for compliance with established company policy or industry benchmarks is often referred to as operational auditing. Internal auditors are often called upon by management to assist in the deterrence and investigation of fraud. The profession is generally unregulated, however, which causes confusion as to what role an internal auditor is expected to play. To help provide clarity, organizations such as the Institute of Internal Auditors have been established to supply some of the needed guidance.

The Regulatory Environment

An external auditor of any publicly held company registered with the Securities and Exchange Commission (SEC) must design the audit process to render two opinions specifically for internal controls. The opinions that must be issued are regarding: (1) the auditor's appraisal of management's assessment of the effectiveness of internal controls over financial reporting, and (2) the auditor's own assessment of the effectiveness of those same internal controls. These requirements, brought about by Sarbanes-Oxley, increase the auditor's responsibility to test (and report upon) the internal controls of their client.

Audits of nonpublic entities have limited responsibility to regulatory oversight. Exceptions to this observation would include recipients of federal money, financial institutions, and insurance companies. In these cases the auditors would report their findings to specifically designated outside oversight boards. However the requirements for internal control testing for such clients vary depending upon the oversight requirements in the particular industry.

Therefore, since most companies are not publically held, there has been little to no regulatory oversight. Such businesses, even if audited for loan or other purposes, generally have little internal control requirements. Auditors of nonpublic entities often rely only upon a check of the ending financial statement balances. Criminal and civil penalties could possibly serve as deterrents to fraudulent actions on the part of employees, but in many cases involving employee fraud, it is up to the business itself to catch and prosecute offenders. Obviously, nonpublic companies have the need for a good set of owner or management implemented internal controls to prevent or reduce fraud.

Elements of Fraud

Management has the ability to significantly influence or to mitigate an opportunity to commit fraud. The first component of the Committee of the Sponsoring Organizations Internal Control–Integrated Framework (COSO, 1992) report named this the control environment, but it is commonly referred to as the tone at the top of the organization. Management's embrace of the internal control system is essential for an effective control structure.

A properly designed control environment is one that ensures an individual does not have the ability to access the custody of assets, the ability to process the information necessary to cover up the removal of assets, or the authority to actually remove the assets. This is known as the segregation of duties and is a critical part of the control activities of an organization. One example of such an activity is the assigning of bank reconciliation duties to a person who does not write the checks, increasing the likelihood that a check written to an inappropriate party will be caught. A second example of segregation of duties is to prevent a sales person from being allowed to grant credit approval to a purchaser. A credit department would be more independent in making credit determinations than a salesperson with a potential commission on the line.

The implementation of such controls, however, generally comes at a cost. Accordingly, the tradeoff between the costs of such implementations versus the benefits of reducing losses due to fraud (risk/rewards) must be considered. For example, surveillance equipment costing thousands of dollars would not be installed to monitor a $100 petty cash box. Generally this determination of cost/benefit is evaluated according to two critical elements: the probability of an irregularity (an act with intent) occurring, and the probability of the financial impact or magnitude of such an event. The most money and effort can then be spent to ensure that the propriety of controls are in place to mitigate the risk of an irregularity that has a high probability of occurring, and a high probability that the irregularity will involve a significant or material dollar amount.

SAS 99, *Consideration of Fraud in a Financial Statement Audit*, was issued in October 2002 (AICPA, 2002), partly in response to the accounting scandals at Tyco, WorldCom, and Enron. As mentioned earlier in this chapter, there are two types of fraud that SAS 99 addresses: (1) the misappropriation of assets (fraud against the organization) and (2) fraudulent reporting (fraud on behalf of the organization). The statement further points out intention as the balancing point between an error and fraud. Specifically, errors are those misstatements or events that are considered to be unintentional, whereas fraud is an intentional act of wrongdoing.

The pursuit of the legal remedies for dealing with fraud may go the route of seeking a civil action, a criminal conviction, or both. Civil torts are wrongful acts that cause harm to another individual. The party suffering the loss can claim compensation. Civil trials do not result in imprisonment. Criminal fraud, on the other hand, involves a violation of law. A less serious crime is a misdemeanor; a more serious crime is a felony. Criminal fraud may result in fines, restitution, and/or a prison sentence for the perpetrator. Since external auditors must remain independent from their client in fact and appearance, it is imperative that management is the party responsible for prosecuting any fraud that is found, even if that fraud was discovered during an audit.

As previously discussed, external auditors have only a limited responsibility for the detection of fraud. They do have a clear responsibility, however, for the reporting of any fraud detected. Auditors are required to perform their job with due professional care, which means informing management and/or the board of directors (whichever is appropriate for the company involved) of any fraud discovered during the audit. Management, not the auditors, must make any prosecutorial decisions and pursue available remedies. The auditors can only inform management of their findings.

In addition to the definitions set forth in SAS 99 (AICPA, 2002), the "fraud triangle" is an important component which initially appeared in Joseph Wells' book *Occupational Fraud and Abuse* (Wells, 1997). The triangle is comprised of three elements: (1) incentive, (2) opportunity, and (3) the ability to rationalize the propriety of the action. Incentive to commit fraud may come in the form of desires or needs, or it may arise from pressures to improve economic performance. Economic crisis at either the personal level or the organization level will generally cause an individual to take a second look at an opportunity. Opportunity can cause temptation. Finally, an attitude that can rationalize the fraudulent behavior as being acceptable, or maybe even necessary, in a given situation is generally the last element resulting in the execution of fraud. An illustration of the fraud triangle in relation to a misappropriation of assets situation is set forth in figure 5.2.

Fig. 5.2. Fraud triangle

Financial Incentive
External pressures on employees
that leads to misappropriation of
cash or other assets of the
organization.

Opportunity
Environment that allows an
employee to carry out the
misappropriation of cash or
other organizational assets.

Rationalization
Employee mindset to justify
unethical behavior to
misappropriate cash or other
assets of the organization

Note that the fraud triangle elements are applicable to malfeasance at any dollar amount. Further, while there may be a cost/benefit tradeoff for addressing lower level employee fraud, such as padding an expense account, the aforementioned elements are nevertheless applicable. In sum, management should always carefully consider the potential for fraud, misappropriation, or abuse and should exercise every preventative measure necessary to attenuate the risk. Later, we will discuss six actual cases of misconduct covering a range of materiality and that address both misappropriation of assets and fraudulent financial reporting in relation to the fraud triangle.

Financial incentive can range in dollar amount, and applies whether or not the misappropriation is a simple small-dollar or complex large-dollar fraud. An assistant store manager may have fallen behind on household bills and thus see a financial incentive to pocket some cash from a few unrecorded sales or perhaps to steal a few inventory items to bring home for personal use; or the controller of a company may have succumbed to a gambling addiction and need a large sum of money to settle debts. Either would be embezzling corporate assets to cover personal needs. Financial incentives of this kind come in all amounts and for all kinds of reasons. In any case, it is important to note that the incentives are external to the organization, and accordingly, management should be vigilant of the fact that they are ever present and most likely undetectable.

Rationalization naturally follows the need. Whether the employee justifies pocketing a few sales in response to an immediate financial situation or because of feeling underappreciated or under compensated, rationalization is what legitimizes the misconduct. The employee may commit an isolated small-dollar act of theft or numerous thefts that aggregate as much larger amounts. The employee may also have access to accounting records or control of assets that could lead to misappropriations of even larger amounts. Logic and value judgments at this point are not applicable; rationalization is an emotional mechanism that facilitates the internal approval allowing the employee to engage in the malfeasance. He or she is someone who justifies his or her inappropriate actions. As in the case with financial incentives, rationalization is also external to the organization, and thus management should be ever vigilant, knowing that these internal thoughts can be present and most likely undetectable.

As mentioned, financial incentives and rationalization are both external to the organization and therefore generally uncontrollable in the workplace. However, management does have the ability to influence workplace opportunity through the establishment of an appropriate control environment that serves to minimize or even mitigate all types of employee fraud. According to the AICPA auditing standards SAS 99, "Neither fraudulent financial reporting nor misappropriation of assets can occur without a perceived opportunity to commit and conceal the act" (AICPA, 2002). Essentially, opportunity is the only variable that management can control. Therefore, internal control procedures (checks and balances) must be implemented and constantly monitored and updated to reduce opportunities for employee malfeasance.

Discussion

We opened our chapter with the highly publicized case of WorldCom and identified several other high profile cases of corporate fraudulent financial reporting. While these cases may be both fascinating and insightful, such large frauds are not widespread. The odds are more likely that most managers will face lower level cases of fraudulent financial reporting and misappropriation of assets on a smaller dollar scale. Understanding the nature of these cases and their related financial impact is therefore important. Here, we have selected actual client cases that involve both types of fraud and range from thousands to millions of dollars. After the facts of each case, we will discuss how the act was perpetrated, how it was discovered, the financial impact, the potential financial impact had the act not been discovered, and the lessons learned. These are more typical of the cases that most managers will encounter; at the same time, management should always be aware of the possibility of fraud regardless of the dollar amount involved. While the earlier cases of misappropriation of assets presented here may appear small in terms of dollar amounts, the potential overall financial impact on the organization, and the need at all times for management to maintain a heightened awareness, must be considered

Cases

The following six cases illustrate various examples of employee fraud. Each case is based upon actual events encountered in client engagements. Given the personal nature of each case and the related client confidentiality, the names have been changed; however, the actual details are provided. The first four cases involve misappropriation of assets or "fraud against the organization." The last two cases are relatively larger examples of fraudulent financial reporting or "fraud on behalf of the organization."

1. Misappropriation of Cash Sales

Incoming cash from a customer sale is often the target of employee fraud. It is generally easily accessible at the initial point where it is tendered by the customer, and sales transactions are easily voided, reversed or just never entered into the accounting system. Therefore, the opportunity to commit a cash sale fraud is always high. Just because a sale was made, without the appropriate controls in place, there is no guarantee that the transaction will be properly recorded or that the money will make it to the bank. While one or even a few unrecorded sales may go unnoticed in the short run, over time, the aggregate totals may become significant and conspicuous.

The owner of a veterinary clinic noticed a pattern of little to no cash sales being recognized by one of the most tenured and loyal front desk employees. After the owner reviewed the records for several months, he was convinced that at the very least something looked odd, so he decided to investigate.

In order to catch the employee, her shift would have to be properly staged to single her out and thus remove all opportunity to point fingers elsewhere. As the employees traded shifts the cash drawer was properly reconciled to the sales so far that day. The suspected employee was now on her shift with sole access and responsibility for her cash drawer. A secret shopper was sent in to buy dog food and tendered two twenty-dollar bills in payment. The appropriate amount of change was given back to the customer. However, as suspected, a receipt was not provided, and the secret shopper had been instructed not to ask for one. At the close of the employee shift, the office manager (on a surprise basis) counted and reconciled the cash drawer of the employee to the shift sales record. While the credit card and check sales all balanced to the sales for the shift, the cash purchase made by the secret shopper was not reflected as a sale on the register and the related cash was not included in the drawer. As a result, the trusted employee was confronted and soon confessed to taking the money due to her financial circumstances. She was terminated and charges were filed.

This simple type of employee fraud is common. A similar operation was discovered at a dental office where the office manager who collected payments directly from patients held back any cash receipts from the daily bank deposit. There were no controls in place to ensure that all the cash that came in the door actually made it to the bank; thus, the "day sheets" that recorded and receipted patient collections were never reconciled to the bank deposits. It is for such purposes of accountability that many stores require receipts for all transactions. In fact many businesses offer customer incentives to ask for a sales receipt or to call a hot line to report if a receipt is not offered at the time a sale is rung up.

Lessons learned:

No employee should ever be thought of as so trustworthy that he or she is beyond reproach. Business owners, or higher level managers, should always be vigilant to ensure that all sales activity is properly captured and accounted for. The long term pattern of little to no cash sales finally raised suspicion in these cases. The total financial impact of the stolen cash from the dental office amounted to more than $45,000. Due to the poor accounting records associated with the veterinarian's office, the total loss could not be quantified. Consider that a large business with numerous employees responsible for making cash sales may be faced with an even greater exposure to employee misappropriations involving larger dollar amounts.

Since an employer would not know about his or her employees' financial needs or other pressures, nor would the employer know about any employee's ability to rationalize his or her improper behavior, it would be impossible to know exactly which employees to watch. Employers must therefore rely upon preventative or detective internal control procedures. Preventative measures such as installing surveillance cameras or instituting a policy that all sales require a receipt could be implemented. Further detective control measures such as reconciling reductions in inventory levels to corresponding sales or the reconciliation of daily sales to the respective bank deposits could be employed to further ensure all daily activity is properly accounted for. By reducing the opportunity (see the aforementioned fraud triangle discussion) for employees to pocket a cash sale or to modify related accounting records (see discussion regarding segregation of duties), and possibly implementing some additional detection controls, the overall financial health of the organization may improve.

2. Credit Card Fraud

The opportunity was laid out at the feet of Sue, the payables clerk, who was responsible for many of the general office duties. As in most under-staffed organizations, Sue was highly praised for her ability to wear so many hats. Her supervisor did not like being bothered by trivial questions, so Sue just made things happen, which made everyone happy. Unfortunately, Sue was facing a lot of personal financial issues including the fact that her sick mother was now residing with her. During the day, Sue's mother was left at home where she loved to watch home shopping television shows. Unfortunately, Sue's mother had a shopping addiction. Sue was often over-worked and would take work, including her payables work, home to catch up. Her mother was always more than willing to help and was eventually able to gain access to the company credit card number. The card had been entrusted to Sue for the purpose of paying company expenditures. It is still unclear if Sue's mother originally took the number with or without Sue's knowledge, but over time they both saw an opportunity. When Sue's mother started using the number to charge her home shopping purchases, Sue saw these charges come through on the company statement. To cover up the activity, Sue made a copy of the credit card statement, cut out the inappropriate charges, and then recopied the statement prior to making it part of the normal accounts payable package. The doctored package was then provided as support for the payable checks submitted for approval and signing. No one ever questioned why the credit card statement was a copy instead of the original and no one ever checked the statement to ensure that it added up correctly. Once the checks were signed, they were returned to Sue to mail. This process gave Sue the opportunity to mail the original statement payment notice with the properly signed check. Sue would then provide the accounting department with the appropriate jour-nal entry to post. The accounting department was very far behind in the production of monthly financial statements and appreciated the help.

Seeing how well this worked, Sue saw an opportunity to fix her car troubles. After all, most executives in the office had a company car, and she always had to rent cars for visiting executives that came into town for meetings. One day after her car had its last attempt at running, she decided to rent herself a car on the company card. The process that had worked well for the home shopping charges soon worked well in turn to solve her car problems and for numerous other purchases.

This monthly routine succeeded until Sue was out of the office on vacation and the mail began to pile up. Since her boss did not want to see Sue come back and deal with the stress of having to address the large stack of mail, the mail was opened and invoices were sorted and reviewed for payment. It was at this point that the home shopping charges were seen on the original statement. Credit card statements were then ordered for the prior two months. These statements were compared to the ones submitted to accounting to support the prior disbursements, exposing the fact that the statements had been doctored, and more statements were ordered and reviewed. When she finally returned from her vacation, Sue was confronted with the evidence. It was later determined that approximately $40,000 had been stolen over the course of only seven months.

Lessons learned:

While Sue may have perceived herself to be a good person and a hard working employee, personal circumstances created the financial incentive (see fraud triangle discussion) that was significant enough to justify her actions when she could not see another way out of her personal situation. Again, no employee should ever be assumed beyond reproach. Basic process controls could have eliminated the opportunity for Sue to commit fraud. Specifically, payments should always be made from an original invoice rather than a copy. Also, critical accounting functions, such as the posting of general ledger entries, should always be segregated from the independent review and approval process. Unaccountable access to an accounting system is a recipe for trouble. The opportunity to perpetrate erroneous payments from doctored invoices can be reduced by simply segregating the duties between the payables clerk and the authority to charge to a company credit card. In addition, company work should be done at work on company time. Removal of company documents can potentially compromise most corporate access controls. Finally, a company should always provide for the work of an employee to be taken care of while they are out on vacation. This is the exact reason why federally chartered banks require their employees to take a two-week annual vacation and assign someone else to complete the daily work of that employee during the time they are absent.

3. Expense Report Fraud

Expense reports represent an employee's accounting of his or her expenses incurred on behalf of an employer. Unfortunately, the padding of expense reports is a common problem faced by employers. In this particular case, the employee involved was the executive director (ED) of a non-profit organization. Like most non-profit organizations, this employer could not afford to pay high salaries, so employees lived on minimal incomes. The ED herself was in need of additional personal financial resources. She soon realized that the process for submittal of expense reports offered an opportunity to enhance her pay, especially since it did not require further approval. Additionally, the processor of the ED's expense report was her subordinate, and the ED had the authority to fire or otherwise adversely affect her subordinate's job. A final aspect of opportunity was that the ED was only required to supply receipts for expenditures—she was never required to provide any documentation or proof that the expenditures actually took place.

Her favorite way to enhance her expense report was with handwritten receipts. She knew which organizations would issue these types of receipts so she would frequent them often. The handwritten receipts were then altered with a similar pen to increase the face amounts and then attached to the expense report to submit for reimbursement. Her plan worked well until an independent accountant was hired by the board of directors to prepare a set of financial statements for the organization. During the engagement the accountant noticed that certain expense line items did not make sense given the corresponding business activity. An investigation was then conducted whereupon it was found that the ED had stolen more than $17,000. She was convicted and required to pay restitution to the organization.

Lessons learned:

Following the misappropriation, the organization implemented a policy that all expense reports of the ED must be reviewed and approved by a member of the board. Properly segregated duties no longer allowed the executive director to be able to use the power of that position to intimidate subordinates into approving and processing inappropriate claims for reimbursements. Further, a policy was implemented where only in rare exceptions would employees fund corporate expenditures and request subsequent reimbursement. Stronger controls were put in place to ensure that the accounts payable process was also properly segregated from the ability to financially commit the organization or to approve actual payment by the organization.

By implementing sound internal controls, the opportunity to commit this type of fraud was mitigated. An interesting side note to this case is that low pay is often cited as a characteristic that increases the likelihood of employee rationalization for fraud. Employees who feel underpaid for their efforts may rationalize that they are "owed" the fraudulently taken money. An organization can reduce this aspect of rationalization by making sure their employees are properly compensated. Accordingly, the compensation and benefits structure of an organization is very important and should be periodically reviewed and updated. The effect of low pay on rationalization can also be seen in the next example.

4. Sale Back of Vacation Time Fraud

Jack, the ED of a very powerful professional trade association, found himself in a unique situation. Over the course of time, he had become the icon of the very organization for which he was the trusted steward. The membership respected the heavy-handed way in which the support staff was tasked for production. He brought significant national recognition to the organization, and under his watch the sleepy association had become a significant force with which to be reckoned. Jack was praised by his board of directors for running such a large ship with so few employees and such low association membership fees.

To ensure that the public saw him as a caring and fatherly figure, Jack instituted a policy to encourage his employees to take time off to be with their family and regenerate themselves. The policy was simple, employees had to use annual vacation time or lose it. The trouble was that most employees found (assuming that Jack actually approved their vacation request) that they were required to call in daily to see if there were any "fires" that required immediate attention. Jack felt he never asked his employees to do anything that he would not do himself. He ran the association as if it were his personal company, and over time, with the board's praise and trust, Jack began to feel a strong sense of ownership. Board members came and went over the years, but Jack was seen as the cornerstone for decisions and direction. Unfortunately he was undercompensated compared to the other numerous transient board members. Once Jack started feeling underappreciated he started to rationalize acts that he felt would help to even out the scorecard.

Late one year he decided that because of work, and through no fault of his own, he would not be able to take his annual vacation. Since he was not able to take his vacation because of company needs, he felt that the company should compensate him for it. This was quickly taken care of with his personal "request" to payroll and accounting. Jack used his authoritative position to have his next payroll check include the value of the vacation time that he "sold back" in breach of the organization's stated policy of "use or lose it." Unfortunately for Jack, he did not realize that he had made more than a few enemies during his rise to the top, and ultimately the external auditors were tipped off by disgruntled employees. During the investigation, in addition to the vacation compensation override, other acts of management override that personally benefited Jack were discovered. Jack, the ED and cornerstone of the organization, was asked by the board of directors to step down.

It was subsequently discovered that Jack had converted approximately $80,000 of corporate funds to his personal use over the course of approximately eighteen months. Since he ruled with an iron hand with the board's blessing, internally no one was in a position to challenge him. Anyone going to the Board would have been dismissed as a disgruntled employee trying to cause trouble.

Lessons learned:

The trade association learned that the unchecked opportunity for management overrides leaves a company vulnerable to malfeasance. Management overrides are acts of using one's position of authority, either implied or actual, to move from following standing corporate policies and procedures. Often the overriding of internal controls is couched as being "efficient" in cutting through red tape. Such an individual often is also taking the stage to publicly display his or her situational power and demonstrate corporate stature (see Elias, Gibson, and Barney's chapter on power and deviance/crime in this volume). If gone unchecked or unchallenged by the process environment, such activity may become de facto acceptable and an approved procedure. In short, as discussed earlier, the third leg of the fraud triangle—opportunity—has come into play. By overriding process controls, a manager completely eliminates the effectiveness of such controls that had been established to mitigate the risk of unauthorized expenditures. In this case, the trade association, as well as its board of directors, learned that it had lost perspective on the ED, and as a result had turned a blind eye to the situation. No longer was the monitoring system objective. If Jack had been watched a little closer, and not allowed to override the accounting system, the fraud might have been prevented. While appreciated for all his hard work and dedication, like any other employee, Jack should never have been seen as beyond reproach. The board should also have anticipated that Jack's below-market pay scale might create a certain level of financial incentive. Despite the board having no awareness of external pressures or even any rationalization on Jack's part, internal controls should have been in place to reduce the opportunity for fraud. Given Jack's position, the organization unfortunately provided him with the clear opportunity to steal. Much of this problem could have been detected sooner had something as simple as an anonymous employee fraud hotline been available to all employees. While the board may have had a blind eye to the situation, it is certain the subordinating employees were aware of Jack's actions.

5. Adjusting Journal Entry (AJE) Fraud

Fraud takes many forms: it may be misappropriation of assets (such as the taking of cash or other assets) or it may be fraudulent financial reporting (such as a cover up of key information to avoid being the bearer of bad news). Due to the significant regulatory reporting requirements facing financial institutions, their books are often vulnerable to being "cooked" as the three elements of the fraud triangle take root and surface. As addressed earlier in the chapter, fraud of this nature is often rationalized as being done on behalf of the organization as opposed to against it. But does that make it any more acceptable?

During a routine analysis of published information conducted by a bank's internal audit department, interest expense as a percent of actual funds borrowed by that bank appeared to be higher than reasonable, which was taken as a signal that the bank might have improperly reported its borrowings. Interestingly, the interest expense reported by the bank's internally generated income statement showed that the actual interest expense was very much in line with the management-created budget for that same time period. The detailed backup for the journal entries affecting that specific expense account were then requested and reviewed in search of a logical explanation, such as a general ledger posting error. Through this process it was discovered that the bank was experiencing significant liquidity problems caused by underperforming assets. The Federal Reserve had actually closed the Federal Reserve Discount Window on the bank, meaning that the Federal Reserve would no longer provide a weekly vehicle for the bank to borrow enough cash to meet its federally mandated liquidity requirements, forcing the bank to seek alternative sources of liquidity. Without the liquidity available to satisfy the federal requirements, the bank had become vulnerable to a takeover by the federal bank examiners.

In order to obtain the needed funds to meet the required liquidity position, management of the bank had begun drawing down on their "uncollected funds" held by other banks and then reporting these funds as available to meet liquidity needs. In this action meant to get around their reporting problems, however, it should be noted that uncollected funds represent the corporate equivalent of taking immediate cash back on a bank deposit made up only of out of state checks. Generally, banks will put a three-day hold on such checks to ensure that they are actually going to be funded by the bank they are issued on before the receiving bank will actually issue the cash to a third party. Otherwise the bank is assuming the risk of loss associated with those checks that are not ultimately funded. Just as a bank customer who overdrafts his or her respective checking account is generally charged a penalty by that bank, a financial institution that introduces an overdraft from another bank into its account is treated no differently. In this case, penalties were charged and collected against the bank for drawing down on uncollected funds.

Management attempted to cover up the situation by accounting for the penalty as a charge to interest expense. Since the dollar amount being expensed was within budget, the periodic review by the board of directors of the monthly actual to budget activity did not raise any red flags.

The messenger, also known as the corporate controller, had no interest in the board being potentially unhappy with his cash flow and/or money management skills. As he saw it, the reporting "problem" had been fixed, so what was the harm? His action was on behalf of the organization and was saving it from an unfriendly takeover by the "bad" bank examiners. Through the controller's rationalization, meanwhile, the board was kept unaware of the significance of the liquidity problem facing their institution. The corporate controller considered that he had found the opportunity to save the bank since he had the ability to post to the general ledger and was also the independent reviewer of all journal entries there. No one questioned his authority to make journal entries, and no one else was responsible for reviewing the entries made there. No controls to prevent acts of fraudulent reporting, or to detect fraudulent reporting that had been done, were in place. Key members of senior management knew it, and knew also that their jobs would be at risk if news of the actual circumstances got out. The fraudulent situation was thus allowed to go undetected by the board and the examiners for some time. For investors, the result was a false confidence in the organization's ability to continue as a viable business. Ultimately, these same investors lost their investment when the bank was closed by federal examiners due to problems with profitability and lack of necessary capital.

Lessons learned:

For a control to be effective, it must possess two primary characteristics. First, the control must bring attention to the situation (i.e. diagnostic ability) and second it must capture the attention of an objective individual who will act on the information without bias.

Fraudulent reporting might have been prevented if appropriate and objective process controls were in place to ensure the propriety of the journal entries recording the penalty as interest expense. However, since it was the fraudster and not an impartial observer in charge of the control process, it would have been more effective to use a detective control method in this situation. A detective control method is one that will raise a flag and call attention to a problem that has already occurred. In this case, had the treasurer of the board been better trained regarding financial reporting and analytical procedures—such as the interest expense going up in the absence of an increase in debt—he might possibly have detected the fraudulent act.

6. Earnings Boosting Fraud

In the 1987 movie *Wall Street*, Gordon Gekko, an influential corporate raider, coined the phrase "greed is good." The qualities of greed are beyond the scope of this chapter, but clearly greed is the cornerstone of many fraudulent activities. Companies often face incredible pressure to meet short-term earnings projections or potentially face losing market capitalization value. Capitalization value represents the number of shares of outstanding stock multiplied by the current trading value of that stock. Stakeholders will often look at the difference between capitalization value and net book value as an indicator of the value of the company. The act of a dividend declaration and the ability to make dividend distributions helps to drive the market value of stock.

A new local company was launched a number of years ago. Its stock was not listed on the New York Stock Exchange, but was traded via over-the-counter (OTC) markets. While not a major stock exchange, OTC shares are nevertheless publicly traded, and therefore subject to the rules of the SEC and other regulatory bodies. Thus, they are subject to widespread scrutiny by stakeholders. The officers of the company negotiated all aspects of the start-up capital needs by tying prospective vendors to stock purchase agreements. The potential rewards were high, and many agreed to purchase stock in exchange for future lucrative contracts. Many of these investors did not have the available cash to purchase the stock, so they borrowed the money by pledging the stock shares as collateral. Loans of this nature generally required the fair market value of the stock to exceed the borrowed amount by a certain set percentage. If the value of the stock declined, additional collateral was required or the loan would need to be paid down in order to bring the outstanding balance into compliance.

The officers of the company had a significantly vested interest in the company's ability to keep its investors happy. Happy investors in this case were those investors who received regular dividends to make interest payments on their stock loans, and whose stock held value enough to avoid loan collateral calls or loan pay downs. When the company started to experience financial difficulties, it turned to "cooking" the books to meet published earning projections. The scam that created the strongest bottom line and instant cash flow was to sell off its branch locations at escalated prices and then lease back the same locations. In addition to recognizing gains and receiving cash, operations were not interrupted as the previously owned facilities were now rented. Buyers were willing to do this because they had entered into simultaneous agreements to lease the building(s) back to the company at above market rental rates. The leases were structured as operating leases to keep the debt off the books of the selling company and to allow the selling company to immediately recognize the gain on the asset sale instead of deferring it. Had this transaction instead been recorded as a capital lease, it would have required all the related lease obligations to be registered and the gains from the selling company would be deferred. This in turn would have increased the overall liabilities and highlighted the fact that the bank now had taken on more debt, which may have impaired key ratios monitored by regulators.

Further, to cinch the deal, the company also agreed to buy back the building for the current selling price adjusted for inflation in ten years. Greed won out and for a while the undisclosed business transactions worked well until the company found itself in need of more revenue and more cash. Operations were still not as profitable as projected, and as the company experienced difficulties in meeting the inflated monthly rent obligations the landlords began suing for back rent payments, causing the system to crash and, the exposing of the secret side of the buy back agreements.. Defrauded shareholders were outraged to find themselves holding bank loans to pay off as well as worthless stock. Upon final assessment, all the contractors who had purchased stock as part of this "pay to play scheme" lost their investment along with all the other shareholders, and in total approximately $300,000,000 in capital was lost. As in the cases of Enron and WorldCom, an untold amount was lost by individuals whose shares were held by retirement accounts or who purchased the stock after the initial public offering.

Lessons learned:

In this situation, officers of the company were not subject to individual accountability for their actions and corruption was therefore unfortunately not punished. While many of the employees suspected wrongdoing and malfeasance, there was no clear way to expose the issues without personal retaliation. Had the board of directors implemented the use of an anonymous employee hot line to report fraud and suspected corruption, it might have helped to expose the fraud sooner, and because trustees are responsible for serving as watchdogs over stakeholders' money, they clearly had further responsibility to ensure that corporate business practice polices were in place and properly adhered to.

As indicated here, the means available to management at a high level to override internal controls, through their access both to the company's books and to company assets themselves, makes clear how difficult it can be to bring such situations of fraud to light. A strong corporate governance structure must be in place where high-level management is under the purview of the board of directors, with the board clearly charged to act on behalf of the stakeholders and to take an oversight role toward management in its implementation of internal controls.

Commonalities among the Cases

Throughout all six cases, fraud is the common theme. Fraud can occur when individuals who are faced with personal financial incentives, and can rationalize their feelings, are presented with an opportunity to benefit themselves—the three aspects of the fraud triangle we have explored. Also demonstrated here is the fact that opportunity is the one aspect of the fraud triangle most controllable by an organization. When fraud occurs, it is most likely to be due to the organization's lack of internal controls or a breakdown in the internal controls ordinarily implemented. When the opportunity for fraud occurs, it is recognized either as the ability to gain inappropriate access to an organizational asset, to inappropriately affect an accounting for the asset, or to inappropriately authorize acquisition of the asset. In all such circumstances the opportunity results from an improper segregation of duties associated with business transactions. It is the duty and function of management, owners, and boards of directors to be aware of the potential for fraudulent activities in these areas and to provide appropriate controls for keeping any such opportunity to a minimum.

Conclusions and Implications

Fraud is an aspect of the business environment that is often not discussed or recognized. Fraud makes people uncomfortable. Reporting fraud involves feelings of betrayal of fellow employees or acquaintances. The discovery of fraud pits human interests against those of the seemingly inanimate organization. In such a situation, it is often the organization that is left to fend for itself. Therefore, managers (and those in control of the organization) need to recognize that fraud exists, and accordingly, should always strive to implement controls to protect the organization, stakeholders and other (innocent) employees from fraud. Further, organizational environments are continually changing, thereby requiring that internal controls are always monitored and updated as deemed necessary.

In this chapter we have discussed the three elements of the fraud triangle: incentive, rationalization, and opportunity. Each relates to both misappropriation of assets and fraudulent financial reporting. External financial pressures faced by an employee as well as rationalization that justifies fraud are generally undetectable and therefore uncontrollable by an organization. The organization can only control opportunity, which is greatly reduced by implementing the proper internal controls.

Designing business processes that appropriately segregate conflicting duties is an example of an effective control. Other examples of beneficial controls can include fraud hotlines and mandatory vacations, to name a few. It would not be feasible to provide an exhaustive listing of all possible internal controls as no two organizations or situations are identical; the common theme here is simply the need for management to reduce the opportunity for employees to perpetrate fraud. In all six cases discussed in this chapter opportunity is shown to be the critical component in the ability of a person or group of people to commit fraud. In each case we have highlighted the additional controls that could mitigate the occurrence of fraudulent activities under the described circumstances if they were put into place. The resulting evidence indicates that management in any organization must be ever vigilant in implementing and maintaining appropriate internal controls to reduce the likelihood that fraud will occur. Preventing or even reducing employee fraud will allow the organization to better serve its customers, as well as protect its owners, employees, and stakeholders.

REFERENCES

American Institute of Certified Public Accountants (1988). *Rule 101, Code of Professional Conduct,* New York: AICPA.

American Institute of Certified Public Accountants (1997). *Statement of Auditing Standards 85, Management Representations,* New York: AICPA.

American Institute of Certified Public Accountants (2002). *Statement of Auditing Standards 99, Consideration of Fraud in a Financial Statement Audit,* New York: AICPA.

American Institute of Certified Public Accountants (2006). *Statement of Auditing Standards 110, Performing Audit Procedures in Response to Assessed Risks and Evaluating the Audit Evidence Obtained,* New York: AICPA.

Association of Certified Fraud Examiners, (2008). *Report to the Nation on Occupational Fraud and Abuse*, Austin, TX: ACFE.

Association of Certified Fraud Examiners, (2010). *Report to the Nation on Occupational Fraud and Abuse*, Austin, TX: ACFE.

Bayot, J. & Farzad, R. (August, 2005). WorldCom executive sentenced, New York Times. Retrieved August 30, 2009 from: http://query.nytimes.com/gst/fullpage.html?res=9C00 EFD6143EF931A2575BC0A9639C8B63&sec=&spon=&pagewanted=all.

Beltran, L. (July, 2002). WorldCom files largest bankruptcy ever, CNN Money, retrieved August 30, 2009 from: http://money.cnn.com/2002/07/19/news/worldcom_bankruptcy.

Committee of the Sponsoring Organizations of the Treadway Commission, (1992) Internal Control–Integrated Framework report.

Hayes International (2009). Employee theft survey. Retrieved May 16, 2010 from http://www.hayesinternational.com/thft_srvys.html.

International Auditing and Assurance Standards Board (2008). *International Standard on Auditing (ISA) 580*.

Jonesington, J., (March 2007). WorldCom scandal: A look back at one of the biggest corporate scandals in U.S. history, Associated Content. Retrieved August 30, 2009 from: http://www.associatedcontent.com/article/162656/worldcom_scandal_a_look_back_at_one.html.

Sarbanes–Oxley Act. (2002). Public Law No. 107-204.

Sherr, I. (July 2009). U.S. retailers continue struggle with employee theft. Retrieved December 21, 2009 from: http://www.reuters.com/article/idUSTRE56957N20090710.

Wells, J. T. (1997). *Occupational Fraud and Abuse*, Austin TX: Obsidian.

6

Human Resource Management and Deviant/ Criminal Behavior in Organizations

PHILIP G. BENSON, GLENNIS M. HANLEY, AND WESLEY A. SCROGGINS

> *A disgruntled employee fired a shotgun at his former workplace because of 14 years of "harassment and bullying," a court has heard. Paul Anthony Stewart, 49, of Monash, had pleaded guilty to two counts of endangering life over the incident at Glossop, near Barmera, in November. In sentencing him yesterday to a suspended jail term, District Court Judge Dean Clayton read a psychologist report which described Stewart as snapping after being "unfairly dismissed" by the company. "It was a destructive, combative relief of nearly 14 years of built-up anger at being bullied and harassed in the workplace," the report says. Judge Clayton sentenced the fitter and turner to 16 months and two weeks' jail, but suspended that because of the "circumstances surrounding the incident" and his "good prospects" of rehabilitation.*
>
> *—(Adelaide) Advertiser, 2010*

Human resource management (HRM) emerged as a profession, formally recognized in work organizations, about a century ago. It is generally agreed that since emerging as an organizational function, HRM has evolved through a variety of approaches, starting as an administrative discipline and eventually becoming a potential strategic partner to top management of a work organization. Modern HRM is a way to strategically manage the human aspects of an organization, to align policies and practices and to utilize the employees in an organization to achieve high performance in attaining organizational goals.

Modern HRM has a much greater theoretical orientation than was found in the original profession; indeed, early HRM (usually referred to as "personnel management" until late in the 20th century) was a form of business practice, developing out of organizational needs and showing little theoretical or research basis. More recently, the theoretical basis of modern HRM has come to the fore, and often borrows from other disciplines in the social sciences. Blended with such complementary fields as organizational behavior/psychology, industrial psychology, and organizational sociology, modern HRM is a serious academic discipline as well as an applied field within management disciplines.

Disruptive Behavior at Work: What Is the Domain of Interest?

The realm of disruptive/dysfunctional behavior in the workplace is vast. Behaviors that fall into this general category can be relatively mild (such as passive-aggressive behavior at work and workplace incivility) to extremely impactful and even illegal (workplace violence possibly including murder, large-scale sabotage, and major forms of theft). Robinson and Bennett (1995) performed multidimensional scaling of questions about deviant workplace behaviors, and found that two dimensions seem to capture the domain (minor vs. serious and interpersonal vs. organizational). Thus, they define deviant workplace behavior as being production deviance, property deviance, political deviance, and personal aggression. More recently other researchers have broadened the concept, and today a wide variety of behaviors can fall into the general category of disruptive, dysfunctional, or deviant workplace behavior.

Such behavior has been referred to as the "dark side" of organizational behavior (Furnham & Taylor, 2004). Some of these topics have a long history of interest to HRM scholars (such as theft in the workplace), while others have a much more modern origin (such as organizational citizenship behavior and workplace bullying). Given the extremely wide latitude that dysfunctional workplace behavior can entail, specific HRM practices to reduce and manage such behavior can be equally variable. We first need to discuss the kinds of behaviors that are in question.

Workplace Incivility. Andersson and Pearson (1999, 475) defined workplace incivility as "low-intensity deviant behavior with ambiguous intent to harm the target, in violation of workplace norms for mutual respect. Uncivil behaviors are characteristically rude and discourteous." Such behaviors are clearly of a mild nature when compared to other forms of workplace deviance and dysfunctional behavior. The two key defining elements in this definition are that the behavior is relatively mild in impact, and it assumes an ambiguous role for intentionality. Finally, incivility is really little more than a violation of basic norms of decency in dealing with other people.

Numerous varieties of specific behavior can fall within this definition. Simple rudeness, hyper-critical or sarcastic comments, or simple benign hostility all fall within this realm, and it is likely that very few workers have never experienced such forms of treatment from coworkers.

Anger. Workplaces have been identified as one of the most interpersonally frustrating contexts that people encounter in their lives (Fitness, 2000), so it is not unreasonable that anger-eliciting and obnoxious workplace events will be experienced by many workers. Anger, it should be noted, is emotional in character; however, anger often leads to outbursts that can include everything from verbal abuse to actual workplace violence. Fitness (2000) notes that anger is found in energized and tense feelings, a desire to attack the anger object, and in some cases actual physical attacks. Lower status individuals, however, recognize that the anger object may control future organizational rewards and other outcomes, and often anger in low-status employees is accompanied by a submissive stance.

Given the emotional content of workplace anger, Fitness (2000) considered the kinds of psychological "scripts" people enact when they experience anger at work. Importantly, she found two distinct sets of such scripts, enacted typically by high power and low power employees. High power individuals feel moderate anger, but tend to not feel humiliated and to not hate the target. They often take constructive steps to resolve the situation, and feel afterward that the situation has been resolved. Low power individuals, in contrast, tend to feel a clear sense of unfairness in the situation, often experience moderate to high levels of hate for the person angering them, are inclined to take retaliating actions in the name of "revenge," and typically do not feel that the situation has been satisfactorily resolved when over.

It is also notable that these responses in themselves represent a variety of outcomes. While anger can be discussed as a form of dysfunctional behavior at work, and as an emotional response in a work organization, it is also true that anger is connected to other forms of dysfunctional behavior, potentially including violence. Thus, while different types of dysfunctional behavior can be identified, it is not clear that they are distinct, unrelated phenomena, a point to which we will return shortly.

Workplace Bullying. Numerous authors have addressed the issues of workplace bullying in the last few decades. As with other forms of dysfunctional workplace behavior, no single definition is agreed upon for these actions, but it is clear that there is a cluster of behaviors relevant to organizational life.

Bullying is a dynamic, interactive phenomenon with myriad underlying inter-related causes and effects; no adequate explanation is mono-causal. Bullying can be experienced across multiple levels of a workplace, and not isolated or contained in a dyadic silo. Workplace bullies have been described as *conquerors* only interested in power and control, *performers* who enjoy belittling subordinates, or *manipulators* who lie, cheat, take the credit of others, and never assume responsibility for their errors (Hornstein, 1996).

Nevertheless, bullying is not easily defined, as it is a broad, typically imprecisely used term, encompassing a wide variety of phenomena. Salin (2003, 1217) proposes "bullying is seldom explained by one factor alone, but is rather a multi-causal phenomenon." It has been described as "internal" violence, yet forms of "internal" violence are known by different names. In the European Union (EU) and Australia for instance, bullying is a commonly used term to describe lower-level violence, whereas in the United States the terms harassment, mistreatment, or emotional abuse are preferred. Horizontal violence and mobbing (group bullying) are other descriptors used to explain hostile and aggressive behavior by individual or group members toward another person (Hastie, 2001).

The multi-causal nature of bullying underscores the difficulty of definitional consensus (Agervold 2007; Djurkovic, McCormack & Casimir, 2005) and it is known that different targets experience different types of bullying (Notelaers, Einarsen, De Witte & Vermunt, 2006). Nonetheless, a common denominator of most definitions is a perceived power imbalance. One explanation proposed by Einarsen (1999, 16) describes bullying as an activity that "occurs when someone is systematically subjected to aggressive behavior from one or more colleagues or superiors over a long period of time, in a situation where the target finds it difficult to defend him or herself or to escape the situation." Generally, it is agreed that bullying is aggressive behavior, typically repeated, and demonstrating an imbalance of power making it difficult for victims to defend themselves. It is germane to point out some distinguishable differences between bullying and harassment, terms sometimes used synonymously. One key difference is that behavior which constitutes harassment is viewed as discriminatory in nature because it is related to a social identity basis, whereas bullying is usually emotional or psychological abuse (Labor Relations Agency, 2007).

Counterproductive Workplace Behavior. Various authors have begun using the term "counterproductive workplace behavior" (CWB) to refer to a wide variety of employee misbehaviors. This terminology is a reflection of this being the opposite of what has been referred to as "organizational citizenship behavior" (OCB), a construct with a longer history in the HRM and management research literature. The literature on CWBs in the workplace leads to the notion of a "syndrome" (Furnham & Taylor, 2004, 83), suggesting that there is a pattern of related but multiple and distinct behaviors that create an overall form of negative behavioral pattern in the workplace. Researchers seem to agree in this notion of a cohort of behaviors. What is agreed is that these behaviors are indicative of hostility toward authority, are intentional, are contrary to the interests of the employing organization, and lead to counter-productivity in the organizations where they occur. To be classified as a CWB, behavior need not be uncommon; for example, taking sick leave when not sick may be so commonplace as to be normative, but still can be viewed as a form of CWB (Furnham & Taylor, 2004).

Sackett (2002) has created a typology of CWBs, and finds that such behaviors fall into eleven categories of conduct. These include theft, destruction of property, information misuse, time/resource misuse, unsafe activities, attendance and tardiness issues, poor work quality, alcohol use, drug use, verbal abuse and other such misbehavior, and inappropriate physical actions.

However, even if CWBs can be thought of as a syndrome, or a collection or pattern of behaviors, it does not necessarily follow that these are the opposite of OCBs. At least one study (Kelloway, Loughlin, Barling & Nault, 2002) has found that these behaviors represent two independent clusters, and are not opposite ends of the same spectrum. In contrast, Spector and Fox (2002) see OCBs and CWBs as both resulting from emotional states of employees, albeit the directions are opposite. They suggest that OCBs and CWBs are in fact two sides of the same phenomenon.

Violence in the Workplace. In recent years, numerous studies have been done on the occurrence of actual violence in the workplace (Griffin, O'Leary-Kelly & Collins, 1998; VandenBos & Bulatao, 1996). When violence occurs, it is of potentially profound organizational impact, even perhaps including such serious felonies as rape or murder in the workplace. Violence in the workplace also carries significant legal consequences for employers (Paetzold, O'Leary-Kelly & Griffin, 2007).

Specifically, workplace violence often results in charges of negligent hiring or negligent retention (Viollis, Roper & Decker, 2005). These differ primarily in the timing that the employer did or should have become aware of the potential problems that an employee could cause for others in the workplace (including non-employees, such as customers). Because workplace violence is typically not in accordance with the employer's workplace objectives, direct tort claims are difficult to establish, but negligence is a common legal argument. We return to this issue later in this chapter.

Summary of Dysfunctional Workplace Behaviors

While numerous forms of dysfunctional behavior have been noted, at some point the construct seems to begin to be "crushed under its own weight." Many of these behaviors seem to be inter-related, and it is unlikely that the categories previously discussed even remotely approach the standard of being independent constructs. While certain dimensions seem to recur (severity, intentionality, and physical vs. emotional responding), it seems that there is a cluster of behavior, generally negative and disruptive, and that there is a "parallel world" of positive behaviors as a contrast (organizational citizenship behaviors in particular). As Rotundo and Sackett (2002) note, the discussion of counterproductive workplace behaviors "is becoming burdened with numerous definitions and conceptualizations of employee deviance" (69).

Even so, the implications of such forms of behavior have serious consequences in work organizations, and the role of HRM in managing such problems cannot be ignored. We next discuss some of the functions of HRM, and their potential application to the problems of dysfunctional workplace behavior.

HRM: Functions and Potential Managerial Actions

Although virtually all modern texts on HRM discuss the strategic role to be played in the broader management of an organization, it is still the case that certain functional areas have been identified within the profession. Several of these have implications for management of workplace deviance, and it is also possible to place the entire HRM function within broader strategic perspectives. We will address the issues from both perspectives.

First, what are the functions of HRM, especially those that are most relevant to managing workplace deviance? We describe the HRM system using a framework proposed by Cascio and Aguinis (2010), where they posit that the relevance of HRM can be more apparent when one takes a systems view. They specifically suggest that relevant HRM functions include job analysis/evaluation, workforce planning, recruitment, initial screening, selection, training/development, performance management, and organizational exit. We find most of these HRM functions relevant to the present discussion, and will emphasize those that are most germane in our discussion.

Recruitment. In the last decade and a half, the literatures of management and marketing have found an area of commonality; specifically, marketing concepts have been applied to organizations and their HRM, especially in recruiting and in the concept of employee branding. Employee branding has rapidly emerged as a key HRM concept, rising from relative obscurity in a little over a decade (Edwards, 2010). Edwards suggests that employer branding "is an activity where principles of marketing . . . are applied to HR activities in relation to current and potential employees" (6).

Essentially, an employer brand is useful in distinguishing one employer from another (Moroko & Uncles, 2009). Employers can brand themselves into distinct market segments, thereby creating a distinct set of expectations for potential employees. When this branding takes place, it is effective through impacts on the psychological contract of employees, both current and future (Edwards, 2010).

While the avoidance of dysfunctional and counterproductive workplace behaviors has not been the focus of employer branding efforts, certain dimensions of brands are related. For example, Berthon, Ewing, and Hah (2005) looked at dimensions of employer brands. They found five factors that account for employer attractiveness, three of which have implications for the kinds of behaviors engaged in by coworkers in the organizations studied. Specifically, they included "social value" (the provision of positive workplace interactions, especially noting good collegial relationships and a team atmosphere), "development value" (which includes the extent to which an employer provides recognition and self-worth), and "application value" (whereby employees can apply themselves and what they have learned, to teach others, and most notably to do so in an environment that includes a customer orientation and humanitarianism).

While the emphasis in employer branding is on deliberately creating a positive brand image, it is also notable that negative brand images are also possible. For example, organizations which have patterns of sexual harassment in the workplace develop a negative brand image, and these negative brands result in reduced attractiveness of the firms as an employer (Sierra, Compton & Frias-Gutierrez, 2008). A firm that receives negative publicity for things like workplace violence can easily create a negative employer brand, which in turn can make it difficult to recruit employees who value positive workplace environments. Indeed, anecdotally the use of the phrase "going postal" in reference to violence (especially using weapons) as a reaction to numerous incidents involving the U.S. Postal Service is an indication of how insidious such negative branding can be in practice. Such generalized societal perceptions can have a basis in the reality of organizational functioning (see Baxter & Margavio, 1996).

While managing employer brands is a new and emerging area of HRM, clearly it is worth consideration by practitioners. While virtually nothing has been specifically written on the brand of low levels of dysfunctional workplace behavior, it would seem relevant to this discussion.

Initial Screening and Selection. Traditionally, the general model of employee staffing has been to focus on identifying those applicants who will demonstrate desired behaviors once hired. As Schmitt and Kim (2007) note, however, there is also a role to be played by screening out from consideration those applicants who will display dysfunctional and counterproductive behaviors if hired.

Various techniques have been proposed for staffing over the years, and one that is briefly noted even in early texts on the subject is the use of background information on an applicant to assess suitability for employment.

This takes various forms, but at a minimum includes the use of reference checks, investigative background reports, and applicant credit information (or credit reports). Other techniques that can be used for screening for basic "character" include drug testing, polygraphs (or lie detectors), and written honesty tests, and these various methods of screening are usually considered to be pre-screening measures of applicant integrity.

The use of such methods has a long history, but some of these methods, especially the use of credit reports, have seen very little empirical scrutiny. For example, according to the classic text by Guion (1965), "The local credit bureau is a reference source that is frequently overlooked. Credit bureaus usually have rather full information on any applicant who has been known to the community for any length of time. Frequently an applicant who appears promising in the employment office seems less desirable when it is learned that he habitually neglects financial responsibilities" (14). However, even though Guion's text cites numerous research studies in support of virtually all of the other staffing methods he promotes, the use of credit reports has no empirical data referenced in support of its veracity. Guion does, however, suggest that empirical validation of such methods cannot be overlooked in the proper conduct of staffing, and that credit information "is just as much subject to empirical validation as is any other; armchair logic is not enough" (384). Little was written of an empirical sort prior to 1965, and a search of published data in the four-plus decades since then likewise turns up very little in the way of recent empirical scrutiny of the practice of using credit reports in hiring. Data in support of other background screening methods vary, but many times these techniques seem to be used without serious scrutiny and evaluation.

In this chapter, we describe some of the screening methods under consideration, and define their nature and assumptions. After describing the methods, we turn to a series of methodological and professional issues in their use, and the implications for firms using such selection methods. Three areas of concern are especially addressed: first, what are the psychometric questions relevant to the use of these methods; second, what are the legal issues in the use of these methods for staffing; and third, what are the cultural, ethical, and moral questions such methods raise, including especially issues involving procedural justice and other models of fair treatment of employees?

Measures for Background Screening. While there is no single source that defines precisely the screening measures discussed in this chapter, there are some common characteristics that typify this set of selection methods. They deal in general with background information about applicants, and deal with questions of employee character and the presumed responsibility of the applicant.

Measures for background evaluation of job candidates typically include drug testing, reference checking (especially with former employers, but this can also include others who know the applicant), credit reports and investigations, use of criminal records and checks of such records, motor vehicle records, and outside investigations of character or past behavior toward employers (including services that will search databases of employees, using things like social security numbers to determine public records of past court actions, workers' compensation claims, and lawsuits filed regarding fair employment issues).

These measures have a common thread in that all deal with potentially damaging, personal information, and often involve finding things about the employee or applicant that the person investigated does not necessarily know the employer can find; moreover, the employee being investigated would often have objections to the use of this information. All of these measures have at least implicit, if not explicit, moral overtones and implications.

Psychometric Considerations: How Should We Validate Such Tests? The use of such tests as credit reports, criminal background files, other third-party reports, drug tests, and other such measures of "character" of an applicant raises a fundamental staffing issue: how is one best able to validate such a procedure? In staffing, we have long recognized various models of test validity, and the general view is that we can use content, construct, or criterion-related models (see Cascio & Aguinis, 2010, or Guion, 1998, for a review). However, although the criterion-related approach to test validation, in particular the predictive model, has long dominated practical use of selection tests, the "tripartite" view of validity has seen criticism (Schmitt & Landy, 1993). Essentially, Schmitt and Landy argue that truly understanding a test requires more than a mere reported correlation between a test score and some (often readily available) simple measure of job performance or other job-related outcomes. Instead of simplistic correlational models, they argue that "we must develop and articulate theories of job performance and define logically the constructs that are central to those theories" (285).

Thus, what is needed for the use of credit reports, drug tests, reference checks, and other background measures in employee screening is a coherent theory as to why such measures are related in meaningful ways to broadly-defined job performance. What exactly is it that such measures capture, and how does this translate into meaningful aspects of employment behavior? Without a clear statement of the "nomological network" (Cronbach & Meehl, 1955) for such predictors, their use becomes at best hypothetical, and at worst detrimental, to the overall functioning of the organization.

Note that from a construct or content validity perspective, background information may well be entirely valid, and yet still lack predictive validity in a specific setting. For example, consider the case of credit reports as screening methods. The information in such documents needs to be correct, and indeed, improving the accuracy of credit reports was one objective of the 2003 amendments to the Fair Credit Reporting Act in the United States (along with improved consumer access to reports, efforts to prevent identity theft, and others) (Taft & Poulon, 2004). The argument that information presented in a credit report is inaccurate, while possible, is not the greatest concern in the use of such assessments for staffing decisions. The fundamental question is whether a person's history of credit worthiness is related to other, meaningful job behaviors, and whether there is thus any economic value added by using such a test. As Guion (1965) points out, in a job where pay for performance is clearly present, a person with financial difficulties may well be more motivated to perform than one who is not experiencing such difficulties.

The potential for inaccuracy of the polygraph, or lie detector, is one reason that it has been largely banned from use in employment settings in the United States, through passage of the Federal Employee Polygraph Protection Act (Bennett-Alexander & Hartman, 2007). Indeed, the polygraph does result in some proportion of false positives in selection (all methods that are less than absolutely perfect do), but the ability of the polygraph to detect attempts at deception likely has far more validity (measured as accuracy of the results) than other routinely used selection methods, such as the employment interview. While the reason for singling out the polygraph are not certain, and could be tested empirically, we would suggest that at least in part it is because the method is dealing with moral questions (lying), is used potentially to harm the applicant (to screen people out of jobs rather than to include them), and has a degree of "believability" or face validity that likely makes it easy for the layman to over interpret the accuracy of the results of such tests. However, the true predictive validity of the measure is likely not that inaccurate, although imperfect.

Thus, what kinds of job-related behaviors are likely to be predicted from the use of employee background information? It appears that the implicit model of the validity of employment screening techniques is based heavily in practitioners' implicit use of a construct validity model, and an implicit belief that these measures tap into a wide variety of negative on-the-job behaviors in a nomological network (Cronbach & Meehl, 1955). These behavior patterns are generally those discussed earlier in this chapter, in form of counter-productive workplace behaviors (CWBs) among employees (Furnham & Taylor, 2004), the presumed flip-side to organizational citizenship behaviors (OCBs; Organ, 1988). There is an implicitly (if not explicitly) held model that a host of behavior patterns are inter-related, and that selection standards that tap into such psychological realms will give a good prediction of employee quality, defined in a broad sense. Empirical support for such hypotheses about human nature would be necessary in the application of such assumptions to the employee staffing process.

The debate over the related or distinct nature of OCBs and CWBs and the subcomponents of each is particularly relevant for this discussion. If these are indeed part of a "syndrome," a collection of important and related behaviors, there is a higher likelihood that measures such as credit reports, background investigations, or drug tests will tap into this construct. If in contrast these represent a group of independent behaviors, it is less likely that specific background measures will tap into a wide variety of behaviors, and in this case the relevant research question is to develop the criterion behavioral constructs in a way to theoretically understand and predict which selection methods are useful in reducing or increasing which kinds of behaviors. In short, to use background screening methods to staff organizations, we need to understand the nature of the dysfunctional workplace behavior, and develop theories that explain how these behavioral issues relate and interact.

In addition, even if the criterion measures (OCBs and CWBs) in this model form a syndrome of related behaviors, it is still not proven that the predictors do likewise. Perhaps canonical models of predictors and job behavior are needed to see the potentially complex inter-relationships among these measures, if the constructs represented are to be truly understood.

Often times we make such assumptions about character, or other related variables, and assume that tests used in selection will almost certainly give us a better quality of employee. This intuitive argument has a certain degree of plausibility, but may not work out in practice. For example, White, Nicholson, Minors, and Duncan (2001) studied a sample of recreational users of illicit drugs, and found that those who were occasional users were not problem employees. Indeed, in their sample such workers proved to be successful, from a wide variety of occupational groups, about as likely to participate in voluntary community activities as Americans overall, far more likely to vote than Americans overall, happy with their marital status, and in general, not the kinds of potential employees one would want to necessarily screen out from employment. Lastly, their drug-using sample was more secular than the American population overall, and less likely to attend regular religious services.

In addition, if an employer adopts a policy for such screening as use of drug tests, it will be mandatory to follow the results without favoritism. At least one source (Brockett, 2006) has indicated that one-third of UK citizens have used marijuana; an employer using drug screening may have to face some serious HR issues regarding dismissals and retention. Thus, it is unclear whether the expense of screening out such applicants is worth the investment in testing.

One type of employment screening that is relevant here is the use of criminal background investigations. These evaluations, however, may well be required due to the problems of negligent hiring (Ryan & Lasek, 1991). Even so, there are distinct limits on the use of criminal background investigations (Howie & Shapero, 2002), and even when limited to considering the United States, there are especially notable differences in local and state regulations in this regard. In addition, just how such information is used is important to consider; a conviction for an offense only marginally related to the job, and ten years prior, is obviously not as relevant as a conviction directly related to the job in question, and only two years prior. In short, the use of criminal background information is not a simple process.

Training and Development

As facilitators and change agents of organizations, an important function of HRM practitioners is to strengthen the psychological capital of employees and social capital within organizations. One way to do so is to use employee training and development (T&D) programs as a conduit to help create a civil and respectful work environment (Estes & Wang, 2008).

Employee training and development (T&D) programs are an integral element of an organization's HRM practices, and in some industries, a critical component of an organization's risk management strategy. In the British health care industry for example, workplace violence is acknowledged as a serious and ongoing issue. The management of aggression training is now firmly entrenched as part of an organization's health and safety response to the phenomenon of workplace violence (Beach & Leather, 2006). Indeed, as Beach and Leather (2006, 33) suggest, violence/aggression training programs underpin a battery of diverse organizational preventative strategies such as selection and screening of staff, information and guidance giving, work organization, defusing incidents, and post-incident de-briefing.

Given the extent of the problem, an obvious question is whether there are discrete or desirable elements of successful anti-workplace violence T&D programs? Chappell and Di Martino (2000) propose three principal elements. The first of these is training to instill interpersonal and communication skills to help defuse threatening situations. Secondly, they suggest training to improve an individual's ability to identify potentially violent situations/people; and thirdly, training to prepare mature and specifically competent staff to take responsibility for complicated interactions (Chappell & Di Martino, 2000, 114).

Mentoring is one training and development method that has the potential to reduce counterproductive workplace behavior. Organizational mentoring programs match experienced, senior employees with less-experienced or new employees, usually for the purpose of employee development. However, mentoring programs can also be a means by which organizational policies, values, and ethical principles are communicated. Organizations can take a proactive step in the management of counterproductive work behaviors by establishing formal mentoring relationships through which values and ethics are clearly communicated, reinforced, and compliance rewarded.

Mentoring relationships can enable organizations to create and maintain ethical cultures and climates, by serving as a socialization mechanism by which new employees are socialized into the current organizational culture. Mentors can create specific perceptions and expectations regarding the nature of ethical behavior, organizational policies regarding such behavior, and the consequences of acting unethically in that organization. Research indicates that employee perceptions of culture and climate can affect their intentions to behave ethically or unethically (Crossen, 1993). Mentors may reduce the likelihood of counterproductive workplace behavior by clearly communicating policies and value systems to mentees.

Mentors can also communicate desired organizational values and principles to employees by their behavior. Studies indicate that managerial behavior can impact the willingness of employees to engage in ethical behaviors (Trevino & Brown, 2005). Therefore, it is imperative that mentors and other influential organizational members model desired ethical behavior and decision making, respond appropriately to organizational critical incidents, and appropriately reward and punish those behaviors that either comply or fail to comply with the organizational value system.

Mentoring can also help reduce counterproductive workplace behaviors by facilitating the development of positive, trusting relationships within the organization. Mentoring relationships can foster the development of more accurate and realistic psychological contracts, which are psychologically implied agreements that develop between employers and employees. Psychological contract fulfillment is often related to perceptions of distributive, procedural, and interactional organizational justice, which have a strong effect on employee behavior (Cropanzano, Bowen & Gilliland, 2007). Mentoring can also increase employee perceptions of increased organizational and psychosocial support. Research indicates that employee perceptions of such support are strongly related to employee organizational commitment (Allen & Meyer, 1996), which makes it less likely that they will violate organizational values and principles by engaging in counterproductive work behaviors.

Put simply, the purpose of any T&D program is to provide employees with skills and attributes to help them best fulfill the mission of their organization. However, in addressing the multi-factorial components of toxic workplaces, the development and implementation of T&D programs is a complex and emotional undertaking. There is no "one size fits all" program; rather as Beach and Leather (2006) remind us, a total organizational response is needed with duties and responsibilities for all organizational members clearly delineated.

Performance Management

As with other human resource management functions, an organization's performance management system can also impact employee motivation to perform counter-productive organizational and other unethical behaviors. Performance management refers to a series of activities that involve defining and communicating performance standards, measuring and evaluating performance, and motivating performance through the use of reward systems (Mathis & Jackson, 2008). As managers conduct performance management activities, they can affect employee motivation to engage in counter-productive or deviant behavior in several ways. First, the performance management process and outcomes can violate employees' sense of organizational justice, or their perceptions of being treated fairly by the organization. Secondly, deviant or unethical behavior is more likely to occur when valued and desirable job outcomes are contingent on goal achievement. Therefore, managers must be careful to ensure that performance management activities are perceived as fair and job relevant. Managers must also closely monitor the performance management system to make certain it does not motivate employees to engage in undesirable behaviors in order to meet performance expectations that lead to desirable job outcomes.

Research conducted over the past two decades has identified numerous distributive and process factors that affect employee perceptions of the fairness of performance management systems, and more specifically, performance evaluations. Given that much evidence exists that indicates that perceptions of injustice are related to deviance behaviors, withdrawal behaviors, and decreased job performance (Cohen-Charash & Spector, 2001; Colquitt, Conlon, Wesson, Porter & Ng, 2001), it is imperative that managers give attention to these factors in performance management activities. It is important that managers obtain performance information prior to the evaluation and use that information during the evaluation. Performance criteria that form the basis of the evaluation must be valid and must be perceived as job relevant by the employee (Dipboye & de Pontbriand, 1981). Furthermore, the manager should solicit job relevant information from multiple sources, such as other managers who might be familiar with the employee's performance, peers, customers, and maybe the employee in the form of a self-assessment (Greenberg, 1986; Litzky, Eddleston & Kidder, 2006). It is important that the employee believe that the manager is familiar with his or her work and performance levels. To the extent that managers give attention to these factors, it is more likely that the performance evaluation will be perceived as fair and accurate and will be accepted by the employee.

The frequency with which evaluations are conducted and performance feedback provided also affects employee perceptions of the fairness and accuracy of the performance evaluation. Landy, Barnes, and Murphy (1978) found that employees' perceptions of fairness and accuracy increased with increased frequency of evaluation. They also found that perceptions of fairness and accuracy increased when managers helped the employees develop plans for eliminating performance problems identified in the evaluation. Other process variables important for positive fairness perceptions of the appraisal process include two-way communication between manager and subordinate during the interview, the opportunity for employees to state their own side of the issues, the ability to challenge/rebut the evaluation, and the consistent application of standards (Cropanzano, Bowen & Gilliland, 2007; Dipboye & de Pontbriand, 1981; Greenberg, 1986).

Distributive outcomes also affect the perceived fairness of the performance management system. Greenberg (1986) found that perceptions of fairness increased when it was believed that the performance rating received was based on the performance level achieved, and when recommendations for pay increases or promotions were based on the rating received.

Given the factors previously discussed, human resource management professionals can definitely contribute to the management of unethical and deviant workplace behaviors that result from organizational justice violations by incorporating awareness of these factors into the performance management system.

Goal setting is often included in performance management systems in order to clarify performance standards and expectations, as well as motivate employees toward desirable performance levels. Although goal setting has had positive effects on performance motivation, it also has the potential to motivate unethical and deviant behaviors in some situations. Schweitzer, Ordonez, and Douma (2004) found that when performance goals were unmet, employees were more likely to engage in unethical behaviors in order to reach those goals. Furthermore, they found the goal setting–unethical behavior relationship was strongest when employees fell just short of goal achievement. This tendency to engage in unethical behavior may also be greater for individuals with certain personality types, such as Type A personality profiles or those high in achievement need. The reason for this is that the psychological consequences of failure may be greater for such individuals in regard to self-concept and esteem.

This goal setting–unethical behavior relationship has implications for the use of goal setting in performance management systems. When using goal setting, managers need to make sure that goals are both specific and moderately challenging (Litzky, Eddleston & Kidder, 2006). Goal specificity increases the likelihood that the goal and performance expectations connected with it are clear, increasing the likelihood that the employee will perform at standard. Moderately challenging goals provide motivation to perform, but are not likely to create a perception of risk or failure that is great enough to decrease motivation for the task or motivate the employee to engage in deviant behaviors due to the threat that they cannot achieve the desired performance level.

Organizational Exit

One of the least pleasant aspects of working in HRM is the process of employee termination. While never a fun task, work organizations engage in this process frequently. Unfortunately, these terminations occasionally turn violent; when this occurs, it is generally deemed worthy of national news coverage, making these events seem riskier than they in fact are.

It is important to think of employee terminations in a longer time frame, not as a distinct event. A terminated employee is just as likely to show up in the workplace with a gun six months after termination, as to show up with a gun one week after termination (Anonymous, 2001). Indeed, a model has been proposed for proper terminations, outlining a nine-step process for terminations (Johnson, King & Kurutz, 1996). In addition, the steps include events before and after the actual termination interview, recognizing that the process is broader in scope than a simple event where the actual termination takes place.

The Role of Overall HRM Strategy

Modern HRM has increasingly recognized the "big picture" that emerges from a strategic view of the role of HR. In this context, the overall climate of a work organization sets the tone for employee behaviors in general.

For example, theft is one form of deviant behavior, and one that employers take seriously. We know that one cause of employee theft is dissatisfaction, but not every dissatisfied worker engages in theft. Kulas, McInnerney, DeMuth, and Jadwinski (2007) have shown that the connection between dissatisfaction and theft is moderated by the organization's climate for theft, and attention to the contextual variable is thus important. Likewise, Everton, Jolton, and Masatrangelo (2007) suggest that a wide variety of dysfunctional workplace behaviors (theft, incivility, violence, and others) are impacted by employee perceptions that managers are fair and supportive. Thus, what kinds of HRM practices and strategies are most relevant to these issues?

The Impact of General and Strategic HRM Practices

While specific HRM practices can impact employee behavior and organizational outcomes, it is also interesting to look at the impact of broad management practices. In particular, recent work in strategic HRM has emphasized the use of high performance work systems (HPWS), and such approaches have been shown to have a wide impact on various organizational outcomes (see Ichniowski, Levine, Olson & Strauss, 2000, for a review).

Snape and Redman (2010) considered the impact of various HPWS practices from an HRM perspective, and looked at impacts on organizational citizenship behaviors. They used a summated scale of varied HRM practices, generally consistent with HPWS, and found that utilization of such practices led to positive impacts on OCBs. In particular, they found that impacts of HRM practices impacted employee behavior by first influencing employee perceptions that they had great job influence. Employees who feel that their employing organization cares about them tend to engage in greater amounts of altruistic behavior at work.

One practice that is often tempting to HRM practitioners is to engage in surveillance at work, to monitor activities as a means of "early detection" of undesirable employee behavior. Surveillance is especially attractive for employers dealing with such disruptive behavior as employee theft, on-the-job drug use, and other illegal activities (see Nelson & Tyson, 2010, for a discussion). Such practices, while technologically feasible, often present unique challenges and difficulties.

Generally, employee surveillance, especially using devices such as video cameras, can raise the specter of invasion of employee privacy. One issue to be addressed in such monitoring is whether or not to inform employees that such surveillance is being done. While some practitioners advocate secrecy, we recommend otherwise. The greatest argument for secrecy is that people are more likely to be caught, but if the organizational goal is to reduce unwanted behavior, publicly stating a policy of surveillance (with associated reductions in negative behavior) seems preferable. It is generally argued that many employees will avoid the negative behavior (theft) if they perceive a high probability of being caught. Thus, secrecy may allow managers to detect (and punish) more unwanted behaviors, but we would argue that it's better to reduce the unwanted behavior than to simply let it occur and then punish it.

Indeed, the whole issue of surveillance raises the possibility of negative impacts on workplace morale. As Nelson and Tyson (2010) note, managers may find "that trying to eradicate theft or drug use by implementing what may be perceived as heavy-handed security measures can destroy the fabric of good will and trust often necessary to create a productive work environment" (108).

Legal Issues in Background Screening for Employment

Screening workers and applicants for issues related to dysfunctional work-place behaviors can raise a whole host of legal issues. These especially include things like discrimination and the issues associated with negligent hiring. Negligent hiring is a form of tort law in the United States, based in common-law principles of master-servant relationships (Levashina & Campion, 2009). Several conditions must be met for this legal doctrine to apply, but essentially, the action questioned must result within an employment relationship where the perpetrator has negative characteristics, or a background that constitutes unfitness for the position held, and the employer knew or should have known that the employee was unfit. These conditions must precede a situation where the employee then caused injury to a third party, while the negligent hiring was the proximate cause of the inappropriate behavior, and all of this resulted in actual damage to the victim.

In simpler terms, an employer has a duty to screen for background char-acteristics of employees, especially when the employee is in a position where he or she could inflict harm on others. Failure to properly screen is poten-tially a source of tort liability for the employer (Levashina & Campion, 2009; Viollis, Roper & Decker, 2005; Woska, 2007).

While academics have discussed the legality of background screening techniques within the United States, less attention has been given to this topic in other countries, or the role of legal regulation in the multi-national company. The laws regarding personal information and its protection vary substantially even within the EU (Buxton, 1995), and when other world loca-tions are considered, issues of information privacy can become very complex (see Milberg, Smith & Burke, 2000).

One legal issue that cannot be ignored in this discussion is the relative standing of privacy rights in various countries and settings. Because we are discussing inherently negative information about employees, those about whom this information is gathered may well feel they have been imposed upon in less-than-fair ways. (Further, issues of fairness raise broader social and ethical issues, ones that we will return to in the next section of this chapter.) Privacy is a broad legal concept, but one that cannot be ignored in this context.

In Europe, most countries' constitutions protect the right to privacy, unlike the legal status of privacy in the United States (George, Lynch & Marsnik, 2001). Indeed, in Europe it is generally held that personal information belongs to the person about whom it refers, and such information is given the status of intellectual property protection. Thus, George et al. (2001) point out that the use of such information (including use for employment decisions, but also, for instance, credit card transactions) can be problematic for American companies doing business in Europe, or sending employees overseas to work in the EU.

Beyond the Law: The Ethical Issues of Background Screening

Legal regulation sets specific parameters on behavior, but beyond questions of legality, it is necessary to consider reactions of parties involved in such interactions. A firm operating in legal ways can still alienate employees and applicants, and by doing so, may still suffer serious negative impacts from otherwise legal decisions.

Ethical views on this topic are tempered by cultural factors (Milberg et al., 2000). The cultural values held by a country impact both the concerns raised by the populace, and the regulatory approach taken by the country. Thus, ethical and cultural values, the regulations established and used in a country, and the desired privacy protections in a country are all inter-related in complex ways.

Selection and recruitment have the potential for negatively impacting applicant views of the hiring organization, and these views in turn can impact the likelihood that an applicant will accept an offer of a job, if one is made (Gilliland, 1993, 1994; Rynes, Bretz & Gerhart, 1991; Smither, Reilly, Millsap, Pearlman & Stoffey, 1993). In addition, interpretations of procedural justice of selection methods have been studied in international contexts, and it has been found that culture does relate to the kinds of procedures that are seen as fair and appropriate in the eyes of applicants (Marcus, 2003; Phillips & Gully, 2003; Scroggins, Benson, Cross & Gilbreath, 2004; Scroggins, Benson & Cross, 2005; Steiner & Gilliland, 1996). In general, methods of staffing that allow an applicant to show his or her ability, that are based on face validity and predictive validity in suggesting future job performance, entail fair and reasonable interpersonal treatment, and ask appropriate kinds of questions are seen as more fair in most cultural settings.

Conclusion

Employee misbehavior at work, under any of myriad names, can create serious difficulties for employers. Some of the damages are tangible, others are not. Still, it is in the best interest of any organization to manage and minimize such unwanted behaviors.

While many techniques can be used to screen, train, or evaluate employees, it is paramount that employers pay attention to legal and conceptual issues in such practices. The practices available to the modern HR professional are less than perfect, and do carry significant legal and ethical obligations.

Background investigations, as used in staffing, are fraught with methodological, legal, and ethical issues, and these issues are magnified when placed into an international context. In addition, the payoffs of using such techniques are questionable; when one considers the talent requirements of international firms (Scullion & Collings, 2006), it is not clear at all that these techniques should be expected to have a major payoff in staffing the successful international firm. By carefully considering these issues, a more reasoned approach to staffing the multi-national enterprise may be found.

REFERENCES

Agervold, M. (2007). Bullying at work: A discussion of definitions and prevalence, based on an empirical study. *Scandinavian Journal of Psychology, 48*, 161–172.

Allen, N., & Meyer, J. (1996). Affective, continuance, and normative commitment to the organization: An examination of construct validity. *Journal of Vocational Behavior, 49*, 252–276.

Andersson, L. M., & Pearson, C. M. (1999). Tit for tat? The spiraling effect of incivility in the workplace. *Academy of Management Journal, 24*, 452–471.

Anonymous (2001, March). Prevent employee dismissals from turning violent. *Security Director's Report, 1*, 10–11.

Baxter, V., & Margavio, A. (1996). Assaultive violence in the U.S. Post Office. *Work and Occupations, 23*, 277–296.

Beach, B., & Leather, P. (2006). Workplace violence in the healthcare sector: A review of staff training and integration of training evaluation methods. *Aggression and Violent Behavior, 11*, 27–43.

Bennett-Alexander, D. D., & Hartman, L. P. (2007). *Employment law for business* (5th ed.). New York: McGraw-Hill.

Berthon, P., Ewing, M., & Hah, L. L. (2005). Captivating company: Dimensions of attractiveness in employer branding. *International journal of Advertising, 24*, 151–172.

Brockett, J. (2006). Does testing work? *People Management, 12*, 13.

Buxton, L. (Ed.). (1995). *Employment law in Europe: A country by country guide for employers* (2nd ed.) Hampshire, England: Gower.

Cascio, W. F., & Aguinis, H. (2010). *Applied psychology in human resource management* (7th ed.). Upper Saddle River, NJ: Prentice Hall.

Chappell, D., & Di Martino, V. (2000). *Violence at work* (2nd ed.). Geneva: International Labour Organisation.

Cohen-Charash, Y., & Spector, P. E. (2001). The role of justice in organizations: A meta-analysis. *Organizational Behavior and Human Decision Processes, 86*, 278–321.

Colquitt, J. A., Conlon, D. E., Wesson, M. J., Porter, C. O. L. H., & Ng, K. Y. (2001). Justice at the millennium: A meta-analytic review of 25 years of organizational justice research. *Journal of Applied Psychology, 86*, 425–445.

Cronbach, L. J., & Meehl, P. E. (1955). Construct validity in psychological tests. *Psychological Bulletin, 52*, 281–302.

Cropanzano, R., Bowen, D. E., & Gilliland, S. W. (2007). The management of organizational justice. *Academy of Management Perspectives, 21*, 34–48.

Crossen, B. R. (1993). Managing employee unethical behavior without invading individual privacy. *Journal of Business and Psychology, 8*, 227–243.

Dipboye, R. L., & de Pontbriand, R. (1981). Correlates of employee reactions to performance appraisals and appraisal systems. *Journal of Applied Psychology, 66*, 248–251.

Djurkovic, N., McCormack, D., & Casimir, G. (2005). The behavioral reactions of victims to different types of workplace bullying. *International Journal of Organization Theory and Behavior, 8*, 439–461.

Edwards, M. R. (2010). An integrative review of employer branding and OB theory. *Personnel Review, 39*, 5–23.

Einarsen, S. (1999). The nature and causes of bullying at work. *International Journal of Manpower, 20*, 16–27.

Estes, B., & Wang, J. (2008). Workplace incivility: Impacts on individual and organizational performance. *Human Resource Development Review, 7*, 218–240.

Everton, W. J., Jolton, J. A., & Mastrangelo, P. M. (2007). Be nice and fair or else: Understanding reasons for employees' deviant behaviors. *Journal of Management Development, 26*, 117–131.

Fitness, J. (2000). Anger in the workplace: An emotion script approach to anger episodes between workers and their superiors, coworkers and subordinates. *Journal of Organizational Behavior, 21*, 147–162.

Furnham, A., & Taylor, J. (2004). *The dark side of behaviour at work: Understanding and avoiding employees leaving, thieving and deceiving.* New York: Palgrave Macmillan.

George, B. C., Lynch, P., & Marsnik, S. J. (2001). U.S. multinational employers: Navigating through the "safe harbor" principles to comply with the EU data privacy directive. *American Business Law Journal, 38*, 735–783.

Gilliland, S. W. (1993). The perceived fairness of selection systems: An organizational justice perspective. *Academy of Management Review, 18*, 694–734.

Gilliland, S. W. (1994). Effects of procedural and distributive justice on reactions to a selection system. *Journal of Applied Psychology, 79*, 691–701.

Greenberg, J. (1986). Determinants of perceived fairness of performance evaluations. *Journal of Applied Psychology, 71*, 340–342.

Griffin, R. W., O'Leary-Kelly, A., & Collins, J. (1998). Dysfunctional work behaviors in organizations. In C. L. Cooper & D. M. Rousseau (Eds.), *Trends in organizational behavior* (pp. 65–82). Chichester, England: Wiley.

Guion, R. M. (1965). *Personnel testing.* New York: McGraw-Hill.

Guion, R. M. (1998). *Assessment, measurement, and prediction for personnel decisions.* Mahwah, NJ: Erlbaum.

Hastie, C. (2001). Horizontal violence in the workplace. www.acegraphics.com.au/articles. Accessed 2 February 09.

Hornstein, H. A. (1996). *Brutal bosses and their prey: How to identify and overcome abuse in the workplace.* New York: Riverhead.

Howie, R. M., & Shapero, L. A. (2002). Pre-employment criminal background checks: Why employers should look before they leap. *Employee Relations Law Journal, 28*, 63–77.

Ichniowski, C., Levine, D. I., Olson, C., & Strauss, G. (2000). *The American workplace: Skills, compensation, and employee involvement.* Cambridge: Cambridge University Press.

Johnson, D. L., King, C. A., & Kurutz, J. G. (1996). Safe termination model for supervisors. *HR Magazine, 41*, 73–74.

Kelloway, E., Loughlin, C., Barling, J., & Nault, A. (2002). Self-reported counter-productive behaviours and organizational citizenship behaviours. *International Journal of Selection and Assessment, 10*, 143–151.

Kulas, J. T., McInnerney, J. E., DeMuth, R. F., & Jadwinski, V. (2007). Employee satisfaction and theft: Testing climate perceptions as a mediator. *The Journal of Psychology, 141*, 389–402.

Labor Relations Agency (2007). www.lra.org.uk/index/employment-questions-and-answers/bullying_and_harassment.htm. Accessed 17 February 09.

Landy, F. J., Barnes, J. L., & Murphy, K. R. (1978). Correlates of perceived fairness and accuracy of performance evaluation. *Journal of Applied Psychology, 63*, 751–754.

Latham, G. P. (2001). The importance of understanding and changing employee outcome expectancies for gaining commitment to an organizational goal. *Personnel Psychology, 54*, 707–716.

Levashina, J., & Campion, M. A. (2009). Expected practices in background checking: Review of the human resource management literature. *Employee Responsibility and Rights Journal, 21*, 231–249.

Lim, S., Cortina, L. M., & Magley, V. J. (2008). Personal and workgroup incivility: Impact on work and health outcomes. *Journal of Applied Psychology, 93*, 95–107.

Litzky, B. E., Eddleston, K. A., & Kidder, D. L. (2006). The good, the bad, and the misguided: How managers inadvertently encourage deviant behaviors. *Academy of Management Perspectives, 20*, 91–103.

Marcus, B. (2003). Attitudes towards personnel selection methods: A partial replication and extension in a German sample. *Applied Psychology: An International Review, 52*, 515–532.

Mathis, R. L., & Jackson, J. H. (2006). *Human resource management* (11th ed.). Mason, OH: South-Western, Thomson.

McGregor, K. (2010, May 22). "Bullying" sparked shotgun incident. *(Adelaide) Advertiser*, 18.

Milberg, S. J., Smith, H. J., & Burke, S. J. (2000). Information privacy: Corporate management and national regulation. *Organization Science, 11*, 35–57.

Moroko. L., & Uncles, M. D. (2009). Employer branding and market segmentation. *Brand Management, 17*, 181–196.

Nelson, C. H. Jr., & Tyson, L. (2010). HR undercover: Factor in privacy rights before rolling out surveillance programs. *HR Magazine, 55*, 107–110.

Notelaers, G., Einarsen, S., De Witte, H., & Vermunt, J. K. (2006). Measuring exposure to bullying at work: The validity and advantages of the latent class cluster approach. *Work & Stress, 20*, 289–302.

Organ, D. W. (1988). *Organizational citizenship behavior: The good soldier syndrome*. Lexington, MA: Lexington Books.

Paetzold, R. L., O'Leary-Kelly, A., & Griffin, R. W. (2007). Workplace violence, employer liability, and implications for organizational research. *Journal of Management Inquiry, 16*, 362–370.

Phillips, J. M., & Gully, S. M. (2003). Fairness reactions to personnel selection techniques in Singapore and the United States. *International Journal of Human Resource Management, 13*, 1186–1205.

Robinson, S. L., & Bennett, R. J. (1995). A typology of deviant workplace behaviors: A multi-dimensional scaling study. *Academy of Management Journal, 38*, 555–572.

Rotundo, M., & Sackett, P. R. (2002). The relative importance of task, citizenship, and counterproductive performance to global ratings of job performance: A policy-capturing approach. *Journal of Applied Psychology, 87*, 66–80.

Ryan, A. M., & Lasek, M. (1991). Negligent hiring and defamation: Areas of liability related to pre-employment inquiries. *Personnel Psychology, 44*, 293–319.

Rynes, S. L., Bretz, R. D. Jr., & Gerhart, B. (1991). The importance of recruitment in job choice: A different way of thinking. *Personnel Psychology, 44*, 487–521.

Sackett, P. (2002). The structure of counterproductive work behaviors. *International Journal of Selection and Assessment, 10*, 5–11.

Salin, D. (2003). Ways of explaining workplace bullying: A review of enabling, motivating and precipitating structures and processes in the work environment. *Human Relations, 56*, 1213–1232.

Schmitt, N., & Kim, B. (2007). Selection decision-making. In P. Boxall, J. Purcell, & P. Wright (Eds.), *The Oxford Handbook of Human Resource Management* (pp. 300–323). Oxford: Oxford University Press.

Schmitt, N., & Landy, F. J. (1993). The concept of validity. In N. Schmitt, W. C. Borman, and Associates (Eds.), *Personnel selection in organizations* (pp. 275–309). San Francisco: Jossey-Bass.

Schweitzer, M. E., Ordonez, L., & Douma, B. (2004). Goal setting as a motivator of unethical behavior. *Academy of Management Journal, 47*, 422–432.

Scroggins, W. A., Benson, P. G., Cross, C., & Gilbreath, B. (2004, September). *Reactions to selection methods: An international comparison*. Proceedings of the annual conference of the Irish Academy of Management, Trinity College Dublin.

Scroggins, W. A., Benson, P. G., & Cross, C. (2005). A cross-cultural comparison of employee reactions to selection methods. Paper presented at the annual meeting of the Irish Academy of Management, Galway, Ireland, September 2005.

Scullion, H., & Collings, D. G. (2006). International talent management. In H. Scullion & D. G. Collings (Eds.), *Global staffing* (pp. 87–116). London: Routledge.

Sierra, J. J., Compton, N., & Frias-Gutierrez, K. M. (2008). Brand response-effects of perceived sexual harassment in the workplace. *Journal of Business and Management, 14*, 175–197.

Smither, J. W., Reilly, R. R., Millsap, R. E., Pearlman, K., & Stoffey, R. W. (1993). Applicant reactions to selection procedures. *Personnel Psychology, 46,* 49–76.

Snape, E., & Redman, T. (2010). HRM practices, organizational citizenship behavior, and performance: A multi-level analysis. *Journal of Management Studies, 47,* 1219–1247.

Spector, P. E., & Fox, S. (2002). An emotion-centered model of voluntary work behavior: Some parallels between counterproductive work behavior and organizational citizenship behavior. *Human Resource Management Review, 12,* 269–292.

Steiner, D. D., & Gilliland, S. W. (1996). Fairness reactions to personnel selection techniques in France and the United States. *Journal of Applied Psychology, 81,* 134–141.

Taft, J., & Poulon, C. (2004). The FACT Act: The latest attempt at overhauling the Fair Credit Reporting Act and the fairness and accuracy of consumer reports. *Banking Law Journal, 121,* 194.

Trevino, L. K., & Brown, M. E. (2005). The role of leaders in influencing unethical behavior in the workplace. In R. E. Kidwell & C. L. Martin (Eds.), *Managing organizational deviance.* Thousand Oaks: Sage Publications.

VandenBos, G. R., & Bulatao, E. Q. (Eds.). (1996). *Violence on the job: Identifying risks and developing solutions.* Washington, DC: American Psychological Association.

Viollis, P., Roper, M. J., & Decker, K. (2005). Avoiding the legal aftermath of workplace violence. *Employee Relations Law Journal, 31,* 65–70.

White, J. B., Nicholson, T., Minors, P., & Duncan, D. (2001). A demographic profile of employed users of illicit drugs. *Current topics in management, 6,* 353–370.

Woska, W. J. (2007). Legal issues for HR professionals: Reference checking/background investigations. *Public Personnel Management, 34,* 79–89.

PART IV

The Role of (In)Justice and Social Power in
Deviant Workplace Behavior

7

Hazards of Justice

Egocentric Bias, Moral Judgments, and Revenge-Seeking

RUSSELL CROPANZANO AND CAROLINA MOLINER

> *Mike has been working at the same national chain restaurant for 7 years. He*
> *is becoming frustrated because even though he has seniority over most of the*
> *other employees at the restaurant, he is consistently passed over for promo-*
> *tions. To make matters worse, Mike's supervisors do not follow the policy*
> *and procedure manual meant to be implemented at all chain locations.*
> *When asked about his supervisors, Mike typically gets upset and begins*
> *to frantically curse and makes accusations about the supervisors engaging*
> *in inappropriate relationships with other members of the staff, who inevi-*
> *tably get promotions. Recently, Mike confided in some friends that he has*
> *begun stealing money from the bar at the restaurant, and that he frequently*
> *engages in time theft by going on "extremely long smoke breaks" behind the*
> *restaurant. After informing his friends about this inappropriate behavior,*
> *Mike tried to justify the behavior by saying, "If they can do what they want,*
> *I can do what I want."*

Research has long documented a relationship between workplace fairness
and organizational deviance. When individuals are treated unjustly, they
tend to retaliate by harming others (for reviews, see Folger, 1993; Folger &
Baron, 1996; Tripp & Bies, 2009). This can have pernicious effects on organizations. In one study, Skarlicki and Folger (1997) surveyed 167 manufactur-
ing workers. Those who felt that their jobs lacked fair outcome (distributive
justice), fair allocation policies (procedural justice), and fair interpersonal
treatment (interactional justice) were more likely to report engaging in a
number of retaliatory behaviors. These activities included such behaviors as
damaging equipment, taking supplies home, and spreading rumors (see also
Skarlicki & Folger, 2004). Other studies have reported similar results. People who perceive that they were unfairly treated are prone to commit acts of
sabotage (Ambrose, Seabright & Schminke, 2002) and vandalism (DeMoore,
Fisher & Baron, 1988). They may also become more aggressive toward others
(Hershcovis, Turner, Barling, Arnold, Dupré, Inness, LeBlanc & Sivanathan,
2007).

The predicament is even worse than it sounds, for the effects of injustice need not be localized. Trouble may extend to innocent people who were not involved in the original difficulties. Unfairness extends its reach through "trickle-down" effects (Masterson, 2001). Injustice can flow "downward" through the organizational hierarchy, with pernicious consequences at multiple levels. Aryee, Chen, Sun, and Debrah (2007) surveyed a group of 47 supervisors who oversaw the work of 178 subordinates. When the supervisors felt that they were being abused by their bosses, they were in turn more likely to mistreat their own subordinates. Such abuse caused the workers to feel they were not receiving interactional justice, thereby reducing citizenship behaviors and job performance.

The relationship between injustice and workplace deviance has been established in the literature, but where does all this injustice come from? There are many sources, of course, but we would like to explore a topic that has not been given enough research attention. We argue that, in a manner of speaking, employees may sometimes show too much concern with fairness. Most people wish to behave ethically and to be treated with justice. As a result employees may sometimes (a) make self-serving judgments as to the merits of their own positions, (b) judge the morality of other people so harshly that redemption is difficult, and (c) seek revenge when they observe inappropriate conduct. When these three tendencies go too far they can create difficulties for organizations. Below, we explicate each of these three issues, but only after we first make some general comments regarding the nature of justice.

Justice, Rationality, and Human Judgment

It is important to make a distinction between two traditions of scholarship that are pertinent to justice. Best known is the *normative* tradition, usually explored by philosophers. This approach seeks to determine what *really is fair* by reasoning about some standard of conduct or set of moral principles (Blackburn, 2001). This approach is prescriptive; it helps us behave ethically by providing workable guidelines. We can illustrate this by considering two well-known examples (for a more detailed review, see Thompson, 2003). Deontological ethicists, such as Immanuel Kant, argue that we should always treat other people as ends in themselves, never as means to our personal ends. Taking a different approach, the consequentialists, such as the utilitarians Jeremy Bentham and John Stewart Mill, maintain that we should seek to do the greatest good for the greatest number. Notice that these two sets of ethicists do not always agree. Depending on the specifics of the situation, these philosophical models can yield different prescriptions for fair conduct (Sandel, 2009).

The normative approach to fairness is venerable and influential, but it is not the paradigm used by most social scientific inquiry into justice. Social scientists take a *descriptive* approach to fairness. This area of study seeks to determine what people *believe to be fair* through the use of scientific theory and empirical exploration (Cropanzano, Byrne, Bobocel & Rupp, 2001). This approach answers a different set of questions than does the normative tradition. Social scientists are concerned with how people form fairness judgments, as well as the consequences of these evaluations. This empirical paradigm supplies most of the material for this chapter. At its core, the descriptive approach treats "justice" as if it were a judgment or evaluation (see van den Bos & Lind, 2002; van den Bos, Lind & Wilke, 2001). Something is fair or unfair because a person or group deems it to be.

This creates a problem for organizations. Just as philosophers do not always agree as to what constitutes fairness, workers will not all agree when a given policy or resource allocation is just. Furthermore, human judgments often depart from rationality (Shafir & LeBoeuf, 2002) and our thinking can be biased in systematic ways (Moore & Flynn, 2008). Given all this, we would expect certain problems to emerge in judgments of fairness and for these to create subsequent disagreements among employees. Everyone will not be of the same mind. We do not all use the same standards and our thinking may not be careful and deliberate.

To explore how these issues create workplace deviance, we will here consider three sets of research findings. First, we argue that there is a self-serving and egocentric bias that causes us to believe that our preferred positions are fairer than others deem them to be. Second, when individuals are making person perception judgments they often weigh bad behaviors quite heavily. Hence, we are slow to revise our (negative) opinions of others. Third, we argue that people often respond to injustice by seeking revenge, even though doing so may not be economically rational.

Egocentric Biases in Justice Judgments

Man prefers to believe what he prefers to be true.
—Francis Bacon

According to Francis Bacon, we often see things as we wish they were rather than as is objectively the case. This has been especially well documented in judgments pertaining to the self (Kruegar, 1998). For example, most people consider themselves to be better leaders, more intelligent, and less prejudiced than the average person (Gilovich, 1991). It is not surprising that we carry these self-serving biases into our fairness judgments. People tend to view themselves as more fair-minded than are their peers (see Liebrand, Messick & Wolters, 1986; Messick, Bloom, Boldizar & Samuelson, 1985).

Other evidence is consistent with these egocentric fairness perceptions. For example, a meta-analytic investigation by Cohen-Charash and Spector (2001) aggregated findings from a number of previous research studies. Among laboratory research participants, those who perceived high outcome negativity tended to believe that they had experienced significantly less distributive and procedural justice. In field settings, the meta-analytically derived correlations were −.49 and −.41, for distributive and procedural justice respectively. A second meta-analysis conducted by Skitka, Winquist, and Hutchison (2003) also found that the quality of one's outcomes predicted fairness evaluations.

Self-serving fairness perceptions can create workplace deviance for a simple reason—People need to cooperate effectively. If each person is making egocentric justice judgments, then differences over interests can transform into disagreements over morality (see Ury, Brett & Goldberg, 1989). These conflicts may be difficult to resolve because no one enjoys being treated unfairly (Fisher, Ury & Patton, 1991). Disputants may harden their positions, sacrificing other interests in order to ensure (what they see as) a fair outcome. To illustrate this possibility, consider a well-known experimental study by Messick and Sentis (1979).

Messick and Sentis (1979) asked research participants to make a pay allocation decision involving two workers—one that had worked for seven hours and another than had worked for ten hours. Sometimes the research participant was the individual who worked for seven hours, but other times it was another individual. Also, the seven-hour worker always earned $25 (U.S. currency). Participants were asked how much the ten-hour worker should be paid. When the subjects (who were the people rendering the judgment) had worked ten hours, they indicated that they should be paid an average of $35.24. However, when the subject had worked for only seven hours, and the other person had worked for ten, then the participants felt that the other ten hour worker deserved only $30.29. Both sets of subjects agreed that a worker who puts in ten hours of effort deserves more than a worker who puts in only seven. However, the ten-hour worker seems to "deserve" more when it is the person assigning pay and less when it is not. Such judgments are inconsistent, and this inconsistency violates a rule of procedural justice (Leventhal, 1976, 1980; Leventhal, Karuza & Fry, 1980). In an actual organization the potential for conflict is obvious.

Self-Serving Justice Perceptions and Negotiation

If we each see fairness egocentrically, then it could make it difficult for us to find common ground with others. The literature on justice and bargaining demonstrates this point. Potential disputants often enter into negotiations with the belief that their position is the just one. As a consequence, parties may fail to reach timely agreements. This could cause conflicts to escalate (see Pruitt, 2008), bringing costs to both sides.

Thompson and Loewenstein's (1992) Studies of Labor-Management Negotiation. Thompson and Loewenstein (1992, Study 1) illustrate this point. These researchers had twenty-one pairs of MBA students simulate a collective bargaining exchange between a steel company and its workers. One student was to represent the union; the other was to represent management. The two counterparts had two (simulated) days to reach an agreement; otherwise a costly strike would be said to ensue. Their costs accelerated as the strike continued. The key issue was employee wages. The workers' representatives reported that a higher wage was just, whereas the management representatives thought that a lower wage was just. The greater the difference between the two parties perceptions, the longer it took for them to reach an agreement.

In a second experiment, pairs of research subjects, in part, simulated a labor-management negotiation between a teacher's union and the board of education. Thompson and Lowenstein (1992, Study 2) extended the findings from their initial study. After reading the case, individuals were more likely to differentially recall facts from the case that buttressed their position. Participants rated a settlement advantageous to themselves as more fair. As in Experiment 1, the union representatives saw a high wage rate as more just, whereas board of education representatives saw a lower rate as more just. These initial differences were related to the length of simulated strikes—the more the two parties disagreed, the longer the strike.

Notice that these two experiments modeled the behavior of an organization that was bargaining with its workforce. When the negotiations broke down, a strike could result. Egocentric judgments of fairness delayed settlements. These delays had the potential to cause work stoppages. Thus, conflict was escalated because the negotiators were seeking justice on terms that were favorable to themselves.

Babcock, Wang, and Loewenstein's (1996) Field Study. Babcock, Wang, and Loewenstein (1996) examined this issue in a field setting. These authors studied collective bargaining between a teacher's union and a number of Pennsylvania school districts. In order to set salaries, both sides selected districts that they believed were comparable to their own. These comparison districts were chosen to provide a standard or baseline in order to appropriately situate the teachers' earnings. Interestingly, the school boards and the unions tended to choose different sets of comparison districts. Moreover, these differences favored their own side. The average pay in the school boards' list was $27,000. For the union's list it was $28,060. As found by Thompson and Lowenstein (1992, Study 2), the greater the difference in the comparable districts, the higher became the strike rate. Strike duration was not significantly impacted, however. In any case, we see that individuals interpret ambiguous evidence in a way that is favorable to their own position. This can cause conflict to escalate and have dysfunctional consequences for organizations.

Limits of Information During Negotiation

Conflict resolution researchers propose a solution to these sorts of problems that we have been discussing. Both parties should share information (Weeks, 1992). This has the potential to build up trust, while promoting mutually advantageous win-win solutions (Malhotra & Bazerman, 2007). Much economic theory would agree. Bargaining should become more efficient in a market when both negotiators have perfect knowledge about one another's preferences and payouts (cf. Camerer & Loewenstein, 1993; Roth & Murnighan, 1982). This sounds reasonable enough, and it is often true. But there are times when more knowledge is not a good thing. The provision of information about another person's outcome can cause disputants to believe that they are being treated unfairly. When individuals are monitoring the fairness with which they are being treated, additional knowledge about the other party's payouts or preferences can create a sense of injustice. Once a sense of injustice exists then agreements break down and conflicts escalate (Allred, 1999; Pruitt, 2008).

Roth and Murnighan (1982) and the Pitfalls of Information. Roth and Murnighan (1982) presented dyads of research participants with 100 lottery tickets. The subjects' shared job was to negotiate a mutually agreeable division. There was one catch—the tickets were worth different amounts to each disputant. One player could win $20 for winning the lottery; the other could only earn $5. If neither party knew the prize amounts, then the tickets were fairly easy to divide. Over 85% of the negotiators reached a solution, usually a 50/50 split. The matter became more exciting when the negotiating dyads had full information regarding their respective payouts. Now two defensible solutions present themselves:

Solution #1: Equalize the number of tickets. This suggests a 50/50 split.
Solution #2: Equalize the expected values. This suggests an 80/20 split. (.80 X
   5 = 4 and .20 X 20 = 4).

Each participant seems to have responded egocentrically. The player with
a $20 payout was more likely to prefer the 50/50 split, whereas the player
with the $5 payout was more likely to prefer an 80/20 split. Disagreements
roughly doubled when players had *more* information. In other words, people
got on better when they knew *less* about one another's preferences.

*Camerer and Loewenstein (1993, Study 1) and a Second Examination of
Information.* Consistent findings were reported in a later experiment by
Camerer and Loewenstein (1993, Study 1). These scholars had dyads of MBA
students negotiate the sale of a plot of land. One individual played the role of
the Appletons, who were the sellers. The other individual played the role of
the Bakers, who were the buyers. The Appletons were said to have an outside
offer of $5,000. The amount the Bakers were willing to pay varied—in one
condition it was $18,000, while in the other it was raised to $24,000. Individuals first bargained without knowing one another's reservation points.
In a first round of negotiating, every dyad reached a settlement, which was
straightforward given the wide and overlapping bargaining zones.

After achieving these agreements, participants were given additional
information about the other paper. Specifically, they were informed of their
counterpart's reservation price. With this knowledge in their possession,
they were then instructed to bargain a second time. Once individuals knew
the value of the land or the sale to the other party, this often changed their
estimate of a fair settlement. Those who reached advantageous settlements
wished to maintain their original agreements. Others, who had received less
favorable terms, preferred to split the difference between the value and cost
of the land, or even to reverse the original agreement so as to make things
more fair overall. As one would expect, the additional information caused
more disagreements in the second round.

Self-Serving Justice Perceptions and Conflict Resolution

Thus far the picture we have painted is somewhat less than completely opti-
mistic. Our egocentric interpretations of fairness may lead us to become
tougher negotiators, and this can produce impasses (Babcock et al., 1995;
Loewenstein et al., 1993), which allow conflicts to escalate (Babcock et al.,
1996; Thompson & Loewenstein, 1992). Firms might prevent some of these
troubles by withholding information (see Camerer & Loewenstein, 1993,

Study 1; Roth & Murnighan, 1982), but secrecy creates problems of its own. There is at least one other reason for caution. Egocentric biases do more than create conflict; they also make existing conflicts more difficult to resolve.

Loewenstein, Issacharoff, Camerer, and Babcock (1993) on Self-Serving Judgments during Litigation. Loewenstein, Issacharoff, Camerer, and Babcock (1993) had pairs of research subjects role-play a lawsuit. One partner in the pair played the role of a plaintiff, the other of a defendant. While riding a motorcycle, the plaintiff had been struck by the defendant's automobile. As a consequence, he or she was seeking damages. The defendant, on the other hand, was claiming that the accident was the plaintiff's fault. The two parties were given thirty minutes to review their case.

Loewenstein and his colleagues (1993) found strong evidence of self-serving bias. Both plaintiffs and defendants recalled more arguments favoring their own positions and fewer arguments favoring the position of their counterpart. Likewise, both parties weighted arguments favorable to themselves as more decisive, while arguments favorable to the other person were viewed as less important. These tricks of memory and judgment were related to other outcomes.

Each party saw a fair settlement as one that was favorable to themselves. As one might imagine, when plaintiffs and defendants had very different views of fairness then they were less likely to reach a settlement. Similar results were obtained when individuals were asked to predict a judge's decision. Even though all parties were provided with a financial incentive to correctly estimate a judge's settlement, plaintiffs predicted that the judge would offer more money, while defendants predicted that the judge would offer less. As this difference became greater, then a settlement became less likely.

Camerer and Loewenstein's (1993, Study 2) Replication and Extension. It is tempting to suspect that Loewenstein and his colleagues' (1993) aforementioned findings were due to determined role-playing. That is, the participants were fully aware that they were exaggerating their positions; they simply viewed this as the best tactic to effectively settle the disagreement. It is noteworthy that Loewenstein et al. (1993) paid subjects a bonus for correctly guessing the judge's award. Thus, if the participants were exaggerating for effect, they would have had to believe that the benefits of misrepresenting themselves would outweigh the lost bonus. Other studies have similarly compensated participants for accuracy, without successfully reducing the self-serving bias (Camerer & Loewenstein, 1993; Thompson & Loewenstein, 1992).

A second experiment by Camerer and Loewenstein (1993, Study 2) belies this possibility. As with Loewenstein et al., Camerer and Loewenstein had subjects role-play plaintiffs and defendants in a legal case. Once again, research participants read the story of a motorcycle accident. After attempting to reach a mutually satisfying agreement each subject indicated what he or she believed a fair settlement to be, predicted a judge's actual award, and rated the importance a "fair judge" would give to sixteen possible arguments. Eight of these arguments were favorable to the plaintiff, while eight others were favorable to the defendant.

However, there was one additional independent variable. In the "known-role" condition, individuals were told in advance whether they would act as plaintiffs or as defendants. Subsequent to this assignment they studied the case. In the "unknown-role" condition, unassigned participants studied the case. Subsequent to this reading they were later assigned to their roles. Notice that all participants, regardless of whether they were plaintiffs or defendants, saw the same material. The difference was that about half of the subjects read the case with their role in mind, while the other half did not.

When participants were aware of their roles while reading the case, they showed the same biases that their fellow subjects demonstrated in the Loewenstein et al. (1993) study. That is, they claimed that the fair settlements were those that were favorable to them, while predicting that the judge would see things their way. Participants also saw arguments favorable to themselves as more important than were the arguments favoring their counterparts. However, these effects were greatly reduced when participants did not learn of their roles until after reading the case. That is, subjects in the unknown-role condition were more similar to their counterparts in the size of a fair settlement, in their predictions regarding a judge's award, and in their importance ratings. As one might imagine, there were more settlements when individuals learned of their roles after examining the stimulus materials, and fewer settlements among those who learned of their roles in advance.

Babcock, Loewenstein, Issacharoff, and Camerer's (1995) Third Study of a Legal Case. A third look at the motorcycle case was provided by Babcock, Loewenstein, Issacharoff, and Camerer (1995). These findings were generally consistent with those of Camerer and Loewenstein (1993). Participants again read about a motorcycle accident in which litigation was pending. They also indicated what they believed would be a fair settlement, predicted a judge's actual award, and rated the importance that a judge would give to sixteen arguments regarding the case. Once again, half of the participants were assigned their roles before reading the case, and half were assigned them after. The two individuals then attempted to reach an agreement. Babcock and her colleagues imposed fictional "legal fees." After exchanging offers for six rounds, money was taken from the earnings of both the plaintiff and the defendant.

Once again, participants who knew their role in advance suggested that a more advantageous settlement (to themselves) was also a fair one, predicted a judge would concur with the case in a way that was advantageous to them, and thought that a judge would view favorable arguments as more important. These differences were greatly reduced when participants learned their roles only after learning the specifics of the case. Finally, when subjects learned their role before the case and showed the requisite biases, they took longer to reach a settlement, were less likely to come to agreement, and had settlements that earned less money for them.

Closing Thoughts: What Can Be Done?

Lowenstein et al. (1993) found evidence of egocentric processing, such that our own position seems also to be the fair one. These findings were replicated by Camerer and Loewenstein (1993) and Babcock et al. (1995), who provided further evidence that this processing is not necessarily intentional. That is, the self-serving bias was most strongly felt when individuals learned their roles before studying their stimulus materials. The knowledge of their position seems to have impacted how they viewed the specific facts of the case. When they learned their assigned roles after reading the material then they could not process it in a biased fashion. Hence, they were less partial to self-serving information. This result suggests that the egocentric perceptions were not a deliberate negotiating ploy—we may really come to believe in the merits of our position.

This is a serious problem, though not an unsolvable one. Thompson and Loewenstein's (1992, Study 2) findings suggest one possibility—go ahead and negotiate. As it happens, these scholars found that people enter into negotiations with a relatively strong egocentric bias. However, after bargaining with another person this bias is subsequently reduced; we come to see things in a manner that is more similar to our counterpart. Self-serving judgments may work against negotiation, but negotiation can also work against self-serving judgments. This may not be a complete solution, but it should help individuals move in a positive direction.

Moral Judgments of Other People

Judge not, and ye shall not be judged: Condemn not, and ye shall not be condemned, forgive, and ye shall be forgiven.
—Luke 6:37

While we are very generous in judging the fairness of our preferences, we are somewhat harder when evaluating others. This could make us slow to forgive the transgressions of other people. There is evidence that once a severely unethical behavior is exhibited, then this "worse case" sets an upper bound on how moral a person can come to be seen. Even subsequent acts of decency may be incapable of erasing this unfortunate impression. At times this could make us overly negative in our assessment of others. In the early 1970s an interesting set of experiments by Birnbaum (1972, 1973) captured this idea.

Birnbaum (1972) and the Limits of Additive Judgments. Birnbaum (1972) was originally interested in understanding how people combine attributes in order to make a morality judgment. In two experiments, he presented undergraduate research participants with pairs of potentially negative behaviors. These ranged from the relatively trivial ("Keeping a dime you find in a telephone booth," "Player poker on a Sunday," "Cheating at solitaire") to the relatively severe ("Habitually borrowing small sums of money from friends and failing to return them," "Spreading rumors that an acquaintance is a sexual pervert," "Poisoning a neighbor's dog whose barking bothers you"). After reading each pair of items the subjects provided their overall evaluation on a nine-point scale.

When making their ratings, Birnbaum (1972) discovered that individuals did not simply add the two behaviors together. Rather, there was a significant interaction between the severity of the first item in the pair and the severity of the second. Specifically, when the second item was highly questionable, this produced high ratings of immorality from the subjects. For other sets of items the second item was only moderately unethical. These moderate actions had a weaker impact on the overall morality judgment than did the severely unethical items. These findings can be visualized as a sort of "fan spread," whereby the egregious offenses have a larger-than-expected impact on ethicality ratings. Given that an additive model could not fully account for his findings, Birnbaum (1972) explored two other possibilities—a range model or an averaging model with differential weights. Trying to distinguish between these two sorts of intuitive composites will bring us to the heart of the matter.

A *range model* proposes that the mean judgment of stimuli, the negative behaviors in these two experiments, has a standard deviation around it. The participant's judgment task is to combine the two items into an overall rating. To the extent that the standard deviations differ, then the composite score will be pulled toward the mean of the item with the smaller standard deviation. Since very extreme behaviors tend to have smaller standard deviations (much consensus and certainty), while less extreme behaviors have larger standard deviations (smaller consensus and uncertainty) then the overall rating is pulled toward the mean of the more severe item. A *differential weighting model* is easier to explain. For sundry reasons, people might alter the importance given to a particular behavior. Birnbaum (1972) suggests that higher values are viewed as having greater weight than are lower values. Thus, the more dubious the behavior the more it is likely to influence the overall judgment. If one assumes differential weighting but adds the assumption that very immoral acts are given a higher weight, then this model could explain the obtained findings. In his first two experiments, Birnbaum (1972) could rule out an additive model but could not fully distinguish between a range model and a differential weighting model. As we shall see in a moment, this was the topic of a later experiment (Birnbaum, 1973). As shall soon be apparent, either of these models fared well, and immoral acts may be harder to rectify than at first appears.

Birnbaum (1973) on Combining Good and Bad Deeds. In his third experiment, Birnbaum (1973) tested the same three models—additive (not supported by Birnbaum, 1972), range, and differential weighting. In order to distinguish between the latter two possibilities, Birnbaum (1973) included both negative and also positive behaviors in his list of stimulus materials. An extremely negative behavior was "Putting razor blades in children's apples on halloween." An extremely positive behavior was "Preventing a forcible rape." Research participants were told that "Your task is to read each set of actions and then judge how 'good' or 'bad' it would be to carry out all of the actions" (396).

These items were presented to subjects in bundles of three sizes—two actions to rate, three actions, and four actions. Additionally, these sets could be homogenous (positive *or* negative items of the same magnitude) or heterogeneous (positive *and* negative actions of different magnitudes). Undergraduate research participants judged 66 sets of items. Birnbaum (1973) compared the overall judgments made by the respondents for these various collections of actions. The results did not unambiguously support either the range model or the differential weighting model.

Birnbaum (1973) argued that his data are consistent with a possible "configural effect" (399). He puts it this way: "Having committed an L [highly immoral] deed, the person cannot be considered moral no matter how many good deeds he performs" (399). Elsewhere in the same paragraph, Birnbaum suggest that extremely egregious acts place "an upper bound on the overall impression." In this way, Birnbaum has separated an appraisal of the acts from an appraisal of the person. When someone does something that is very unethical, he or she becomes a bad *person,* and it is difficult to change this impression. Birnbaum's configural effect is important, because it suggests that once one is labeled negatively, it is difficult to recover.

Riskey and Birnbaum (1974) and the Configural Effect. In a fourth experimental study, Riskey and Birnbaum (1974) directly tested the configural effect. These scholars again had subjects rate collections of good and bad deeds. Participants read thirty-seven sets of actions in all. These bundles were either homogeneous (either all very moral or all moderately moral) or heterogeneous (moral items followed by either moderately or very immoral items). The sets of actions were of varying lengths. This approach allowed Birnbaum to ascertain how many ethical behaviors were necessary to compensate for negative deeds.

The results supported Birnbaum's (1973) configural model. Following immoral acts, moral deeds could improve one's rating. Highly moral deeds produced more improvement than actions of only moderate morality. However, an asymptote was reached. Once a questionable action has been committed there seems to be an upper limit on how ethical an individual can be viewed. As Riskey and Birnbaum (1974, 171) put it, "Data suggest that performance of very immoral deeds limits the highest level of morality that a person can achieve." What's done is difficult to undo. Such a judgment also has ramifications for the firm as a whole. None of us is perfect. If we continue to look askance at our colleagues, even after they have performed numerous acts of decency, then the social fabric could be torn by distrust and mutual acrimony.

Another interesting feature of these findings has to do with the homogeneous sets of actions. Recall that these deeds were all positive, though some were extremely positive and some were moderately so. The homogeneous bundles, since they were exclusively positive, contained no negative behaviors to set an upper bound. In the case of these homogenous and positive sets of deeds, there is evidence that the subjects' ratings showed linearity. That is, the more positive one's deeds the more positive were the overall judgments. Consequently, positive deeds seem to have been aggregated through an additive model, while negative and positive deeds were aggregated together through a configural model. This helps to explain why poor behavior hurt more than beneficent behavior helped.

Closing Thoughts: What Can Be Done?

Birnbaum's (1972, 1973) research poses a problem. Once a person makes a mistake, especially a serious mistake, it is difficult for that individual to recover. The worst behavior may put a ceiling on how decent that co-worker could come to be seen. Since none of us are free from error, and all of us have our failings, the configural model implies that distrust could spread through a work team. Scholars have not provided a complete answer to this problem, but we would recommend beginning with an apology. When people make mistakes they should admit their blunder. Doing so can restore good feelings toward the transgressors (Kim, Ferrin & Cooper, 2004; McCullough, Bellah, Kilpatrick & Johnson, 2001; McCullough, Rachel, Sandage, Worthington, Brown & Hight, 1998; McCullough & Worthington, 1995; McCullough, Worthington & Rachel, 1997) and reduce the desire for future revenge (Ohbuchi, Kameda & Agarie, 1989; Tripp, Bies & Aquino, 2007). This may be the best place to begin.

Restoring Fairness, Deonance, Altruistic Punishment, and Revenge

Fiat justitia, ruat coelum. (Let justice be done, though the heavens fall.)
—attributed to Lucius Calpurnius Piso Caesoninus

We now turn our attention to our third and final concern. As we shall see, there is a tendency for people to strike back when they are treated unfairly, and this can be disruptive in and of itself. In his *deontic* model of justice, Folger (1994, 1998, 2001) argued that justice is intrinsically valuable (Folger & Salvador, 2008). People desire fairness for its own sake. The name "deontic" alludes to ethical duty (*deon* = obligation). Folger asserts that experiencing an injustice (or even witnessing an injustice) can produce a *deontic state*. This deontic state includes strong emotions, such as resentment and disgust (Folger, Cropanzano & Goldman, 2005; Folger & Skarlicki, 2008), which push our behavior in certain ways (Cropanzano, Goldman & Folger, 2003). For example, our feelings often drive us to seek revenge against those that have treated us inappropriately (Folger & Cropanzano, in press).

Evidence favoring deontic justice was obtained in a series of four experimental studies by Turillo, Folger, Lavelle, Umphress, and Gee (2002). In each experiment, Turillo et al. invited a research participant to allocate a reward between themselves and another person. (This was a cover story. The other person did not actually exist.) The subject was told that the other party had behaved fairly or unfairly at a previous experimental session. Turillo and his colleagues then gave the participant an opportunity to penalize this person, but only if they gave up some of their own earnings to do so. Notice that it is not economically rational for an individual to forfeit his or her own profits so as to punish someone who harmed a stranger (see Shafir & LeBeouf, 2002). Regardless, the results were consistent across the four experiments. Participants tended to punish those who were alleged to have been unfair, while rewarding those who were supposedly fair. This occurred even when the alleged victim was an outgroup member (Studies 2 and 4). Of course, in the four Turillo et al. experiments the subject could never meet the transgressor (because that person did not exist) and there was no chance of future interaction. These studies suggest that justice is an important concern for many individuals. As Turillo and his colleagues discovered, once we believe that an injustice has occurred we are motivated to strike back.

Altruistic Punishment

Fehr, Fishbacher, and Gächter (2002) concur with Folger (1993, 1998, 2001) that retaliation often follows unfair behavior. These authors use the term "altruistic punishment" to describe the phenomena. Retaliatory sanctions are "punishment," of course, because they are intentionally directed at another person in order to reprimand inappropriate conduct. However, these behaviors can also be "altruistic" to the extent that they are costly to the actor but beneficial to others. Consistent with this, evidence suggests that altruistic punishment has a deterrence effect that pushes all group members to effectively contribute. Thus, it is positively associated with cooperation (Camerer & Fehr, 2006; Fehr & Fishbacher, 2004a) and negatively associated with shirking (Fehr & Fishbacher, 2004b; Fehr & Gächter, 2002).

We can illustrate this thinking with an experiment by Fehr and Gächter (2000). In this study, teams of research subjects participated in a mixed-motive game. If they choose to do so, subjects could attempt to "free ride." That is, working less and letting their teammates carry the load. As is typical for these sorts of games, the maximum payout occurs when all parties work together for a period of time. However, cooperation has a downside. If one person defects, the defector can still do well, but the non-defectors—the cooperators—suffer a stiff financial penalty.

Fehr and Gächter's (2000) experiment went for twenty rounds. Sometimes the subjects had the power to castigate free riders but other times they did not. When individuals had the power to punish the offender, they often did so. Indeed, they even tailored the size of the punishment to the size of the offense. This turned out to be effective. There was less free riding and more cooperation when retribution was allowed. Payouts were also impacted. In the short run, those teams that punished paid a penalty. The reprimands were costly, and this cut into earnings. But over time penalizing the shirkers paid off. In the long run, the heightened cooperation promoted higher earnings. Retaliation rebounded to the benefit of the team.

Understanding the Revenge Process

Research on deontic justice and altruistic punishment suggests that, when employees perceived that they are unfairly treated, then they will often wish to restore fairness by retaliating against the transgressor (Tripp, Bies & Aquino, 2007). Workers may come to believe that retribution will alter the consequences for the offender and thereby restore fairness to a relationship. These retaliatory actions are partially instrumental, people wish to be compensated for losses, but they are not only so. Retaliation also serves to reaffirm the moral principles (Reb, Goldman, Kray & Cropanzano, 2006). From the employees' point of view, acts of revenge are informal strategies for dealing with resentment by punishing the offenders and thereby producing fairness. As Tripp and Bies (2009, 13) put it: "revenge should be seen as actions intended to restore a sense of justice." Such responses are probably not unusual. Thomas and Schmidt (1976) report that managers spend as much as 20% of their working time dealing with conflict.

The Revenge Process. In their thorough review of the retribution literature, Tripp and Bies (2009) identify three critical participants in a retaliatory episode: the avenger (the person seeking revenge in response to the perceived harm), the offender or transgressor (the individual alleged to be responsible for the harm), and bystanders (guiltless people that could be impacted by the vengeful action). In a typical episode the avenger strikes out at an offender, perhaps managing to harm this transgressor. However, in so doing, an innocent bystander could be inadvertently hurt. Accordingly, most acts of vengeance are intentional and directed responses; they are motivated by a sense of injustice. Even so, they often lack a careful consideration of the secondary consequences and potential for injury to blameless parties.

The lack of concern for the well-being of bystanders poses something of a paradox. In a fervent quest for fairness an avenger may seek retribution, though perhaps at the hazard of hurting an innocent party. It is as if avengers become so concerned with the ill-treatment that they received, that they may overlook an injustice toward a bystander. To explain how this could occur, Tripp and Bies (2009) offer a conceptual model of revenge. Their framework analyzes the avenging employees' thoughts, emotions, and behaviors.

The process begins with a workplace provocation. Such provocations often involve the violation of justice norms. If the offender is held responsible for the unfortunate event, then the victim experiences strong emotions, such as anger or resentment (Folger et al., 2005; Folger & Cropanzano, in press; Frank, 1988). These powerful emotions motivate the victim to inflict damage on the transgressor (Bies & Tripp, 1996). The more severe and intentional was the harm, the greater the sense of injustice and the stronger will be the emotional "push" for revenge (Aquino, Tripp & Bies, 2001). Bies and Tripp's framework is important, for it illustrates at least two places where careful judgment can be compromised—in the attributions of the other party's behavior and in one's own emotional reactions.

Attributions for Wrongful Behavior. To understand why these attributions of blame can be disruptive, it is important to consider retribution in view of our earlier comments on self-serving biases. An individual can honestly believe that he or she has been treated unjustly *even when most people do not believe this is so.* Still, to the extent that we act on our own perceptions, retaliation could follow. Bies, Tripp, and Kramer (1997) have found that people often make overly personalistic attributions, believing that a deliberate harm was done to them when it may have instead been an accident. This can amplify the blame toward the offender more than an objective third-party would do. As such, this sort of attribution error can augment the desire for revenge.

Now we need to consider the victim's perspective. This targeted party could be viewing things egocentrically as well. Believing in the merit of his or her own position, the victim could now feel wronged. Thus, the targeted individual may also seek revenge (Allred, 1999). Concisely put, what is righteous indignation to one party appears to be irrational antagonism to another. This sets off a process called "biased punctuation" (see Bies, Tripp & Kramer, 1997; Pruitt, 2008). Biased punctuation escalates the conflict beyond the original harm, as each party struggled to right (what they view as) a moral wrong.

Emotion and Revenge. It is also important to emphasize that revenge is an emotional process, and these emotions help to motivate action (Bies & Tripp, 2002). Since emotions increase the motivation for retribution, then the avenger may not carefully deliberate about the costs and benefits of this action. Blind acts of "lashing out" can occur. For example, individuals who are frustrated by powerful superiors will sometimes "displace" their hostility at blameless, but less threatening, bystanders (Marcus-Newhall, Pedersen, Carlson & Miller, 2000). In a field study, Mitchell and Ambrose (2007) surveyed 427 American workers. As anticipated, those who had been subjected to abusive supervision reported more deviance directed toward their boss. However, these individuals also showed displaced deviance directed at their coworkers and their organization. As such, bystanders may be caught in a maelstrom of unintentional conflict, as the act of vindictiveness escalates past the original disagreement.

Revenge Behavior. It bears mention that everyone who is wronged does not necessarily seek revenge. Usually, we do not do so. Mikula (1986, Study

1) had respondents recall an injustice. Only about 18% of the respondents reported retaliation and a higher number—roughly 20%—resigned themselves to the unfair event. In a later study, Crombag, Rassin, and Horselenberg (2003) found that 71% of their respondents did not engage in revenge following an unfair transgression.

Closing Thoughts: What Can Be Done?

Though the settling of scores can be harmful, this is not universally true. A positive vision of revenge is also possible. In this sense, Tripp and Bies (2009) conceive revenge as an indicator of a dysfunctional organization (see also, Ury et al., 1988). When the work environment has broken down, then informal acts of retaliation could be a practical option for preventing injustice at work and discouraging future acts of abusive behavior (see Frank, 1988). Going further, retribution can act as an important motivator for organizational change. As the altruistic punishment literature illustrates, vengeful acts can even encouraging cooperation (Camerer & Fehr, 2006; Fehr & Fishbacher, 2004a). While acknowledging this good news, we should remember that such phenomena as biased punctuation and displacement of aggression can be hurtful. The challenge for organizations is to pay attention to how employees are treated, gain knowledge and skills on how to encourage justice in organizations and use this knowledge to establish mechanisms that restore justice and prevent for the escalation of the conflict (Pruitt, 2008).

It is noteworthy that individuals often decide to take a vindictive action after perceiving an injustice. Hence, if justice is repaired either by the organization or the offender, there is no need for getting even. This is an opportunity for organizations to lessen the amount of revenge-seeking by increasing constructive conflict resolution (Bendersky, 2003). When properly conducted, both formal (Olson-Buchanan & Boswell, 2008) and informal (Goldman, Cropanzano, Stein & Benson, 2008) interventions can be useful for resolving problems and thereby reducing conflict (Ury et al., 1988).

Conclusion

In this chapter we have argued that the peoples' concern with justice can sometimes cause problems. There are three ways that this can transpire. We first examined egocentric self-perceptions. We found that individuals have systematically distorted judgments, which tend to favor allocations that are to their advantage. As a result of these self-serving perceptions it is sometimes difficult to achieve agreements, and this can lead to conflict escalation.

Additionally, conflict resolution is harder when disputants are firmly wedded to a position that each sees as just. We then turned our attention to the literature on moral judgment. We observed that ethical evaluations of others can sometimes be unforgiving. A person's worse negative act seems to create a ceiling on moral judgment. Even multiple ethical deeds may not fully eliminate this effect. Such an unyielding judgment can lay the groundwork for future conflict. Finally, we discussed the individual's tendency to punish injustice. This can even occur when it is personally costly. At times this can be a good thing, since angry aggression can deter counter-normative behavior and thereby increase cooperation. But this does not mean that revenge is always beneficial. Given the egocentric bias in our judgments, the victim may view that retaliatory action as unwarranted. This, in turn, could create a conflict spiral that creates even a worse problem (Pruitt, 2008).

The influential philosopher of ethics John Rawls (1971, 3) famously remarked that "Justice is the first virtue of social institutions, as truth is of systems of thought." For Rawls justice was a high priority, even the top priority, for society. This is a lofty goal, and one that will sometimes have to be approached with caution. Organizations should endeavor to treat their employees with decency and fairness. However, they should also recognize that doing so may be difficult and, at least for some, thankless. We will not all agree on what constitutes fairness. But we can at least seek justice with principled intentions and open eyes.

REFERENCES

Allred, K. G. (1999). Anger and retaliation: Toward an understanding of impassioned conflict in organizations. In R. J. Bies, R. J. Lewicke, & B. H. Sheppard (Eds.), *Research on negotiation in organizations* (pp. 27–58). Greenwich, CT: JAI.

Ambrose, M. L., Seabright, M. A., & Schminke, M. (2002). Sabotage in the workplace: The role of organizational injustice. *Organizational Behavior and Human Decision Processes, 89*, 947–965.

Aquino, K., Tripp, T. M., & Bies, R. J. (2001). How employees respond to personal offense: The effects of blame attribution, victim status, and offender status on revenge and reconciliation in the workplace. *Journal of Applied Psychology, 86*, 52–59.

Aquino, K., Tripp, T. M., & Bies, R. J. (2006). Getting even or moving on? Status variables and procedural justice as predictors of revenge, forgiveness and reconciliation in organizations. *Journal of Applied Psychology, 91*, 653–668.

Aryee, S., Chen, Z. X., Sun, Y-Y., & Debrah, Y. A. (2007). Antecedents and outcomes of abusive supervision: Test of a trickle-down model. *Journal of Applied Psychology, 92*, 191–201.

Babcock, L., Loewenstein, G., Issacharoff, S., & Camerer, C. (1995). Biased judgments of fairness in bargaining. *American Economic Review, 85*, 1337–1343.

Babcock, L., Wang, X., & Loewenstein, G. (1996). Choosing the wrong pond: Social comparisons in negotiations that reflect a self-serving bias. *Quarterly Journal of Economics, CXI*, 1–19.

Bendersky, C. (2003). Organizational dispute resolution systems: A complementarities model. *Academy of Management Review, 28,* 643–656.

Bies, R. J. & Tripp, T. M. (1996). Beyond distrust: "Getting even" and the need to revenge. In R. M. Kramer, T. Tyler (Eds.), *Trust and organizations* (pp.246–260). Sage, Thousand Oaks, CA:

Bies, R. J. & Tripp, T. M. (2001). A passion for justice: the rationality and morality of revenge. In R. Cropanzano (Ed.), *Justice in the workplace: From theory to practice (Vol. 2)* (pp. 197–208). Mahwah, NJ. Lawrence Erlbaum Associates.

Bies, R. J. & Tripp, T. M. (2002). Hot flashes, open wounds: injustice and the tyranny of its emotions. In S. W. Gilliland, D. D. Steiner & D. Skarlicki (Eds.), *Emerging perspectives on managing organizational justice* (pp. 202–223). Greenwich, CT: Information Age.

Bies, R. J., Tripp, T. M., & Kramer, R. M. (1997). At the breaking point: Cognitive and social dynamics of revenge in organizations. In R. A. Giacalone & J. Greenberg (Eds.), *Antisocial behavior in organizations* (pp. 18–36). Thousand Oaks, CA: Sage.

Birnbaum, M. H. (1972). Morality judgments: Tests of an averaging model. *Journal of Experimental Psychology, 93,* 35–42.

Birnbaum, M. H. (1973). Morality judgment: Test of an averaging model with differential weights. *Journal of Experimental Psychology, 99,* 395–399.

Blackburn, S. (2001). *Being good: A short introduction to ethics.* Oxford: Oxford University Press.

Camerer, C., & Fehr, E. (2006). When does "economic man" dominate social behavior? *Science, 311,* 47–52.

Camerer, C. F., & Loewenstein, G. (1993). Information, fairness, and efficiency in bargaining. In B. A. Mellers & J. Baron (Eds.), *Psychological perspectives on the justice: Theory and applications* (pp. 155–179). Cambridge: Cambridge University Press.

Cohen-Charash, Y., & Spector, P. E. (2001). The role of justice in organizations: A meta-analysis. *Organizational Behavior and Human Decision Processes, 86,* 278–321.

Connolly, T., & Hardman, D. (2009). "Fools rush in": A JDM perspective on the role of emotions in decisions, moral and otherwise. In D. M. Bartels, C. W. Bauman, L. J. Skitka, & L. D. Medin (Eds.), *The psychology of learning and motivation* (Vol. 50, pp. 275–306). Burlington, VT: Academic.

Crombag, H., Rassin, E. & Horselenberg, R. (2003). On vengeance. *Psychology, Crime and Law, 9,* 333–344.

Cropanzano, R., Byrne, Z. S., Bobocel, D. R., & Rupp, D. E. (2001). Moral virtues, fairness heuristics, social entities, and other denizens of organizational justice. *Journal of Vocational Behavior, 58,* 164–209.

Cropanzano, R., Goldman, B., & Folger, R. (2002). Deontic justice: the role of moral principles in workplace fairness. *Journal of Organizational Behavior, 24,* 1019–1024.

Cropanzano, R., Goldman, B. M., & Folger, R. (2003). Deontic justice: The role of moral principles in workplace fairness. *Journal of Organizational Behavior, 24,* 1019–1024.

DeMoore, S. W., Fisher, J. D., & Baron, R. M. (1988). The equity-control model as a predictor of vandalism among college students. *Journal of Applied Social Psychology, 18,* 80–91.

Fehr, E., & Fishbacher, U. (2004a). Social norms and human cooperation. *Trends in Cognitive Science, 8,* 185–190.

Fehr, E., & Fishbacher, U. (2004b). Third party punishment and social norms. *Evolution and Human Behavior, 25,* 63–87.

Fehr, E., Fishbacher, U., & Gächter, S. (2002). Strong reciprocity, human cooperation and the enforcement of social norms. *Human Nature, 13,* 1–25.

Fehr, E., & Gächter, S. (2000). Cooperation and punishment in public goods experiments. *American Economic Review, 90,* 980–994.

Fehr, E., & Gächter, S. (2002). Altruistic punishment in humans. *Nature, 415,* 137–140.

Fisher, R., & Ury, W., & Patton, B. (1991). *Getting to yes: Negotiating agreement without giving in* (2nd Ed.). New York: Penguin Books.

Folger, R. (1993). Reactions to mistreatment at work. In J. K. Murnighan (Ed.), *Social psychology in organizations* (pp. 161–183). Englewood Cliffs, NJ: Prentice Hall.

Folger, R. (1994). Workplace justice and employee worth. *Social Justice Research, 7,* 225–241.

Folger, R. (1998). Fairness as a moral virtue. In M. Schminke (Ed.), *Managerial ethics: Moral management of people and processes* (pp. 13–34). Mahwah, NJ: Erlbaum.

Folger, R. (2001). Fairness as deonance. In S. W. Gilliland, D. D. Steiner, & D. P. Skarlicki (Eds.), *Research in social issues in management* (Vol. 1, pp. 3–33). New York: Information Age.

Folger, R., & Baron, R. A. (1996). Violence and hostility at work: A model of reactions to perceived injustice. In G. R. VandenBos & E. Q. Bulato (Eds.), *Violence on the job: Identifying risks and developing solutions* (pp. 51–58). Washington, DC: American Psychological Association.

Folger, R., & Cropanzano, R. (in press). Social hierarchies and the evolution of moral emotions. In M. Schminke (Ed.), *Managerial ethics: Managing the psychology of morality.* New York: Routledge/Psychology Press.

Folger, R., Cropanzano, R., & Goldman, B. (2005). What is the relationship between justice and morality? In J. Greenberg & J. A. Colquitt (Eds.), *Handbook of organizational justice* (pp. 215–246). Mahwah, NJ: Erlbaum.

Folger, R., & Salvador, R. (2008). Is management theory too "self-ish"? *Journal of Management, 34,* 1127–1151.

Folger, R., & Skarlicki, D. P. (2008). The evolutionary bases of deontic justice. In S. W. Gilliland, D. D. Steiner, & D. P. Skarlicki (Eds.), *Justice, morality, and social responsibility* (pp. 29–62). Charlotte, NC: Information Age.

Frank, R. H. (1988). *Passions within reason: The strategic role of emotions.* New York: Norton.

Gilovich, T. (1991). *How we know what isn't so: The fallibility of human reason in everyday life.* New York: Free Press.

Goldman, B., Cropanzano, R., Stein, J., & Benson, L., III (2008). The role of third-parties/mediation in resolving conflict in organizations. In M. J. Gelfand & C. K. W. De Dreu (Eds.), *The psychology of conflict and conflict management in organizations* [SIOP Frontiers Series] (pp. 291–320). Mahwah, NJ: Erlbaum.

Hershcovis, M. S., Turner, N., Barling, J., Arnold, K. A., Dupré, K. E., Inness, M., LeBlanc, M. M., & Sivanathan, N. (2007). Predicting workplace aggression: A meta-analysis. *Journal of Applied Psychology, 92,* 228–238.

Kim P. H., Ferrin D. L., & Cooper C. D. (2004). Removing the shadow of suspicion: The effects of apology versus denial for repairing competence- versus integrity-based trust violations. *Journal of Applied Psychology, 89,* 104–118.

Kruegar, J. (1998). Enhancement bias in descriptions of self and others. *Personality and Social Psychology Bulletin, 24,* 505–516.

Leventhal, G. S. (1976). Fairness in social relationships. In J. W. Thibaut, J. T. Spence, & R. C. Carson (Eds.), *Contemporary topics in social psychology* (pp. 211–240). Morristown, NJ: General Learning.

Leventhal, G. S. (1980). What should be done with equity theory? In K. J. Gergen, M. S. Greenberg, & R. H. Willis (Eds.), *Social exchange: Advances in theory and research* (pp. 27–55). New York: Plenum.

Leventhal, G. S., Karuza, J., & Fry, W. R. (1980). Beyond fairness: A theory of allocation preferences. In G. Mikula (Ed.), *Justice and social interaction* (pp. 167–218). New York: Springer-Verlag.

Liebrand, W. B. G., Messick, D. M., & Wolters, F. J. M. (1986). Why we are fairer than others: A cross-cultural replication and extension. *Journal of Experimental Social Psychology*, 22, 590–604.

Loewenstein, G., Issacharoff, S., Camerer, C., & Babcock, L. (1993). Self-serving assessments of fairness and pretrial bargaining. *Journal of Legal Studies, 22*, 135–159.

Malhotra, D., & Bazerman, M. H. (2007). *Negotiation genius: how to overcome obstacles and achieve brilliant results at the bargaining table and beyond*. New York: Bantam Books.

Marcus-Newhall, A., Pedersen, W. C., Carlson, M., & Miller, N. (2000). Displaced aggression is alive and well: A meta-analytic review. *Journal of Personality and Social Psychology, 78*, 670–689.

Masterson, S. S. (2001). A trickle-down model of organizational justice: Relative employees' and customers' perceptions of and reactions to fairness. *Journal of Applied Psychology, 86*, 594–604.

McCullough, M. E., Bellah, C. G., Kilpatrick, S. D, & Johnson, J. L. (2001). Vengefulness: Relationships with forgiveness, rumination, well-being, and the big five. *Personality and Social Psychology Bulletin, 27*, 601–610.

McCullough, M. E., Rachel, K. C., Sandage, S. J., Worthington, E. L., Jr., Brown, S. W., & Hight, T. L. (1998). Interpersonal forgiving in close relationships II: Theoretical elaboration and measurement. *Journal of Personality and Social Psychology, 75*, 1586–1603.

McCullough, M. E., & Worthington, E. L., Jr. (1995). Promoting forgiveness: A comparison of two brief psychoeducational interventions with a waiting-list control. *Counseling and Values, 40*, 55–68.

McCullough, M. E., Worthington, E. L., & Rachel, K. C. (1997). Interpersonal forgiving in close relationships. *Journal of Personality and Social Psychology, 73*, 321–336.

Messick, D. M., Bloom, S., Boldizar, J. P., & Samuelson, C. D. (1985). Why we are fairer than others. *Journal of Experimental Social Psychology, 21*, 480–500.

Messick, D., & Sentis, K. (1979). Fairness and preference. *Journal of Experimental Social Psychology, 15*, 418–435.

Mikula, G. (1986). The experience of injustice: Toward a better understanding of its phenomenology. In H. W. Bierhoff, R. L. Cohen, & J. Greenberg (Eds.), *Justice in social relations* (pp. 103–123). New York: Plenum.

Mitchell, M. S., & Ambrose, M. L. (2007). Abusive supervision and workplace deviance and the moderating effects of negative reciprocity beliefs. *Journal of Applied Psychology, 92*, 1159–1168.

Moore, D. A., & Flynn, F. J. (2008). The case for behavioral decision research in organizational behavior. *Academy of Management Annuals, 2*(1), 399–431.

Ohbuchi K., Kameda, M., & Agarie, N. (1989). Apology as aggression control: Its role in mediating appraisal of and response to harm. *Journal of Personality and Social Psychology, 56*, 219–227.

Olson-Buchanan, J. B., & Boswell, W. R. (2008). Organizational dispute resolution systems. In M. J. Gelfand & C. K. W. De Dreu (Eds.), *The psychology of conflict and conflict management in organizations* [SIOP Frontiers Series] (pp. 321–352). Mahwah, NJ: Erlbaum.

Pruitt, D. G. (2008). Conflict escalation in organizations. In M. J. Gelfand & C. K. W. De Dreu (Eds.), *The psychology of conflict and conflict management in organizations* [SIOP Frontiers Series] (pp. 245–266). Mahwah, NJ: Erlbaum.

Rawls, J. (1971). *A theory of justice*. Cambridge: Harvard University Press.

Reb, J., Goldman, B. M., Kray, L. J., & Cropanzano, R. (2006). Different wrongs, different remedies? Reactions to organizational remedies after procedural and interactional injustice. *Personnel Psychology, 59*, 31–64.

Roth, A. E., & Murnighan, J. K. (1982). The role of information in bargaining: An experimental study. *Econometrica, 50*, 1123–1343.

Riskey, D. R., & Birnbaum, M. H. (1974). Compensatory effects in moral judgment: Two rights don't make up for a wrong. *Journal of Experimental Psychology, 103*, 171–173.

Sandel, M. J. (2009). *Justice: What's the right thing to do?* New York: Farrar, Straus and Giroux.

Shafir, E., & LeBoeuf, R. A. (2002). Rationality. *Annual Review of Psychology, 53*, 491–517.

Skarlicki, D. P., & Folger, R. (1997). Retaliation in the workplace: The role of distributive, procedural, and interactional justice. *Journal of Applied Psychology, 82*, 434–443.

Skarlicki, D. P., & Folger, R. (2004). Broadening our understanding of organizational retaliatory behavior. In R. W. Griffin & A. M. O'Leary-Kelly (Eds.), *The dark side of organizational behavior* (pp. 373–402). San Francisco: Jossey-Bass.

Skitka, L. J., Winquist, J., & Hutchinson, S. (2003). Are outcome fairness and outcome favorability distinguishable psychological constructs? A meta-analytic review. *Social Justice Research, 16*, 309–341.

Thomas, K. W., & Schmidt, W. H. (1976). A survey of managerial interests with respect to conflict. *Academy of Management Journal, 19*, 315–318.

Thompson, L., & Loewenstein, G. (1992). Egocentric interpretations of fairness and interpersonal conflict. *Organizational Behavior and Human Decision Processes, 51*, 176–197.

Thompson, M. (2003). *Ethics*. Oxon, UK: Teach Yourself Books.

Tripp, T. M., & Bies, R. J. (2009). *Getting even: The truth about workplace revenge—and how to stop it*. San Francisco: Jossey-Bass.

Tripp, T. M., Bies, R. J., & Aquino, K. (2007). A vigilante model of justice: Revenge, reconciliation, forgiveness, and avoidance. *Social Justice Research, 20*, 10–34.

Turillo, C. J., Folger, R., Lavelle, J. J., Umphress, E., & Gee, J. (2002). Is virtue its own reward? Self-sacrificial decisions for the sake of fairness. *Organizational Behavior and Human Decision Processes, 89*, 839–865.

Ury, W. L., Brett, J. M., & Goldberg, S. B. (1988). *Getting disputes resolved: Designing systems to cut the costs of conflict*. New York: Jossey-Bass.

van den Bos, K., & Lind, E. A. (2002). Uncertainty management by means of fairness judgments. In M. P. Zanna (Ed.), *Advances in experimental social psychology* (Vol. 34, pp. 1–60). Boston: Elsevier.

van den Bos, K., Lind, E. A., & Wilke, H. A. M. (2001). The psychology of procedural and distributive justice viewed from the perspective of fairness heuristic theory. In R. Cropanzano (Ed.), *Justice in the workplace: From theory to practice* (Vol. 2, pp. 49–66). Mahwah, NJ: Erlbaum.

Weeks. D. (1992). *The eight essential steps to conflict resolution: Preserving relationships at work, at home, and in the community*. New York: Putnam Books.

8

The Role of Social Power in Sexual Harassment and Job Discrimination

STEVEN M. ELIAS, LINDSEY A. GIBSON, AND CHET E. BARNEY

> *When I first started, I wanted to learn from the guys, but that led to stuff like ". . . why don't you go out with me? I've really got something to offer you. When are we going on a date? C'mon. Sex between us would be really great." If that didn't get me to leave, somebody would say, "Leave the room so I can tell this joke." One guy finally said, "What are you doing here? You're taking up space where a male could be supporting his family." Now I keep my distance.*

> —Lawson, 2000

Instances of sexual harassment are all too common in the workplace (see Chamberlain et al., 2008). Jokes with sexual content, whistling at a woman in a skirt, and soliciting favors of a sexual nature are just a handful of instances where one employee is inappropriately exercising power over another employee. Because of the wide range of behaviors that can fall into the category of sexual harassment, there is a frequent blurring of the line that separates appropriate from inappropriate behavior in the workplace. Like sexual harassment, it is not uncommon for job discrimination to occur within an organization. For example, while it may be an unlawful employment practice, employers undoubtedly continue to consider certain protected demographics (such as gender and race) when making personnel decisions. The purpose of this chapter is to explore sexual harassment and discrimination in the workplace, its causes and consequences, and its relationship with social power. Possible solutions to reducing sexual harassment and discrimination in the workplace are also explored.

What is social power? Social power can be described as the ability of one person to impact or change the behavior of another, and power bases best describe the ways in which a person exercises this influence (see Elias, 2008). French & Raven (1959) developed a highly influential typology that describes social power through five bases of power: reward, coercive, legitimate, referent, and expert power. Several years later, Raven (1965) added informational power to the taxonomy.

Reward power is said to be at use when a powerholder promises some form of compensation to a target in exchange for compliance. For instance, a supervisor may provide "time off" to a subordinate in exchange for the subordinate completing a task that is not part of his or her job description. *Coercive* power is at use when the threat of punishment is made in order to gain compliance. For example, a manager may threaten to reduce a subordinate's pay should he or she not comply with a certain request. *Legitimate* power stems from one having a justifiable right to request compliance from another individual. For instance, subordinates may comply with a supervisor's request simply because they believe a supervisor has a right to ask them to do their work in a certain way. *Expert* power is at use when one relies on his or her superior knowledge in order to gain compliance. For example, management may follow the advice of consultants because those consultants are perceived as possessing a high-level of expertise in their field. *Referent* power is at use when a target complies with the request of a powerholder due to his or her identifying with the influencing agent. For instance, an employee wishing to receive a promotion will likely comply with requests made by managers due to his or her wanting a similar position as those managers in the future. *Informational* power is at use when an individual provided a rational explanation to a target as to why compliance is desired. For example, a subordinate may complete an undesirable task because his or her supervisor provides a logical explanation as to why the task needs to be completed.

Instances of how these power bases can be leveraged in order to perpetrate sexual harassment, and/or engage in discriminatory practices, are fairly easy to consider. For example, coercive power is at work when an employer threatens to terminate an employee if he or she does not comply with a request to engage in a sexual relationship. A blending of reward and coercive power is at work during instances of quid pro quo. A male employer may use his legitimate power to avoid hiring females. A supervisor may withhold information (informational power) from a certain group of employees (say, minorities) in order to make their jobs more difficult.

It is important to note that power is present in all social relationships, including all relationships observed in the workplace. Also noteworthy is that power and influence do not only occur in situations where the powerholder possesses a higher status or rank than the target of the influence attempt. For instance, Yukl and colleagues (Yukl & Falbe, 1990, 1991; Yukl & Tracey, 1992) have differentiated between upward (as in a subordinate influencing a supervisor), downward (as in a supervisor influencing a subordinate), and lateral (as in peers influencing one another) influence attempts. When taking this into consideration, the potential for sexual harassment and job discrimination to occur via social power need not only occur in a downward fashion. To be certain, harassment and discrimination frequently occur in a lateral fashion, and may potentially occur in an upward fashion as well.

We believe this chapter will make a significant contribution to an understanding of deviant workplace behavior because "the topic of power and deviant behavior has been relatively neglected." (Seabright, Ambrose & Schminke, 2010, 94) Power is important to this topic because power can be seen as control over an organization's resources (see Fiske, 2001), or when dealing with sexual harassment and discrimination, control over employees. Such control over employees is a legitimate concern given that subordinates may very well believe they have no resources available to assist in their resistance against sexual harassment and/or discriminatory practices. Interestingly, this sense of powerlessness on the part of the subordinate may result in the employee engaging in his or her own deviant workplace behavior. For example, a sense of powerlessness has been cited as a major motivation for employees engaging in sabotage (Seabright et al., 2010). Furthermore, research suggests that when employees experience a sense of powerlessness, they may engage in deviant workplace behavior as a mechanism to restore a sense of power (Cropanzano & Baron, 1991; Jones, 2010). While not exclusively in relation to a sense of powerlessness, Jones (2010) has written that individuals often describe their deviant workplace behavior (such as seeking revenge) as an effort to regain power and control within their place of employment.

As mentioned by Hodson and Jensen in the current volume, writings relating power and deviance can be observed in almost every chapter of this book. Social power is certainly one of the most ubiquitous topics in the discussion of deviant workplace behavior. As Edwards and Greenberg (2010, 327) have written, "Beyond various individual characteristics, the positions individuals hold in their hierarchical organizations relative to others also are likely to affect their risk of victimization." While social power is certainly linked to any number of deviant workplace behaviors, we will now turn our attention to power in relation to sexual harassment and job discrimination.

What Is Sexual Harassment?

Women have long been considered the underdog in terms of equality in organizations (Kesselman, 1990) and sexual harassment has tended to receive increasing attention only as occurrences have been addressed in the mainstream media (Ilies, Hauserman, Schwochau & Stibal, 2003). Scholars have struggled to conceptualize what constitutes sexual harassment in the workplace because it can appear in many different forms (Chamberlain,

Crowley, Tope & Hodson, 2008; Browne, 2006; Wilson & Thompson, 2001). However, several scholars have attempted to categorize the domain of sexual harassment and the behaviors that are deemed inappropriate in a workplace setting. Wilson & Thompson (2001) discuss five types of sexual harassment that are recognized by the European Commission. In *non-verbal* sexual harassment, perpetrators use a variety of hand gestures, whistling, or displaying suggestive pictures for the target to see. *Physical* sexual harassment involves one employee unnecessarily touching another employee. *Verbal* sexual harassment encompasses the act of suggesting unsolicited advances. *Intimidation* includes the use of coercive strategies that are targeted at the victim's apparel, on the job performance, or overall appearance. The final form of sexual harassment is *sexual blackmail*. As one of the most treacherous forms of sexual harassment, sexual blackmail involves the agent threatening to reveal sensitive information to others if the target does not comply with the demands for sexual favors.

Chamberlain, Crowley, Tope & Hodson (2008) recognize three types of sexual harassment in organizations ranging from the least severe to the most severe. *Patronizing* includes sexist, albeit nonsexual, comments and actions. *Sexual taunting* consists of behavior that "has crossed the line" and includes gestures, comments, and inquiries of a sexual nature that foster an uncomfortable and hostile workplace. *Predatory sexual harassment*, which is the most threatening form of harassment, includes such coercive sexual behaviors as frequent threats, soliciting sexual favors, and/or aggressive contact.

Two categories of sexual harassment that are frequently observed in the sexual harassment literature are *quid pro quo* and *hostile environment* (see Browne, 2006). With instances of quid pro quo, sexual favors are solicited in exchange for not being terminated or as a means to obtaining an advantage (such as a promotion or increase in salary). Hostile environment focuses on the conditions that make the work environment uncomfortable for the target. This includes, but is not limited to, innuendos and comments that create feelings that are intolerable, resulting in the employee being unable to actively and productively thrive in the workplace.

Popovich & Warren (2010) recognize that a limitation found in the sexual harassment literature is the preoccupation with defining sexual harassment rather than focusing on theory development and the refinement of past theories. While many behaviors have been classified by academics as sexually deviant, it has been suggested that the context in which a potentially inappropriate incident occurs is important to deciding whether or not the behavior is acceptable in a particular work setting (Wilson & Thompson, 2001; Pryor, LaVite & Stoller, 1993; Rospenda, Richman & Nawyn, 1998). To further develop theories of sexual harassment, it is necessary to understand the facilitating conditions preceding an occurrence of sexual harassment (Popovich & Warren, 2010). Because sexual harassment can take many forms, the boundaries between "acceptable" behaviors appear to be blurred from one individual's explanation of what constitutes sexual harassment to another. Likewise, variance may be observed between organizations or industries in terms of their tolerance of what may constitute sexual harassment.

While some cases of sexual harassment have involved a female as the aggressor, research suggests the majority of sexual harassment occurrences involve a male harassing a female (Pryor, La Vite & Stoller, 1993; Wilson & Thompson, 2001). Sexual harassment appears to be a function of gender dispersion among the workplace. Some have suggested that sexual harassment is strongly rooted in gender-based biases (Gutek & Koss, 1993; Uggen & Blackstone, 2004). Wilson & Thompson (2001) and Fitzgerald, Drasgow, Hulin, Gelfand & Magley (1997) suggest that organizations that predominantly employ males create an environment where sexually deviant behavior is more likely to be directed toward female employees. Contrarily, organizations that predominantly employ females create an environment where sexually deviant behavior is less likely to occur.

How Common Is Sexual Harassment?

Sexual harassment has historically been, and continues to be, a major problem confronting individual employees and entire organizations (see O'Leary-Kelly, Bowes-Sperry, Bates & Lean, 2009). Bates, Bowes-Sperry, and O'Leary-Kelly (2006) have written that a review of the sexual harassment literature indicates almost 75% of women surveyed report experiencing unwanted sexual attention, while almost 50% of women surveyed report experiencing gender-related harassment. According to the U.S. Equal Employment Opportunity Commission (EEOC, 2009a), the annual number of sexual harassment claims filed between 1997 and 2008 ranged from 12,025 to 15,889. While victims of sexual harassment at work are typically females, males did account for 11.6% to 16% of the sexual harassment claims filed with the EEOC during the 1997 to 2008 timeframe.

What Are the Consequences of Sexual Harassment in the Workplace?

It has become apparent that sexual harassment's effects are widespread at both the individual and organizational level (Schneider, Swan & Fitzgerald, 1997; Lopez, Hodson & Roscigno, 2009). At the individual level, victims of sexual harassment have reported such effects as emotional and psychological stress, increased occurrences of absenteeism, and subsequent turnover. While incidents of sexual harassment may be viewed and experienced differently by victims, scholars have reported several common consequences of such behavior. For example, victims of sexual harassment tend to experience high levels of psychological distress, drastic decreases in their job performance, diminished relationships with coworkers and peers, and higher rates of turnover. Furthermore, victims are likely to become lax in terms of arriving to work on time and tend to seek out more ways to be absent from work (Chamberlain, Crowley, Tope & Hodson, 2008; Popovich & Warren, 2010).

Not surprisingly, organizations implicated in instances of sexual harassment suffer large monetary losses. From a financial standpoint, the annual disbursement amount paid by organizations to victims of sexual harassment between 1997 and 2008 ranged from 34.3 million dollars to 54.6 million dollars. It is noteworthy that these disbursement amounts pertain to monies paid by employers to avoid legal action and do not include any monies paid to victims as a result of lawsuits (EEOC, 2009a).

Perhaps it comes as no surprise that the intensity of the sexual harassment experienced is directly related to the severity of the consequences for the victim. Exposure to sexual harassment, even on a small scale, has been found to have a negative impact on female employees. Schneider, Swan & Fitzgerald (1997) investigated exposure to sexual harassment on three levels of intensity: low, moderate, and high. The authors found that women exposed to sexual harassment at all three levels reported decreased job performance and negative job related outcomes.

Why Does Sexual Harassment Occur in the Workplace?

Stringer, Remick, Salisbury & Ginorio (1990) suggest that there are two predominant motivating factors behind occurrences of sexual harassment. The first motivating factor is the actual desire to receive sexual favors, while the second motivating factor involves the exertion of power and/or dominance over another individual. Sexual harassment frequently becomes the mechanism by which a perpetrator displays such power and/or authority over another individual. Indeed, a major key to understanding sexual harassment, and the reasons for its frequent occurrence, lies in understanding its links to power. Cleveland & Kerst (1993) suggest that this relationship is one that lacks attention in organizational research and is worthy of a more in-depth investigation.

Power and gender have a close relationship. Research indicates that the mere presence of males in the workplace does not necessarily mean sexual harassment will occur (Pryor, LaVite & Stoller, 1993). In terms of male to female ratios, organizations with an even balance of male and female employees have reported instances of sexual harassment. Fitzgerald, Drasgow, Hulin, Gelfand & Magley (1997, 586) find the culprit lies in a more traditional realm. Specifically, Fitzgerald et al. indicate sexual harassment may result when women work in an environment where there are a large number of male employees, working on traditionally male-oriented tasks.

Schneider, Swan & Fitzgerald (1997) have recognized that close proximity to perpetrators of sexual harassment makes organizational life extremely difficult for those who have been a target of sexual harassment. Negative consequences are present long after the incident has occurred. They report that most women who have fallen victim to sexual harassment try to avoid the perpetrator as much as possible. This is particularly difficult if the sexual harassment has gone unreported. However, it is difficult to do this when the victim's job demands and requirements dictate that there must be some form of interaction with the perpetrator.

Social Power and Sexual Harassment

> Often, women were made to feel that the norms of shipyard behavior were set by men and were violated at one's peril. Doris Avshalomov, for example, told "them very loudly to cut it out" when male workers tried to back her into a corner and touch her. "And then when they'd see me they'd make little noises and catcalls implying that I was a prude." . . . Female sexuality was simultaneously an object of ridicule, fascination, and uneasiness in the shipyards. The pervasive emphasis on sexuality may have been viewed as a method of easing the tensions created by women's presence in the shipyards. While some women recognized that this defusing of tension was at the expense of women's dignity as workers, there was neither the language nor the organizational means to challenge it. (Kesselman, 1990, 63)

Research suggests that sexual harassment is actually a struggle between an individual exercising power and the psychological implications for the target of such power (Chamberlain, Crowley, Tope & Hodson, 2008; Wilson & Thompson, 2001). Therefore, the literature further suggests that the issue is "not just about the sex" but rather is the harasser's interpretation of situational factors, such as the implications of women being present in the organization and the assumptions and/or perceptions of this situation (Chamberlain et al., 2008).

To further complicate matters, Bargh, Raymond, Pryor & Strack (1995) contend that many individuals may be partaking in sexually deviant behavior without consciously knowing it and using power in what they think is an acceptable behavior (Bargh & Alvarez, 2001). Both French & Raven (1959) and Popovich & Warren (2010) recognize that power is in the eye of the beholder. The perception that a particular behavior is sexually motivated can be perceived as completely different from the agent. For example, an employee compliments a fellow employee about the blouse she is wearing that day. While the compliment may have had the best intentions, it could make the woman uncomfortable. If the problem is not addressed, similar situations can occur in the future and begin to snowball.

Implications for Managers

When management did intervene on behalf of a woman who was being sexually harassed by a supervisor or teacher, the solution was to transfer the women to another area or supervisor. When Mabel Studebaker objected to being "petted" by the foreman, who "thought he was a ladies' man," she also was ordered to work in the rain. When she refused, pointing out that new workers were normally given that assignment and she was no longer new, he replied, "'Either work out in the rain or go home.' So I went home." Studebaker returned to work and was reassigned to the same foreman, and finally after reporting the incident to a supervisor, was transferred to another area. When Kathryn Blair's lead man tried to embrace her every morning in their carpool she found his behavior "quite shocking," but aware of her vulnerable situation, she managed as adroitly as she could to hold him off without antagonizing him. (Kesselman, 1990, 62)

The effects of sexual harassment are far-reaching. As shown in this vignette, management's reactions to sexual harassment complaints can be just as frustrating to the victim. In this case, management was essentially imposing another set of punishments to the victim for coming forward and making a complaint. The problem was dealt with in an unsatisfactory manner and brings to light a key point for managers: Issues with power and sexual harassment in the workplace are problems that cannot go unaddressed.

Because common understanding of the ingredients that lead to sexually deviant behavior are not necessarily forthcoming, making all the relevant information, such as organizational policies and procedures for handling complaints as well as knowledge of the consequences, available to all employees is paramount. Thacker & Ferris (1991) suggest that strength resides in this last point. Knowledge of the consequences and understanding what constitutes sexually deviant behavior will give organizations the necessary tools to deal effectively with sexual harassment. Stringer, Remick, Salisbury & Ginorio (1990) further suggest that instances of sexual harassment must be dealt with as separate and specific instances, instead of lumping all cases of sexual harassment into one large category. They also suggest that both power and facilitating conditions play a large part in what determines sexually deviant behavior and recommend to practitioners that a careful investigation into those factors will help create solutions that will be fruitful. Chamberlain, Crowley, Tope & Hodson (2008) suggest that formal policies and procedures are an effective way in which sexual harassment can be reduced within organizations.

Concluding Thoughts on Sexual Harassment in the Workplace

Schneider, Swan & Fitzgerald (1997) found that the effects of sexual harassment linger long after the initial occurrence. Interestingly, when questioned if they had been sexually harassed within the last few years, many respondents did not admit that they had been sexually harassed. They did, however, admit to suffering the consequences of a sexual harassment encounter long after the incident occurred. This evidence places responsibility back on managers to create a work environment where

1. Employees feel comfortable coming to work. They feel safe and secure within their work area and with coworkers. This includes building relationships with employees where they will feel comfortable bringing concerns to management's attention. They must feel that their concerns will be taken seriously and confidentially.
2. Information regarding sexual harassment and its specific behaviors (as indicated by the organization) is available to all employees.
3. Formal grievance procedures for dealing with sexual harassment are widely known by all employees (Chamberlain, Crowley, Tope & Hodson, 2008).
4. Consequences for sexual harassment aggressors are clearly identified.
5. Aggressors are confronted about their behavior by management, as they may not be aware that their behavior is causing harm (Bargh, Raymond, Pryor & Strack, 1995; Bargh & Alvarez, 2001)
6. All policies are strictly enforced. No exceptions.

What Is Job Discrimination?

The Supreme Court on Monday threw out an enormous employment discrimination class-action suit against Wal-Mart that had sought billions of
dollars on behalf of as many as 1.5 million female workers. The suit claimed
that Wal-Mart's policies and practices had led to countless discriminatory
decisions over pay and promotions. (Liptak, 2011)

Two new job discrimination cases have Supreme Court justices considering how broadly federal law protects workers from retaliation after
they complain about bias. Arguments in one of the cases this past week
showed that many of the justices appear ready to retreat from the generous
interpretation of retaliation coverage in a 2005 case with then-justice San-
dra Day O'Connor casting the decisive vote. On Wednesday, justices heard
a case begun by a black Cracker Barrel restaurant worker who was fired
after complaining about a manager's allegedly derogatory remarks. The
arguments showed how much the court is changing from 2005 and, more
conclusively, from prior decades when a majority of the justices broadly
interpreted anti-discrimination laws. (Biskupic, 2008)

Discrimination in the workplace can take on a number of forms—most of
which have been declared illegal.

When one thinks of workplace discrimination, visions of a boss treating
subordinates harshly and unfairly usually appear. However, discrimination can
also be described as something as subtle as making distinctions among employees or coworkers, or playing favorites. In research settings, discrimination has
typically been operationalized as a hardship placed on an individual due solely
to his or her belonging to some form of group (such as gender, ethnicity, or sexual orientation). Most often discrimination can be initiated through the use of
power in order to make distinctions for, or against, a specific person or group.

However defined, it is important to realize that workplace discrimination
can take place in all aspects of the workforce, not just within a direct supervisor—subordinate relationship. Discrimination can take place in the moment
of hire, throughout a career, and even during termination. The widespread
scourge of discrimination has cultivated a channel to allow researchers to
study discrimination and workplace behavior within organizations. In order
to unravel the workplace discrimination phenomenon we must take a look
into what discrimination entails.

Examples of workplace discrimination may include illegal hiring or firing, sexual harassment, unequal pay, and workplace bullying. Furthermore,

demographics have also been used as a basis for discrimination on age, citizenship, disability, gender, marital status, race, and religion to name a few. Discrimination in the workplace has become so widespread that state and federal laws have been implemented to discourage certain types of discrimination.

One of the more famous federal laws passed prohibiting discrimination in the workplace is Title VII—Equal Employment Opportunity of the Civil Rights Act of 1964. Section 704 (a) of the Civil Rights Act states, "It shall be an unlawful employment practice for an employer to discriminate against any of his employees or applicants for employment." The Civil Rights Act of 1964 outlawed several forms of workplace discrimination; however, discrimination in the workplace still persists.

Why Does Discrimination Occur?

Discrimination has been observed since ancient times. Culture, disability, economic status, ethnicity, gender, language, political affiliation, race, religion, and social status have all been a basis of discrimination over the centuries. In today's workplace setting, discrimination can be more often discrete rather than visually open to coworkers. Sometimes discrimination occurs simply when one person refuses to see the point of view of another, perhaps due to empowerment. In essence, this act of superiority lends itself quite easily to discrimination, and relatively often superiors have the mentality that they are indeed superior to subordinate employees. If history is a predictor of the future, people in positions of power will continue to discriminate throughout time.

In the workplace, countless organizations have established diversity training, where employees are taught about different types of discrimination as well as the legalities associated with discriminant behavior. Oftentimes, mandatory diversity training is not favorably received by employees. The reason being, for some, that on the job training dealing with any subject takes time away from tasks at hand. For others, subtle discrimination might be a part of their personal life—and nobody likes to be told that they are doing wrong, especially at work. In any case, as long as there are lawsuits stemming from workplace discrimination, organizations will implement diversity trainings in order to combat prejudices.

Organizational culture may play a role in the amount of discrimination found within an operation. For example, a firm with a lackadaisical view of diversity training may find its employees behaving inappropriately when compared to a firm that places an emphasis on following state and federal laws that deal with workplace discrimination. As such, the culture of the organization will usually dictate the importance of discrimination behavior; however, deviance toward discrimination regulations lay within individuals.

How Prevalent Is Discrimination?

While the EEOC enforces any number of laws meant to curb employee discrimination, such discrimination remains a major problem confronting today's workforce. Indeed, the EEOC (2009b) has recently had to go so far as to remind employers that Title VII of the Civil Rights Act and Title I of the Americans With Disabilities Act make it illegal to discriminate against employees who have been diagnosed with the H1N1 flu virus (Swine Flu).

Although progress has been made in terms of reducing employee discrimination, a review of the EEOC workplace discrimination statistics will reveal how prevalent and costly such discrimination continues to be. For example, according to a recent report (EEOC, 2009b), the annual number of workplace discrimination claims filed between 1997 and 2008 ranged from 75,428 to 95,402. During each of these years, the majority of the claims filed revolved around charges of racial discrimination in the workplace. This is consistent with the belief that discrimination may result when attempts at increasing racial diversity are seen as being unfair to groups who have not historically faced difficulties gaining employment (Harrington & Miller, 1992). In terms of the economic impact associated with employee discrimination, the annual settlement amount paid by organizations to victims of such discrimination between 1997 and 2008 ranged from 169.2 million dollars to 290.6 million dollars (EEOC, 2009c). Consistent with the case of sexual harassment, it is noteworthy that these settlement amounts pertain to monies paid by employers to avoid legal action and do not include any monies paid to victims as a result of litigation.

Social Power and Discrimination

In a supervisor-subordinate relationship, the implementation of power is expected. Supervisors must make sure that employees are working towards the common goals of the organization, thus the enactment of power is a useful tool. However, social power is not always used to align employee work with corporate goals. Social power can be utilized as a method of discrimination. By simply exerting power, one is attempting to influence another to do something that aligns with his or her wishes, sometimes at the expense of a certain group of employees. Examples of power and discrimination can be seen in organizational research. Gender bias (Elias & Cropanzano, 2006; Stainback, Ratliff & Roscigno, 2011), racial bias (Kay et al., 2009), and unequal compensation (Fehr & Kirchsteiger, 1994; Hultin & Szulkin, 1999) are a few examples of where power has played a discriminating role. The basis of these types of discrimination can stem from a variety of individual beliefs held by supervisory personnel. For example, a supervisor may believe that a certain individual should receive a higher compensation package simply because that individual is a different gender or race than other subordinates within the same organization. Social power can be utilized to secure this unequal compensation, usually unbeknown to other members of the organization.

Implications for Managers

Given the plethora of negative ramifications associated with job discrimination, management (including those in human resource management; see Benson, Hanley, and Scroggins of this volume) must take specific actions to curb the occurrence of discrimination. One of the more common methods used in this situation is diversity training. Indeed, with the number of harassment and discrimination lawsuits increasing each year, diversity training has become more and more common in organizations.

Although diversity training is currently widespread among many organizations, past lawsuits have influenced the U.S. Supreme Court to rule that diversity training should be periodically provided to every employee. Failure to provide harassment and discrimination prevention training may expose organizations to punitive damages, as well as forfeit their ability to raise a defense against harassment lawsuits (Johnson, 2004). A failure to provide diversity, harassment, and discrimination training may also conflict with local and state laws. The guidelines set forth by the Equal Employment Opportunity Commission clearly state that liability standards that apply to sexual harassment claims also apply to claims of harassment and retaliation based on race, national origin, age, disability, and other characteristics (Johnson, 2004), thus it is essential that organizations provide training on all types of discrimination. Common components of diversity training include legal awareness, cultural awareness, and sensitivity training (Mathis & Jackson, 2011), yet should not be limited to certain types of awareness.

While Best Practices for Diversity Training (2011) offers noteworthy advice on how to get the most out of diversity training, it should be pointed out that informational power plays an integral role in the implementation of any training program. Specifically, in order for a diversity training program to be successful, management must *explain* how the training program will benefit their employees. Once this explanation has occurred, several "best practices" should be implemented. First, diversity training should include the use of a business case that is relevant to the individuals partaking in the training. Second, training participants should be exposed to experiential learning exercises that develop skills rather than work them through simulations. Third, it should be made clear to everyone involved what would be considered successful diversity training. Fourth, employees should be encouraged to practice using their newly acquired skills. Fifth (and perhaps most important), management should not expect diversity training to provide a miracle cure for discrimination.

Conclusions

Social power is all around us. Some people use their power for good, while others use their power for bad. As has been mentioned several times, most chapters in this volume make reference to ways in which abuses of power can serve as antecedents to deviant and criminal behavior in the workplace. Our intent was to elucidate some of the ways social power can lead to behaviors such as sexual harassment and job discrimination. In addition, we set out to offer some insight into how sexual harassment and job discrimination can be avoided, or at least reduced. These are important issues to address because harassment and discrimination can have drastic, negative effects at the level of the individual employee, as well as for the organization as a whole. Our hope is that by making readers aware of social power's role in deviant and criminal behavior in the workplace, employees may be less likely to be victimized. As the old saying goes, "Knowledge is power."

REFERENCES

Bargh, J. A., & Alvarez, J. (2001). The road to hell: Good intentions in the face of nonconscious tendencies to misuse power. In A. Y. Lee-Chai & J. A. Bargh (Eds.), *The use and abuse of power: Multiple perspectives on the causes of corruption* (pp. 41–55). Philadelphia: Psychology Press.

Bargh, J. A., Raymond, P., Pryor, J. B., & Strack, F. (1995). Attractiveness of the underlying: an automatic power sex association and its consequences for sexual harassment and aggression. *Journal of Personality and Social Psychology, 68, 5,* 768–781.

Bates, C. A., Bowes-Sperry, L., & O'Leary-Kelly, A. M. (2006). Sexual harassment in the workplace: A look back and a look ahead. In E. K. Kelloway, J. Barling, & J. Joseph, Jr. (Eds.), *Handbook of workplace violence* (pp. 381–416). Thousand Oaks, CA: Sage.

Becker, G. S. (1957). *The economics of discrimination.* Chicago: University of Chicago Press.

Best Practices for Diversity Training. (2011). *Workforce Management, 8,* 14.

Biskupic, J. (2008, February 24). Job discrimination cases hit new opposition. *USA Today*. http://www.usatoday.com/news/washington/2008-02-24-court_N.htm.

Browne, K. R. (2006). Sex, power, and dominance: The evolutionary psychology of sexual harassment. *Managerial and Decision Economics, 27*, 145–158.

Chamberlain, L. J., Crowley, M., Tope, D., & Hodson, R. (2008). Sexual harassment in organizational context. *Work and Occupations, 35* (3), 262–295.

Civil Rights Act of 1964 § 7, 42 U.S.C. § 2000e *et seq.* (1964).

Cleveland, J. N., & Kerst, M. E. (1993). Sexual harassment and perceptions of power: An under-articulated relationship. *Journal of Vocational Behavior, 42*, 49–67.

Cropanzano, R., & Baron, R. A. (1991). Injustice and organizational conflict: The moderating effect of power restoration. *International Journal of Conflict Management, 2* (1), 5–26.

Donald, S. G., & Hamermesh, D. S. (2006). What is Discrimination? Gender in the American Economic Association, 1935–2004. *American Economic Review, 96* (4), 1283–1292.

Edwards, M. S., & Greenberg, J. (2010). Issues and challenges in studying insidious workplace behavior. In J. Greenberg (Ed.), *Insidious workplace behavior* (pp. 309–354). New York: Routledge.

Elias, S. M. (2008). Fifty years of influence in the workplace: The evolution of the French and Raven power taxonomy. *Journal of Management History, 14*, 267–283.

Elias, S. M., & Cropanzano, R. (2006). Gender discrimination may be worse than you think: Testing ordinal interactions in power research. *Journal of General Psychology, 133* (2), 117–130.

Fehr, E., & Kirchsteiger, G. (1994). Insider power, wage discrimination and fairness. *Economic Journal, 104* (424), 571–583.

Fiske, S. T. (2001). Effects of power on bias: Power explains and maintains individual, group, and societal disparities. In A. Y. Lee-Chai & J. A. Bargh (Eds.), *The use and abuse of power* (pp. 181–193). Philadelphia: Psychology Press.

Fitzgerald, L. F., Drasgow, F., Hulin, C. L., Gelfand, M. J., & Magley, V. J. (1997). Antecedents and consequences of sexual harassment in organizations: a test of an integrated model. *Journal of Applied Psychology, 82* (4), 578–589.

French, J. R. P., & Raven, B. (1959). The basis of social power. In Cartwright, D. (Ed.), *Studies in social power* (pp. 529–569). Ann Arbor: University of Michigan Press.

Gutek, B. A., & Koss, M. P. (1993). Changed women and changed organizations: Consequences of and coping with sexual harassment. *Journal of Vocational Behavior, 42*, 28–48.

Harrington, H. J., & Miller, N. (1992). Overcoming resistance of affirmative action in industry: A social psychological perspective. In P. Sudfeld & P. Tetlock (Eds.), *Psychology and social policy* (pp. 137–147). New York: Hemisphere.

Hultin, M., & Szulkin, R. (1999). Wages and Unequal Access to Organizational Power: An Empirical Test of Gender Discrimination. *Administrative Science Quarterly, 44* (3), 453–472.

Ilies, R., Hauserman, N., Schwochau, S., & Stibal, J. (2003). Reported incidence rates of work related sexual harassment in the United States: using meta-analysis to explain reported rate disparities. *Personnel Psychology, 56*, 607–631.

Johnson, M. W. (2004). Harassment and discrimination prevention training: What the law requires. *Labor Law Journal, 55* (2), 119–129.

Jones, D. A. (2010). Getting even for interpersonal mistreatment in the workplace: Triggers of revenge motives and behavior. In J. Greenberg (Ed.), *Insidious Workplace Behavior*. New York: Routledge.

Kay, A. C., Gaucher, D., Peach, J. M., Laurin, K., Friesen, J., Zanna, M. P., & Spencer, S. J. (2009). Inequality, discrimination, and the power of the status quo: Direct evidence for a motivation to see the way things are as the way they should be. *Journal of Personality & Social Psychology, 97* (3), 421–434.

Kesselman, A. (1990). Fleeting opportunities: Women shipyard workers in Portland and Vancouver during WWII and reconversion. Albany: SUNY Press.

Lawson, H. M. (2000). Ladies on the lot: Women, car sales and the pursuit of the American dream. Lanham, MD: Rowman & Littlefield.

Liptak, A. (2011, June 20). Justices rule for Wal-Mart in class-action bias case. *The New York Times.* http://www.nytimes.com/2011/06/21/business/21bizcourt. html?_r=1&pagewanted=print.

Lopez, S. H., Hodson, R., & Roscigno, V. J. (2009). Power, status, and abuse at work: general and sexual harassment compared. *The Sociological Quarterly, 50,* 3–27.

Mathis, R. L., & Jackson, J. H. (2011). *Human Resource Management* (13th ed.). Mason, OH: South-Western Cengage Learning.

O'Leary-Kelly, A. M., Bowes-Sperry, L., Bates, C. A., & Lean, E. R. (2009). Sexual harassment at work: A decade (plus) of progress. *Journal of Management, 35,* 503–536.

Polsby, N. W. (1959). The Sociology of community power: A reassessment. *Social Forces, 37* (3), 232–236.

Popovich, P. M., & Warren, M. A. (2010). The role of power in sexual harassment as a counterproductive behavior in organizations. *Human Resource Management Review, 20,* 45–53.

Pryor, J. B., LaVite, C. M., & Stoller, L. M. (1993). A social psychological analysis of sexual harassment: the person/situation interaction. *Journal of Vocational Behavior, 42,* 68–83.

Raven, B. H. (1965). Social influence and power. In I. D. Steiner and M. Fishbein (Eds.), *Current studies in social psychology* (pp. 371–382), New York: Holt, Rinehart, and Winston.

Rospenda, K. M., Richman, J. A., & Nawyn, S. J. (1998). Doing power: the confluence of gender, race, and class in contrapower sexual harassment. *Gender & Society, 12* (1), 40–60.

Schneider, K. T., Swan, S., & Fitzgerald, L. F. (1997). Job-related and psychological effects of sexual harassment in the workplace: Empirical evidence from two organizations. *Journal of Applied Psychology, 82, 3,* 401–415.

Seabright, M. A., Ambrose, M. L., & Schminke, M. (2010). Two images of workplace sabotage. In J. Greenberg (Ed.), *Insidious workplace behavior* (pp. 77–99). New York: Routledge.

Speer, P. W. (2008). Social power and forms of change: implications for psychopolitical validity. *Journal of Community Psychology, 36* (2), 199–213.

Stainback, K., Ratliff, T. N., & Roscigno, V. J. (2011). The context of workplace sex discrimination: Sex composition, workplace culture and relative power. *Social Forces, 89* (4), 1165–1188.

Stringer, D. M., Remick, H., Salisbury, J., & Ginorio, A. B. (1990). The power and reasons behind sexual harassment: An employer's guide to solutions. *Public Personnel Management, 19* (1), 43–52.

Thacker, R. A., & Ferris, G. R. (1991). Understanding sexual harassment in the workplace: The influence of power and politics within the dyadic interaction of harasser and target. *Human Resource Management Review, 1* (1), 23–37.

Uggen, C., & Blackstone, A. (2004). Sexual harassment as a gendered expression of power. *American Sociological Review, 69,* 64–92.

U.S. Equal Employment Opportunity Commission. (2009a). Sexual harassment charges EEOC & FEPAs combined: FY 1997FY 2008. http://www.eeoc.gov/stats/harass.html, August 28, 2009.

U.S. Equal Employment Opportunity Commission. (2009b). Employment discrimination and the 2009 H1N1 flu virus (Swine Flu). http://www.eeoc.gov/facts/h1n1.html, September 2, 2009.

U.S. Equal Employment Opportunity Commission. (2009c). Charge statistics FY 1997 through FY 2008. http://www.eeoc.gov/stats/charges.html, August 28, 2009.

Wilson, F., & Thompson, P. (2001). Sexual harassment as an exercise of power. *Gender, Work and Organization, 8* (1), 61–83.

Yukl, G., & Falbe, C. M. (1990). Influence tactics and objectives in upward, downward, and lateral influence attempts. *Journal of Applied Psychology, 75* (2), 132–140.

Yukl, G., & Falbe, C. M. (1991). Importance of different power sources in downward and lateral relations. *Journal of Applied Psychology, 76* (3), 416–423.

Yukl, G., & Tracey, J. B. (1992). Consequences of influence tactics used with subordinates, peers, and the boss. *Journal of Applied Psychology, 77* (4), 525–535.

PART V

Violence in the Workplace

9

When Employees Turn Violent

The Potential Role of Workplace Culture in Triggering Deviant Behavior

RICKY W. GRIFFIN AND YVETTE P. LOPEZ

> About fifteen years ago, James Davis walked through the doors of the Union Butterfield tool company in Asheville, North Carolina. He had been fired by Union Butterfield just two days before, and now he wanted revenge. To extract that revenge, Davis carried a semiautomatic rifle and a pistol. Once inside the doors he opened fire, getting off about fifty shots and killing three of his former co-workers. After he finished shooting, Davis lit a cigarette and calmly waited for the police to arrive; then he quietly surrendered and was led away in handcuffs. He is currently serving a life sentence in prison, and expresses no regrets for his actions.
>
> A few months later James Daniel Simpson entered his former workplace, Walter Rossler Company in Corpus Christi, Texas and began systematically shooting employees at point-blank range before going out the back door and fatally shooting himself in the head. When Simpson worked for Rossler, the company had reimbursed him for college tuition in return for his agreement to work for the firm for two more years. When he quit prematurely, Rossler Company sued Simpson; Simpson, in turn, was forced to sell many of his possessions in order to repay Rossler. Rossler also provided a poor recommendation, making it difficult for Simpson to find another job. Finally, he pawned his television and bought the gun that ended several lives.

Unfortunately, tragedies such as these are not uncommon in the least. According to recent statistics, an employee is killed at a U.S. workplace by a current or former co-worker an average of once each week. In addition, another twenty-five are seriously injured by violent assaults. Overall, some two million U.S. workers are victims of some form of workplace violence each year. Experts also suggest that U.S. businesses lose billions of dollars each year in lost work time and productivity, litigation expenses, and security measures in the aftermath of workplace violence. Among the more common reasons often given for increasing workplace violence are economic fears regarding job security, heightened concerns for personal safety after the September 11, 2001 terrorist attacks, and generalized stress and anxiety among workers.

Most non-fatal incidents attract little or no media attention. However, workplace homicides are still likely to attract coverage, especially in local media outlets. Most media coverage follows a fairly consistent storyline: (1) what happened, (2) who was killed and/or severely injured, (3) what is the profile of the perpetrator, (4) what in the perpetrator's background and personal life most likely stimulated the violence, and (5) what the company and its employees are doing to recover. Even when there appears to be a specific triggering event, such as a layoff or termination, observers tend to accept such management actions as a regrettable but common business practice and focus their attention almost exclusively on the perpetrator as the sole target for blame. Indeed, it seems only logical to direct blame at the individual who brought the gun to work and shot his (or her) former associates. And in most cases such attributions are absolutely correct. After all, mature and well-adjusted adults should be able to control their impulses and channel their anger and frustration through healthier avenues.

At the same time, however, there seems to be some indirect evidence and anecdotal indicators to suggest that on at least some occasions the organization itself has played a role in the incidence of violence. This organizational role is most likely to be manifested through its culture. By placing the concept of workplace violence into a deviance framework and identifying potential contributing factors for these behaviors associated with individuals and with organization culture separate and apart from one another, it then becomes possible to examine them together in a more meaningful and integrated manner. This is our goal in this chapter.

Definition of Workplace Deviance

The National Institute for Occupational Safety and Health (NIOSH) defines workplace violence as any physical assault, threatening behavior, or verbal abuse that occurs in a work setting. Workplace deviance, a broader concept than violence per se, has been defined as "voluntary behavior that violates significant organizational norms and in so doing threatens the well-being of an organization, its members, or both" (Robinson & Bennett, 1995, 556). This definition of workplace deviance has been widely used in subsequent research dealing with deviance (Bennett & Robinson, 2000; Bennett & Robinson, 2003; Bordia, Restubog & Tang, 2008; Colbert, Mount, Harter, Witt & Barrick, 2004; Diefendorff & Mehta, 2007; Ferris, Brown & Heller, 2009; Henle, Giacalone & Jurkiewicz, 2005; Judge, Scott & Ilies, 2006; Mitchell & Ambrose, 2007; Stewart, Bing, Davison, Woehr & McIntyre, 2009; Tepper, Henle, Lambert, Giacalone & Duffy, 2008).

While this definition focuses on the negative aspects of deviance, others have extended the concept to include more neutral terms resulting in deviant behavior that can be either positive or negative (Warren, 2003). By defining deviance more broadly as simply a departure from norms, it becomes difficult to attribute the value or merit of the underlying behavior (Warren, 2003). As such, deviance can be seen as a departure from norms resulting in negative behavior, as previously described by others (termed *destructive deviance*), or positive behavior that can lead to improvement and potential benefits for the organization, its members, or both (termed *constructive deviance*). Our focus, however, will center on the intentional acts that violate norms of the organization and in this respect potentially result in harm to the organization, its members, or both (Bennett & Robinson, 2003). And as previously implied, we will generally address deviance but use workplace violence as a specific framework for discussion.

Grounded in this form of destructive deviance, Robinson and Bennett (1995, 2003) developed a widely accepted typology of workplace deviance which identifies deviant behavior based on its target (recipient of the harmful behavior—individual/organization) and its severity (the magnitude of the harmful behavior—minor/serious) (Ambrose, Seabright & Schminke, 2002). The combination of these two dimensional configurations results in four distinct categories, or quadrants, of workplace deviance: Property Deviance, Production Deviance, Political Deviance, and Personal Aggression. Two of these quadrants focus specifically on organizational deviance, where the targeted recipient of the deviant behavior is the organization. Robinson and Bennett (1995, 2003) identify these forms of organizational deviance as property deviance and production deviance. Property deviance is presented as the most harmful and serious form of organizational deviance, resulting in such behaviors as sabotaging equipment and stealing from the organization. A more minor form of organizational deviance, production deviance, may result in such destructive behaviors as withdrawal and absenteeism.

The remaining two quadrants focus specifically on what Robinson and Bennett (1995) define as interpersonal deviance, where the targeted recipient of the deviant behavior is another individual such as a coworker or supervisor. Robinson and Bennett (1995, 2003) identify these forms of interpersonal deviance as political deviance, resulting in political backstabbing, the spreading of rumors, favoritism, verbal abuse, and incivility, as well as the more harmful and serious form of interpersonal deviance described as personal aggression, resulting in aggressive behavior, harassment, and violence.

The distinction between organizational deviance and interpersonal deviance has been and continues to be widely used in the literature describing deviant behavior in the workplace (see Ambrose, Seabright, Schminke, 2002; Berry, Ones & Sackett, 2007; Mitchell & Ambrose, 2007; Tepper, Carr, Breaux, Geider, Hu & Hua, 2009). In fact, Ambrose, Seabright, and Schminke (2002) make an interesting association between Robinson and Bennett's (1995) forms of deviant behavior (organizational deviance and interpersonal deviance) and the extant literature on organizational justice. The authors propose similarities between organizational deviance and structural aspects of justice described by distributive justice and procedural justice as well as interpersonal deviance and social aspects of justice (Folger & Skarlicki, 1998; Greenberg, 1993a), or interactional justice. Given that the experience of an injustice can be created by the organizational system or through interpersonal interactions with specific individuals (Ambrose et al., 2002), such sources could be construed as driving forces capable of impacting individual deviant behavior. As such, "research suggests that individuals' responses to injustice are likely to correspond to its source" (Ambrose et al., 2002, 953). Therefore, in describing the causes of workplace deviant behavior it is presumed that specific types of variables may explain the different types of workplace deviance described as organizational deviance and interpersonal deviance. In essence, "organizational variables might be more likely to influence deviance directed at harming organizations, and individual variables may be more likely to explain interpersonal forms of deviance" (Robinson & Bennett, 1995, 567).

With this definition and review as context, we now turn our attention to a discussion of the role of the individual as an instigator of violence, the extreme form of deviance. We will then discuss the role of organizations as a context for instigating or stimulating violence behavior. This will lead to an analysis of how individual and organizational factors may interact to increase or decrease the probability of violent behaviors.

Individual Predispositions for Violent Behavior

Given that the perspective traditionally taken in reporting and discussing workplace violence generally starts with characteristics of the individual, we will likewise begin our discussion with the individual as well. Specifically, we propose that individuals enter an organization with some potential predisposition to exhibit deviant behaviors. We further propose that this predisposition exists in all people even though it may be very low in most individuals. But simply because the predisposition is low does not mean that it does not exist. Indeed, just as it is theoretically impossible to accept a null hypothesis, we cannot confirm that a behavioral trait or predisposition does not exist simply because it does not manifest itself. In those cases where individuals do exhibit deviant behavior, of course, the argument for predisposition becomes more compelling. Hence, we suggest that every person has a predisposition to behave in deviant ways under certain circumstances; for most individuals this predisposition may be very low while for others it may range from modest to very likely.

Examining the fundamental underpinnings of predispositions toward deviant behavior requires a complex analysis of a variety of literatures. For the purposes of this chapter we will only note some of the most logical and significant factors that contribute to a predisposition toward deviance. Evidence suggests that these factors include personality, experiences, and motives. Further, after a person has been in an organization for some period of time, whatever predisposition toward deviance she or he had upon entering may increase or decrease as a result of both direct and vicarious organizational experiences.

Personality Traits

While Henle and Gross address the relationships between personality and deviant workplace behavior in this volume, we provide an overview of personality traits in order to offer some context. Individual predisposition, or the person-based perspective of workplace deviance, postulates that an individual's personality, not the environment he/she operates in, is what dictates individual behavior (Henle, 2005). As such, personality will dictate individual behavior regardless of the existing context or situation. In effect, it is personality that will influence how an individual interprets or responds to different contexts or situations (Henle, 2005). Therefore, individuals with a predisposition for deviant behavior can be presumed to be characterized by a specific profile of traits that lend themselves to this type of behavior (Henle, 2005).

While the belief that personality influences deviant behavior has been widely held, existing research has been slow to support this perspective (Bennett & Robinson, 2003). In fact, the personality traits that have been linked to deviant behavior (Trevino, 1986) have been shown to explain relatively little variance (Robinson & Greenberg, 1998). Exceptions, however, have started to arise related to some of the Big Five Personality traits, dispositional aggressiveness, Machiavellianism, narcissism, and locus of control.

Big Five Personality Traits. Several of the Big Five personality factors have been shown to predict workplace deviant behavior. Research by Lee, Ashton, and Shin (2005) revealed that extraversion played a prominent role in predicting both organizational deviance and interpersonal deviance. Their logic for this relationship stems from the need for individuals to exemplify a certain level of boldness, assertiveness, and activity in order to engage in deviant behavior such as harassment and sabotage, while passive or timid individuals would be lacking this capability.

Support has also been found for the trait of agreeableness in relation to interpersonal deviance (Colbert et al., 2004; Lee et al., 2005). Given that the trait of agreeableness is described by likability, friendliness, warmth, kindness, empathy, trust, and being cooperative (Barrick & Mount, 1991), Lee et al. (2005) proposed that the trait of agreeableness would be more likely to affect interpersonal deviance as opposed to organizational deviance given its relation to social interactions. As such, results indicated a significant negative relationship between agreeableness and interpersonal deviance. Therefore, individuals who tend to be low on agreeableness are more likely to engage in interpersonal deviant behavior than those who are high on agreeableness. This relationship was further supported by Colbert et al. in their 2004 study.

Conscientiousness has also been linked to deviant behavior. More specifically, given that the trait of conscientiousness is often described by such traits as endurance, achievement-oriented, responsible, hardworking, and persevering, it has been proposed that conscientiousness would most likely affect organizational deviance as opposed to interpersonal deviance given its relation to work situations and its impersonal, non-social, description. As such, results indicated a significant negative relationship between conscientiousness and organizational deviance (Colbert et al., 2004; Lee et al., 2005). Therefore, individuals who tend to be low on conscientiousness are more likely to engage in organizational deviant behavior than those who are high on conscientiousness.

Neuroticism, otherwise described as emotional stability or negative affectivity, has also been linked to deviant behavior. Negative affectivity has been described as the frequency or intensity with which one feels distressing emotions such as anger, anxiousness, depression, embarrassment, emotional, fear, hostility, insecurity, and worry (Aquino, Lewis & Bradfield, 1999; Barrick & Mount, 1991; Watson & Clark, 1984). Previous research indicates that individuals who experience high levels of negative affectivity are likely to experience negative moods across all contexts or situations (Aquino et al., 1999; Watson & Clark, 1984). As such, "negative affect has been viewed as the most proximal predictor of aggressive behaviors in various models of aggression" (Lee, Ashton & Shin, 2005, 86). Results indicate negative affectivity is significantly correlated with both organizational deviance and interpersonal deviance (Aquino et al., 1999).

Dispositional Aggressiveness. The personality trait of aggressiveness has been shown to have a significant direct relationship to interpersonal deviance (Aquino, Galperin & Bennett, 2004). Research by Berkowitz (1993) and Geen (1995) indicates that individuals with aggressive dispositions tend to experience "more intense emotional responses to aversive stimuli, hold more aggressive cognitive scripts, and experience weaker internalized constraints against engaging in antisocial behavior than do those who are less aggressive" (Aquino, Galperin, Bennett, 2004, 1004). As a result, aggressiveness has consistently been found to moderate the relationship between aversive stimuli and aggressive response (Geen, 1995).

Machiavellianism. The personality trait of Machiavellianism is another dispositional characteristic shown to be linked to deviant behavior. Machiavellianism has been conceptualized as an individual's propensity to be distrustful, engage in the act of manipulation, cheat, and steal, particularly when there is low risk of getting caught and high opportunity for rewards. Research indicates those who demonstrate high levels of Machiavellianism are more likely to engage in acts of theft (Harrell & Hartnagel, 1976) and more likely to engage in both interpersonal deviance and organizational deviance (Bennett & Robinson, 2000).

Narcissism. Several studies have demonstrated positive correlations between narcissism and deviant behavior, such as counterproductive workplace behavior, hostility, and aggression (Penney & Spector, 2002; Raskin, Novacek & Hogan, 1991; Rhodewalt & Morf, 1995; Wink, 1991). Research suggests that "narcissists may be predisposed to engage in aggressive and other deviant behavior because they are predisposed to see their work environment in negative, threatening ways" (Judge, LePine & Rich, 2006, 764). Therefore, provocation and threats, particularly to one's self-concept (Stucke & Sporer, 2002) and self-esteem (Bushman & Baumeister, 1998) are likely to trigger an aggressive response from those who score high on narcissism. Additionally, while narcissists seem to exhibit increased aggressive behavior, they also have been shown to lack the ability to restrain aggressive behavior. This lack of restraint has been explained by the correlation between narcissism and disinhibiting tendencies (Emmons, 1984).

Locus of Control. Locus of control is a personality trait defined by one's general expectation over whether rewards, reinforcements, or outcomes in life are self controlled or controlled by others (Spector, 1988). In a work setting, individuals with an internal locus of control believe that work outcomes (promotions, salary increases, and career advancement) are a direct reflection of their own actions, behaviors, efforts, and abilities. Individuals with an external locus of control believe that work outcomes are a direct result of external factors or forces, such as luck, chance, fate, or powerful others.

An individual's type of locus of control is likely to influence his or her behavior. As such, those with an external locus of control often experience perceived powerlessness. Perceived powerlessness is frequently associated with a lack of participation, a lack of autonomy, and a lack of freedom (Allen & Greenberger, 1980; Ashforth, 1989; Bennett, 1998). Therefore, in an effort to regain some semblance of control, research indicates that those who experience perceived powerlessness are likely to engage in behavior that will serve as a corrective means for restoring one's sense of control within his/her respective environment (Ashforth, 1989). Deviant behavior is perceived to be a means for restoring such control (Bennett & Robinson, 2003). In fact, perceived powerlessness has been construed as a provocation to deviant behavior (Bennett & Robinson, 2003) and as such has been linked to sabotage (Ambrose et al., 2002; Bennett, 1998; DiBattista, 1991), aggressive behavior (Perlow & Latham, 1993), and destructive behavior (Allen & Greenberger, 1980).

Experiences

Individual experiences have also been frequently studied as a potential precursor or trigger for deviant behavior. Of particular interest have been experiences dealing with frustration and perceived injustice in the workplace. As such, previous research has focused on examining deviance as a potential reaction to an experience of frustration or injustice.

The link between frustration and deviant behavior stems from the proposed interplay of affective antecedents and behavioral responses. Spector and Colleagues (Chen & Spector, 1992; Fox & Spector, 1999; Fox, Spector & Miles, 2001; Spector, 1997; Storms & Spector, 1987) have demonstrated strong empirical support for the link between experienced frustration and deviant behavior. More specifically, experienced frustration is deemed to create an emotional state that results in an affective reaction. This affective reaction has shown significant empirical support for its ability to trigger aggressive responses such as deviant behavior. Often the emotional response of frustration is triggered by the experience of a frustrating job stressor such as interference with goal attainment or goal maintenance (Spector, 1978), or even the felt emotional response to inadequate resources (Taylor & Walton, 1971), which can then serve as the source of frustration and therefore the motivation behind any resulting deviant behavior (Ambrose, Seabright & Schminke, 2002).

Consistent with the writings of several authors in this volume, perceived injustice in the workplace is another individual experience factor linked to triggering deviant behavior. Injustice refers to the belief of having been treated in an unfair manner either through the distribution of outcomes (distributive justice), the procedures used to determine the outcomes (procedural justice), or being disrespected or treated in a demeaning or discourteous manner (interactional justice). Adam's Equity Theory (1965) indicates that when an individual perceives to have been treated unfairly, he or she is likely to respond in a way to try and restore the balance of equity. Research indicates that one means of restoring equity and responding to experienced injustice is to resort to deviant behavior (DeMore, Fisher & Baron, 1988; Greenberg, 1990; Greenberg, 1993b; Greenberg & Alge, 1998).

Generally, injustice has consistently been cited to trigger such deviant behavior as sabotage (Crino, 1994; Crino & Leap, 1989; Neuman & Baron, 1998; Robinson & Bennett, 1997; Skarlicki & Folger, 1997). More specifically, distributive and procedural injustice have frequently been cited for their influence on such deviant behaviors as theft (Greenberg, 1990, 1993b; Greenberg & Alge, 1998), sabotage (Ambrose, Seabright & Schminke, 2002), and aggression (Folger & Baron, 1996; O'Leary-Kelly, Griffin & Glew, 1996; Skarlicki & Folger, 1997). As for interactional injustice, the perception of having been treated in an interpersonally unfair manner has been shown to have a consistent link to deviant behavior, such as retaliation through stealing, even when the stolen item was of no value to the individual (Greenberg, 1996), and revenge (Bies & Tripp, 1998). Whereas individuals are likely to try and restore equity when they have encountered distributive injustice, research indicates retaliation is a far more likely form of response when they experience interactional injustice (Greenberg, 1996). Hence, "interactional injustice (especially lack of interpersonal sensitivity) takes on paramount importance in predicting retaliation and aggression in the workplace" (Folger & Skarlicki, 1998, 43).

A different form of experience that also seems to contribute to an individual's propensity for violence in particular is knowledge of and experience with weapons, especially firearms.

James Davis, for example, grew up in a family environment characterized by violence and aggression—his father routinely beat Davis, his brother, and his mother. After Davis left home he joined the military and saw combat in Vietnam. Later, back in civilian life he bought a .44 Magnum and practiced target shooting in his basement. His experiences in Vietnam were a frequent topic of conversation at work, and he was fired for fighting with a co-worker. James Daniel Simpson was an avid hunter earlier in his life and also knew his way around guns.

Motives

"Behind each form of deviance is a particular motivation produced by a specific provocation" (Robinson & Bennett, 1997, 23). In examining the motivational underpinnings of workplace deviance, prior research indicates that deviant behavior is often a provoked response. This response is motivated most often by perceived inequity or experienced injustice.

Robinson and Bennett (1997) describe two distinct motivations that relate to workplace deviance. One form, termed expressive motivation, "reflects the need to vent, release, or express one's feelings of outrage, anger, or frustration" (Robinson & Bennett, 1997, 16). Expressive motivation thereby focuses more on the ends and can be described as an affective response (Lee & Allen, 2002) to feelings of injustice. In fact, affective responses have been suggested to influence aggressive behavior (Baron, 1993) furthering support for the triggering of deviant behavior. The second form of motivation described by Robinson and Bennett (1997) is termed instrumental motivation. Instrumental motivation "reflects attempts to reconcile the disparity by repairing the situation, restoring equity, or improving the current situation" (Robison & Bennett, 1997, 16). As such, instrumental motivation can be described as a cognitive-judgment-driven response to a perceived inequity whereby "deviant behavior need not be spontaneous in every occasion; individuals may also engage in workplace deviance after cognitive deliberation" (Judge et al., 2006, 127). Thus, instrumental motivation focuses more on the means to an end, in an effort towards obtaining balance and restoring equity. This form of motivation and resulting engagement in deviant behavior "requires employees to think about their work and hence, suggests an emphasis on cognition" (Lee & Allen, 2002, 133).

Organizational Propensity to Elicit Violent Behavior

In ways very similar to that of the individual component of our model and in describing the individual's predisposition for deviant behavior, we also propose that an organization has a propensity to elicit deviance. This propensity construct describes the range of potential influence that an organization can have in contributing to, and eliciting, deviant behavior from individuals (employees). This perspective, of course, has been noted previously. For instance, the situation-based perspective of workplace deviance postulates that the environment an individual operates in is what dictates individual deviant behavior (Henle, 2005). As such, "employees will commit deviant acts at work depending on the work environment they are in regardless of their individual characteristics" (Henle, 2005, 248). This perspective advocates workplace deviance as a sole product of the individual's organizational environment. Therefore, organizations predisposed to employee deviance are likely to exhibit certain characteristics that make organizations vulnerable to employee deviant behavior (Henle, 2005).

For example, if an organization is perceived by individuals (employees) as fair and as intolerant of deviant behavior, of having a warm and nurturing culture, of having an equitable reward system, and treating its employees with dignity and respect, it may reasonably be described as having a low propensity for eliciting deviant behavior from individuals. On the other hand, if an organization tolerates or reinforces deviant behaviors, has a harsh and overly competitive culture, maintains a reward system characterized by arbitrariness and capriciousness, and treats its employees impersonally and as consumable assets, it may be much more likely to have a higher propensity to elicit deviance. As with an individual's predispositions for deviance, we propose the organization's propensity to elicit deviance to be reflected by a continuum ranging from low to high.

Perhaps not surprisingly, numerous workplace killers have placed some or all of the blame for their actions on their former employers. James Davis, for instance, cited a culture that caused worry, stress, and anxiety at Union Butterfield as the cause of his rampage. While such views are, of course, likely to be biased and created to serve as defense mechanisms, independent assessments have also noted organizational conditions that have contributed to violence. The Equal Employment Opportunity Commission, for instance, investigated a shooting at a large defense contractor and concluded that the firm permitted a racially charged atmosphere to exist at one of its factories. Specifically, the EEOC charged that the firm knew that a hostile work environment existed at the facility but did nothing to change things. The propensity of organizations to elicit violence is critical in that we argue that it serves as a likely stimulating or repressing context for the potential emergence of deviant behaviors by its employees. Among the critical elements of an organization that determine its propensity to elicit deviance are its culture, norms and procedures, reward system, and orientation toward employees.

Organizational Culture

Organizational culture is the set of values, norms, assumptions, and beliefs that exists among organizational members which influence employee attitudes, thoughts, feelings, and behaviors. An organization's culture can control the way employees interpret or perceive situations and how they respond to situations. Several studies have examined the value system of organizations which helps create an organization's culture to determine influences on employee deviant behavior. For example, the NCS Workforce Development Group and the Food Marketing Institute conducted the 8th Annual Survey of Supermarket Employees, which served to examine counterproductive behavior by employees ranging from theft, a form of property deviance, to absenteeism, a form of production deviance. Results of the study indicated that organizations with "positive" cultures are less likely to trigger employee deviant behavior than organizations with "negative" cultures. Organizations with "positive" cultures maintain at least seven of the following eight values: (a) fairness with employees, (b) caring and empathy, (c) employee empowerment, (d) career-enriching opportunities, (e) equitable pay and benefits, (f) accurate job-person matching, (g) honesty and ethics, and (h) safe working conditions.

In effect, "employees who described their company as having a 'positive culture' admitted far less theft—$12.23 annually—than employees of organizations with a 'negative culture,' who said they stole more than $90 a year" (Wellman, 1998). Therefore, an organization with a high propensity to elicit employee deviant behavior is likely to have developed a "negative" culture. This type of environment is likely to mold or reinforce deviant behavior. It is also likely to have created an overly competitive culture. On the other hand, an organization with a low propensity to elicit employee deviant behavior is likely to have a value system that creates a "positive culture" described as fair, respectful, warm, trusting, and nurturing. It is also likely to communicate its intolerances of deviant behavior by consistently punishing deviant behavior.

Norms and Procedures

Just like values, norms can have a very powerful effect on behavior (Schein, 1996). Norms are often construed as informal rules of conduct that communicate to members which behaviors are expected of them. Norms serve as a means for controlling behavior and often are enforced through rewards and punishment by the group members within an organization. Norms have often been studied as an antecedent of workplace deviance through various theoretical underpinnings such as social information processing and social learning theory (Robinson & O'Leary-Kelly, 1998).

According to social information processing theory, "individuals, as adaptive organisms, adapt attitudes, behavior, and beliefs to their social context" (Salancik & Pfeffer, 1978, 226). As such, Robinson and O'Leary-Kelly (1998) use social information processing theory to help explain its application to individual antisocial behavior by indicating that "individuals use information from their immediate social environments to interpret events, develop appropriate attitudes, and understand expectations concerning their behavior and its consequences" (659). Therefore, the social context for an individual is likely to be a strong predictor of individual behavior.

Bandura's (1977) social learning theory has also been used to examine such deviant behavior as antisocial behavior. O'Leary-Kelly and colleagues (1996) indicate that through social learning theory, individuals are likely to learn appropriate adaptive responses through social cues in the environment. These environmental social cues may be learned through modeling behavior (Bandura, 1977) or through incentive inducements as explained by positive reinforcement (Bandura, 1977). While some individuals are more prone than others towards deviant behavior, such as violence (Bandura, 1977; Berkowitz, 1993), it is suggested that deviant behavior can be considered a learned response based on the context of one's environment, given the right triggering social cues. Therefore, individuals who operate in the context of coworkers who engage in deviant behaviors are likely to engage in deviant acts (Robinson & O'Leary-Kelly, 1998). Additionally, individuals who receive positive rewards for their deviant behavior are more likely to continue to demonstrate this form of deviant behavior.

As such, research indicates that social norms have been influential in triggering workplace deviance (Robinson & Greenberg, 1998; Robinson & O'Leary-Kelly, 1998), as well as specific deviant behaviors such as sabotage (Giacalone, Riordan & Rosenfeld, 1997), workplace aggression (Greenberg & Alge, 1998), theft (Greenberg, 1998), antisocial behavior (Robinson & O'Leary-Kelly, 1998), and counterproductive behavior (Boye & Jones, 1997). Therefore, given the influence of group norms on individual behavior, it is presumed that social cues that communicate tolerance for deviant behavior are more likely to create an organizational culture with a high propensity to elicit employee deviant behavior. On the other hand, employee deviance can also be constrained by these same social norms that can then serve as informal social controls through primary work-group relationships (Hollinger & Clark, 1982). Therefore, social norms can also be very powerful in inhibiting deviant behavior thereby creating an organizational culture with a low propensity to elicit employee deviant behavior.

Reward System

The organizational environment can contribute to deviant displays of behavior in one of two ways: by creating social conditions that promote this type of behavior and/or by lowering restraints against it (Berkowitz, 1993). According to Berkowitz (1982, 1983), while an individual may have a strong impulsive reaction to deviant behavior such as violence, the actual display of the behavior is "most likely to occur when cognitively based inhibitory restraints are minimal" (Carlson, Marcus-Newhall & Miller, 1990, 622). The organization can therefore become a contributory factor in whether or not deviant displays of behavior are engaged in by the individual, especially when, for example, the threat of punishment from the organization is absent (Berkowitz, 1993).

Reinforcement theory posits that individual behavior is determined by its consequences. Therefore, an organization can influence the behavior of its employees through the use of rewards and punishments. For an organization to maintain a low propensity to elicit employee deviant behavior, it is proposed that the organization must maintain a reward system that is equitable. A fair and adequate reward system is likely to keep employees satisfied and less likely to trigger feelings of frustration towards the organization, potentially resulting in deviant behavior (Boye & Jones, 1997). It is also proposed that the organization maintain a reward system that perhaps even promotes reducing deviant behavior. Boye and Jones (1997) propose the use of a profit sharing system whereby "this method of compensation should help make clear to employees the reward they can obtain by reducing counterproductive behavior and thus helping the company to increase its profitability" (181). This method would communicate the intolerance for deviant behavior and at the same time reward or provide incentive for employees to maintain desired, as opposed to undesired, behaviors.

On the other hand, it would serve organizations well to punish unacceptable counterproductive or deviant behaviors. Boye and Jones (1997) further propose the use of a policy to communicate concerns regarding employee deviant behavior and the organization's intolerance of such behavior. However, punishment is ineffective if organizations engage in weak sanctions for rule or policy violations (Appelbaum, Iaconi & Matousek, 2007). As such, empirical evidence indicates that the severity of sanctions is critical in influencing or deterring deviant behavior. Hollinger and Clark (1982) indicate that while formal sanctions do serve to deter both property deviance and production deviance, the strength of informal sanctions by coworkers is two and a half times greater. Therefore, "employee behavior seems to be constrained more by the anticipated reaction to deviance by one's fellow coworkers than the threatened formal reaction on the part of management" (Hollinger & Clark, 1982, 340). Yet, both formal and informal sanctions are critical in effectively reducing employee deviant behavior, particularly when sanctions against those who engage in deviant behaviors are consistent, severe, and known to all employees (Boye & Jones, 1997).

Organizations that tend to have a high propensity to elicit employee deviant behavior are likely to maintain a reward system characterized by arbitrariness and capriciousness, and that runs counter to generally accepted behavior. That is, organizations often develop *counternorms* (Sims, 1992), which describe generally accepted "organizational practices that are contrary to prevailing ethical standards" (507), such as rewarding secretive and deceitful behavior, encouraging individuals to "pass the buck" and avoid taking responsibility, and communicating to employees to do whatever it takes to get a job done. Organizations, therefore, tend to encourage individuals to maintain a "bottom line mentality" that often occurs at the expense of upholding other values (Appelbaum, Deguire & Lay, 2005).

In the context of workplace deviant behavior, counternorms are thought to result in what has been termed the "effect/danger" ratio (Appelbaum et al., 2005). The "effect/danger" ratio describes deviant behavior that occurs covertly in the workplace and involves an aggressor who engages in behaviors that effectively harm the target (individual/organization) yet allows him or her to incur minimal danger to oneself (Bjorkqvist, Osterman & Hjelt-Back, 1994). Prior research indicates that covert aggression tends to be a preferred method of deviant behavior over overt actions such as physical violence, particularly in the workplace, where one's identity can be more effectively hidden (Baron & Neuman, 1998).

Orientation Towards Employees

An organization's orientation towards its employees can have significant effects on its employees' behaviors. Several theoretical perspectives support this relationship. Social exchange theory (Gould, 1979; Levinson, 1965) and norm of reciprocity (Gouldner, 1960) indicate that individuals will tend to demonstrate reciprocative behaviors directly towards those who benefit or harm them. As such, empirical evidence suggests that individuals who perceive they are receiving supportive and favorable treatment from the organization are likely to engage in positive behaviors such as increased motivation and commitment. On the other hand, individuals who perceive unfavorable treatment by the organization are likely to violate organizational norms and exhibit deviant behavior (Colbert et al., 2004).

The justice and perceived organizational support literatures help to further explain the relationship between an organization's orientation towards its employees and employee behavior. Research indicates that regardless of the form of injustice, when employees are treated in an unjust manner, they are more likely to engage in deviant behavior (Bennett & Robinson, 2003). Distributive and procedural forms of injustice are likely to trigger theft (Greenberg, 1990, 1993b; Greenberg & Alge, 1998), sabotage (Ambrose et al., 2002), and aggression (Folger & Baron, 1996; O'Leary-Kelly et al., 1996; Skarlicki & Folger, 1997). Interactional injustice, on the other hand, is likely to trigger retaliation (Greenberg, 1996) and revenge (Bies & Tripp, 1998). In fact, Bies and Tripp (1998) indicate that interactional justice through interpersonal insensitivity, such as the demeaning treatment of employees, may play a critical role in triggering retaliatory sabotage, or revengeful behavior.

As for perceived organizational support, the employee-organization relationship is determined by their work history and series of exchanges (Eisenberger, Huntington, Hutchison & Sowa, 1996; Wayne, Shore & Liden, 1997). When employees feel a general sense of being valued by the organization and cared for (Rhoades & Eisenberger, 2002), they are likely to feel support from the organization and are less likely to engage in workplace deviance (Colbert et al., 2004). However, when employees perceive low levels of organizational support, when they are "shown disrespect, passed over for promotion, given additional responsibilities with no pay increase, denied adequate resources to do the job, or didn't receive what he or she considered adequate credit for work performed from co-workers or management" (Crino, 1994, 315), then the resulting frustration is likely to result in deviant behavior such as sabotage (Ambrose, Seabright & Schminke, 2002), and potentially, hostility or aggression (Spector, 1997).

Therefore, organizations with a low propensity to elicit employee deviant behavior are likely to treat employees with dignity and respect, to maintain fair and equitable procedures, to treat employees with trust, respect, dignity, and sensitivity as proposed by Boye and Jones (1997). Organizations with a high propensity to elicit employee deviant behavior are likely to treat employees impersonally and as consumable assets, and to maintain unjust environments filled with perceived social and structural injustices (Greenberg & Alge, 1998).

Person-Situation Determinants of Deviant Behavior

In the preceding sections we have developed arguments that two central constructs in understanding workplace deviance are individual predispositions for deviant behavior and organizational propensity to elicit deviant behavior. As noted by Appelbaum, Iaconi, and Matousek (2007), situation-based and person-based predictors of employee deviance have traditionally been considered to be mutually exclusive. More recently, though, cognitive social theorists have come to believe that there is a strong interaction between person-based and situation-based types of deviance. This is because personality is contextual and it modifies how individuals interpret, and thus respond to, particular situations (Henle, 2005). Further, Appelbaum et al. also argue that deviant behavior actually cannot be attributed to personality traits alone. As previously noted, it is more likely that deviant behavior may be best predicted based on a combination of personality variables and the nature of the workplace situation (Peterson, 2002; Caruana, Ramaseshan & Ewing, 2001).

The individual predispositions for violent behavior and organizational propensity to elicit violent behavior constructs provide a useful integrative framework for potentially understanding how situation-based and person-based predictors may interact to influence deviant behavior. Specifically, figure 9.1 presents the organizing elements of a model of person-situation determinants of deviant behavior in organizations. By viewing individual predispositions for deviant behavior and organizational propensities for eliciting deviant behaviors as continuums, and by considering these two constructs as theoretically independent of one another, we can create the 2x2 matrix shown in the figure. This matrix defines four general conditions:

- Condition 1: High individual predisposition for deviance/low organizational propensity to elicit deviance
- Condition 2: High individual predisposition for deviance/high organizational propensity to elicit deviance
- Condition 3: Low individual predisposition for deviance/high organizational propensity to elicit deviance
- Condition 4: Low individual predisposition for deviance/low organizational propensity to elicit deviance

As also illustrated in table 9.1, condition 2 is likely to have the highest incidence of deviant behaviors, given that the individual has a high propensity for deviance and the organization has a high propensity to elicit deviance. Alternatively, condition 4 is likely to have the lowest incidence of deviant behaviors, since the individual has a low propensity for deviance and the organization has a low propensity to elicit deviance. Conditions 1 and 3 are likely to have moderate incidences of deviant behavior.

To illustrate further, consider the case of two hypothetical persons, Sam and Peter, and two hypothetical employers, company A and company B. Assume that Sam has a relatively high propensity for deviance and that Peter

Table 9.1
A Model of Person-Situation Determinants of
Deviant Behavior in Organizations

		Organization Propensity to Elicit Deviant Behavior	
Individual Predespositions for Deviant Behaviors	**High**	1 Moderate incidence of deviant behavior	2 Highest incidence of deviant behavior
	Low	Lowest incidence of deviant behavior 4 Low	Moderate incidence of deviant behavior 3 High

Organization Propensity
to Elicit Deviant Behavior

has a relative low propensity for deviance. Similarly, assume that company A has a relatively high propensity to elicit deviance and that company B has a relatively low propensity to elicit deviance. The highest overall probability for deviant behavior to arise among these four 'actors' would be if Sam were to take a job at company A. Similarly, the lowest overall probability for deviant behavior would be if Peter took a job at company B. Of course, this does not mean that deviance by Sam and no deviance by Peter are certain, but instead simply suggests relative probabilities for the two potential deviant acts.

It is also likely that predispositions and propensities can change over time, resulting in potentially fluid probabilities. For instance, someone with a high predisposition for deviant behavior might achieve some increased measure of personal peace or tranquility, thereby lowering his or her predisposition for deviance. Likewise, a series of major personal setbacks and tragedies could conceivably increase a person's predisposition for deviance. The patterns could also exist in organizations as they alter their cultures, norms and procedures, reward systems, and orientation towards employees in ways that increase or decrease their propensity to elicit deviant behaviors.

Implications and Future Directions

Considerable work, of course, is needed in order for the value of our proposed model to be fully realized. For one thing, a more thorough and comprehensive theoretical development of the key constructs is required. For example, while we focus on such individual factors as personality,

experiences, and motives, other factors such as values and genetic and bio-
logical elements may also need to be included. Similarly, other contextual
factors such as the role of supervision, coworkers, and national culture may
also be relevant.

More precise linkages between the two constructs must also be developed. For instance, there is clearly a wide range of deviant behaviors. Sub-
categories of deviant behaviors may also be differentially affected by different person-specific constructs. Personality differences, for example, may
be more influential on certain deviant behaviors whereas experiences and
motives may be more influential on others. Similarly, certain organization
factors like culture may be more likely to elicit certain kinds of deviance
while reward systems and norms and procedures may elicit other forms of
deviance. Clearly, then, there is room for greater theoretical and conceptual
development and exposition.

Empirical research is also necessary in order to further assess the validity of the model after it is fully elaborated. A combination of laboratory
research, detailed clinical case studies, and organizational field studies may
all be needed in order to provide greater insights into the constructs of individual predispositions for deviance, organizational propensity to elicit deviance, and the interactions between the two. The authors' hope is that the
model can serve as an organizing framework for a more complete perspective on the study of deviant behavior in organizations.

REFERENCES

Adams, J. S. (1965). Inequity in social exchange. In L. Berkowitz (Ed.), *Advances in experi-
mental social psychology* (Vol. 2: pp. 267–299). New York: Academic.
Allen, V. L., & Greenberger, D. B. (1980). Destruction and perceived control. In A. Braun &
J. E. Singer (Eds.), *Advances in Environmental Psychology* (Vol. 2: pp. 85–109). New York:
Academic.
Ambrose, M. L., Seabright, M. A., & Schminke, M. (2002). Sabotage in the workplace: The
role of organizational injustice. *Organizational Behavior and Human Decision Processes,
89,* 947–965.
Appelbaum, S. H., Deguire, K. J., & Lay, M. (2005). The relationship of ethical climate to
deviant workplace behaviour. *Corporate Governance, 5,* 43–55.
Appelbaum, S. H., Iaconi, G. D., & Matousek, A. (2007). Positive and negative deviant workplace behaviors: Causes, impacts, and solutions. *Corporate Governance, 7,* 586–598.
Aquino, K., Galperin, B. L., & Bennett, R. J. (2004). Social status and aggressiveness as moderators of the relationship between interactional justice and workplace deviance. *Journal
of Applied Social Psychology, 34,* 1001–1029.
Aquino, K., Lewis, M. U., & Bradfield, M. (1999). Justice constructs, negative affectivity, and
employee deviance: A proposed model and empirical test. *Journal of Organizational
Behavior, 20,* 1073–1091.

Ashforth, B. (1989). The experience of powerlessness in organizations. *Organizational Behavior and Human Decision Processes, 43,* 207–242.

Bandura, A. (1977). *Social learning theory.* Englewood Cliffs, NJ: Prentice Hall.

Baron, R. A. (1993). Affect and organizational behavior: When and why feeling good (or bad) matters. In J. K. Murningham (Ed.), *Social psychology in organizations: Advances in theory and research* (pp. 63–88). Englewood Cliffs, NJ: Prentice Hall.

Baron, R. A., & Neuman, J. (1998). Workplace aggression—The iceberg beneath the tip of workplace violence: Evidence on its forms, frequencies, and targets. *Public Administration Quarterly, 21,* 446–464.

Barrick, M. R., & Mount, M. K. (1991). The big five personality dimensions and job performance: A meta-analysis. *Personnel Psychology, 44,* 1–26.

Bennett, R. J. (1998) Perceived powerlessness as a cause of employee deviance. In R. W. Griffin, A. M. O'Leary-Kelly, & J. M. Collins (Eds.), *Dysfunctional behavior in organizations: Violent and deviant behaviors* (pp. 221–240). Greenwich, CT: JAI.

Bennett, R. J. & Robinson, S. L. (2000). Development of a measure of workplace deviance. *Journal of Applied Psychology, 85,* 349–360.

Bennett, R. J. & Robinson, S. L. (2003). The past, present, and future of workplace deviance research. In Greenberg, J. (2nd Ed.). *Organizational behavior: The state of the science* (pp. 247–282). Mahwah, NJ: Erlbaum.

Berkowitz, L. (1982). Aversive conditions as stimuli to aggression. In L. Berkowitz (Ed.), *Advances in experimental social psychology* (Vol. 15: pp. 249–285). Orlando, FL: Academic.

Berkowitz, L. (1983). The experience of anger as a parallel process in the display of impulsive, "angry" aggression. In R. Geen & E. I. Donnerstein (Eds.), *Aggression: Theoretical and empirical reviews* (Vol. 1: pp. 103–133). Orlando, FL: Academic.

Berkowitz, L. (1993). *Aggression: Its causes, consequences, and control.* New York: McGraw-Hill.

Berry, C. M., Ones, D. S., & Sackett, P. R. (2007). Interpersonal deviance, organizational deviance, and their common correlates: A review and meta-analysis. *Journal of Applied Psychology, 92,* 410–424.

Bies, R. J., & Tripp, T. M. (1998). Revenge in organizations: The good, the bad, and the ugly. In R. W. Griffin, A. O'Leary-Kelly, & J. M. Collins (Eds.), *Dysfunctional behavior in organizations, Part B: Non-violent dysfunctional behavior* (pp. 49–68). Stamford, CT: JAI.

Bjorkqvist, K., Osterman, K., & Hjelt-Back, M. (1994). Sex differences in covert aggression among adults. *Aggressive Behavior, 20,* 27–33.

Bordia, P., Restubog, S. L. D., & Tang, R. L. (2008). When employees strike back: Investigating mediating mechanisms between psychological contract breach and workplace deviance. *Journal of Applied Psychology, 93,* 1104–1117.

Boye, M. W., & Jones, J. W. (1997). Organizational culture and employee counterproductivity. In R. A. Giacalone & J. Greenberg (Eds.), *Antisocial behavior in organizations* (pp. 172–184). Thousand Oaks, CA: Sage.

Bushman, B. J., & Baumeister, R. F. (1998). Threatened egotism, narcissism, self-esteem, and direct and displaced aggression: Does self-love or self-hate lead to violence? *Journal of Personality and Social Psychology, 75,* 219–229.

Carlson, M., Marcus-Newhall, A., & Miller, N. (1990). Effects of situational aggression cues: A quantitative review. *Journal of Personality and Social Psychology, 58,* 622–633.

Caruana, A., Ramaseshan, B., & Ewing, M.T. (2001), Anomie and deviant behaviour in marketing: Some preliminary evidence. *Journal of Managerial Psychology, 16,* 322–338.

Chen, P. Y., & Spector, P. E. (1992). Relationship of work stressors with aggression withdrawal, theft and substance use: An exploratory study. *Journal of Occupation and Organizational Psychology, 65,* 177–184.

Colbert, A. E., Mount, M. K., Harter, J. K., Witt, L. A., & Barrick, M. R. (2004). Interactive effects of personality and perceptions of the work situation on workplace deviance. *Journal of Applied Psychology, 89,* 599–609.

Crino, M. D. (1994). Employee sabotage: A random or preventable phenomenon? *Journal of Managerial Issues, 6,* 311–330.

Crino, M. D., & Leap, T. L. (1989). What HR managers must know about employee sabotage. *Personnel,* 31–38.

DeMore, S. W., Fisher, J. D., & Baron, R. M. (1988). The equity-control model as a predictor of vandalism among college students. *Journal of Applied Social Psychology, 18,* 80–91.

DiBattista, R. A. (1991). Creating new approaches to recognize and deter sabotage. *Public Personnel Management, 20,* 347–352.

Diefendorff, J. M., & Mehta, K. (2007). The relations of motivational traits with workplace deviance. *Journal of Applied Psychology, 92,* 967–977.

Dollard, J., Doob, L. W., Miller, N. E., Mowrer, O. H., & Sears, R. R. (1939). *Frustration and Aggression.* New Haven: Yale University Press.

Eisenberger, R., Huntington, R., Hutchison, S., & Sowa, D. (1986). Perceived organizational support. *Journal of Applied Psychology, 71,* 500–507.

Emmons, R. A. (1984). Factor analysis and construct validity of the Narcissistic Personality Inventory. *Journal of Personality Assessment, 48,* 291–300.

Ferris, D. L., Brown, D. J., & Heller, D. (2009). Organizational supports and organizational deviance: The mediating role of organization-based self-esteem. *Organizational Behavior and Human Decision Processes, 108,* 279–286.

Folger, R., & Baron, R. A. (1996). Violence and hostility at work: A model of reactions to perceived injustice. In G. R. VandenBos, & E. Q. Bulatao (Eds.), *Violence on the job: Identifying risks and developing solutions* (pp. 51–85). Washington, DC: American Psychological Association.

Folger, R., & Skarlicki, D. P. (1998). A popcorn metaphor for employee aggression. In R. W. Griffin, A. O'Leary-Kelly, & J. M. Collins (Eds.), *Dysfunctional behavior in organizations, Part A: Violent and deviant behavior* (pp. 43–82). Stamford, CT: JAI.

Fox, S., & Spector, P. E. (1999). A model of work frustration-aggression. *Journal of Organizational Behavior, 20,* 915–931.

Fox, S., Spector, P. E., & Miles, D. (2001). Counterproductive work behavior (CWB) in response to job stressors and organizational justice: Some mediator and moderator tests for autonomy and emotions. *Journal of Vocational Behavior, 59,* 1–19.

Geen, R. G. (1995). Human aggression. In A. Tesser (Ed.), *Advanced social psychology* (pp. 383–417). New York: McGraw-Hill.

Giacalone, R. A., Riordan, C. A., & Rosenfeld, P. (1997). Employee sabotage: Toward a practitioner-scholar understanding. In R. A. Giacalone & J. Greenberg (Eds.), *Antisocial behavior in organizations* (pp. 109–129). Thousand Oaks, CA: Sage.

Gould, S. (1979). An equity-exchange model of organizational involvement. *Academy of Management Review, 4,* 53–62.

Gouldner, A. W. (1960). The norm of reciprocity: A preliminary statement. *American Sociological Review, 25,* 161–178.

Greenberg, J. (1990). Employee theft as a reaction to underpayment inequity: The hidden cost of pay cuts. *Journal of Applied Psychology, 75,* 561–568.

Greenberg, J. (1993a). The social side of fairness: Interpersonal and informational classes of organizational justice. In R. Cropanzano (Ed.), *Justice in the workplace: Approaching fairness in human resource management* (pp. 79–103). Hillsdale, NJ: Erlbaum.

Greenberg, J. (1993b). Stealing in the name of justice: Informational and interpersonal moderators of theft reactions to underpayment inequity. *Organizational Behavior and Human Decision Processes, 54,* 81–103.

Greenberg, J. (1996). What motivates employee theft? An experimental test of two explanations. Paper presented at the annual meeting of the Society for Industrial-Organizational Psychology, San Diego, CA (April).

Greenberg, J. (1998). The cognitive geometry of employee theft: Negotiating "the line" between taking and stealing. In R. W. Griffin, A. M. O'Leary-Kelly, & J. M. Collins (Eds.), *Dysfunctional behavior in organizations: Non-violent dysfunctional behavior* (Vol. 23 (B): pp. 147–193). Stamford, CT: JAI.

Greenberg, J., & Alge, B. J. (1998). Aggressive reactions to workplace injustice. In R. W. Griffin, A. O'Leary-Kelly, & J. M. Collins (Eds.), *Dysfunctional behavior in organizations, Part A: Violent and deviant behavior* (pp. 83–117). Stamford, CT: JAI.

Harrell, W. A., & Hartnagel, T. (1976). The impact of Machiavellianism and the trustfulness of the victim on laboratory theft. *Sociometry, 39,* 157–165.

Henle, C. A. (2005). Predicting workplace deviance from the interaction between organizational justice and personality. *Journal of Managerial Issues, 17,* 247–263.

Henle, C. A., Giacalone, R. A., & Jurkiewicz, C. L. (2005). The role of ethical ideology in workplace deviance. *Journal of Business Ethics, 56,* 219–230.

Hollinger, R. C., & Clark, J. P. (1982). Formal and informal social controls of employee deviance. *The Sociological Quarterly, 23,* 333–343.

Judge, T. A., LePine, J. A., & Rich, B. L. (2006). Loving yourself abundantly: Relationship of the narcissistic personality to self- and other perceptions of workplace deviance, leadership, and task and contextual performance. *Journal of Applied Psychology, 91,* 762–776.

Judge, T. A., Scott, B. A., & Ilies, R. (2006). Hostility, job attitudes, and workplace deviance: Test of a multilevel model. *Journal of Applied Psychology, 91,* 126–138.

Lee, K., & Allen, N. J. (2002). Organizational citizenship behavior and workplace deviance: The role of affect and cognitions. *Journal of Applied Psychology, 87,* 131–142.

Lee, K., Ashton, M. C., & Shin, K. H. (2005). Personality correlates of workplace anti-social behavior. *Applied Psychology: An International Review, 54,* 81–98.

Levinson, H. (1965). Reciprocation: The relationship between man and organization. *Administrative Science Quarterly, 9,* 370–390.

Mitchell, M. S., & Ambrose, M. L. (2007). Abusive supervision and workplace deviance and the moderating effects of negative reciprocity beliefs. *Journal of Applied Psychology, 92,* 1159–1168.

Neuman, J. H., & Baron, R. A. (1998). Workplace violence and workplace aggression: Evidence concerning specific forms, potential causes, and preferred targets. *Journal of Management, 24,* 391–419.

O'Leary-Kelly, A. M., Griffin, R. W., & Glew, D. J. (1996). Organization-motivated aggression: A research framework. *Academy of Management Review, 21,* 225–253.

Penney, L. M., & Spector, P. E. (2002). Narcissism and counterproductive work behavior: Do bigger egos mean bigger problems? *International Journal of Selection and Assessment, 10,* 126–134.

Perlow, R., & Latham, L. L. (1993). Relationship of client abuse with locus of control and gender: A longitudinal study in mental retardation facilities. *Journal of Applied Psychology, 78,* 831–834.

Peterson, D. K. (2002) Deviant workplace behavior and the organization's ethical climate. *Journal of Business and Psychology, 17,* 47–61.

Raskin, R., Novaceck, J., & Hogan, R. (1991). Narcissistic self-esteem management. *Journal of Personality and Social Psychology, 60,* 911–918.

Rhoades, L., & Eisenberger, R. (2002). Perceived organizational support: A review of the literature. *Journal of Applied Psychology, 87,* 698–714.

Rhodewalt, F., & Morf, C. C. (1995). Self and interpersonal correlates of the Narcissistic Personality Inventory: A review and new findings. *Journal of Research in Personality, 29,* 1–23.

Robinson, S. L., & Bennett, R. J. (1995). A typology of deviant workplace behaviors: A multidimensional scaling study. *Academy of Management Journal, 38* (2), 555–572.

Robinson, S. L., & Bennett, R. J. (1997). Workplace deviance: Its definition, its nature, and its causes. In R. J. Lewicki, B. H. Sheppard, & R. J. Bies (Eds.), *Research on negotiation in organizations* (Vol. 6: pp. 3–28). Greenwich, CT: JAI.

Robinson, S. L., & Greenberg, J. (1998). Employees behaving badly: Dimensions, determinants, and dilemmas in the study of workplace deviance. In C. L. Cooper & D. M. Rousseau (Eds.), *Trends in organizational behavior* (Vol. 5: pp. 1–30). New York: Wiley.

Robinson, S. L., & O'Leary-Kelly, A. M. (1998). Monkey see, monkey do: The influence of work groups on the antisocial behavior of employees. *Academy of Management Journal, 41,* 658–672.

Salancik, G. R., & Pfeffer, J. (1978). A social information processing approach to job attitudes and task design. *Administrative Science Quarterly, 23,* 224–253.

Schein, E. H. (1996). Culture: The missing concept in organization studies. *Administrative Science Quarterly, 41,* 229–240.

Sims, R. R. (1992). The challenge of ethical behavior in organizations. *Journal of Business Ethics, 11,* 505–513.

Skarlicki, D. P., & Folger, R. (1997). Retaliation in the workplace: The roles of distributive, procedural, and interactional justice. *Journal of Applied Psychology, 82,* 434–443.

Spector, P. E. (1978). Organizational frustration: A model and review of the literature. *Personnel Psychology, 31,* 815–829.

Spector, P. E. (1988). Development of the work locus of control scale. *Journal of Occupational Psychology, 61,* 335–340.

Spector, P. E. (1997). The role of frustration in antisocial behavior at work. In R. A. Giacalone & J. Greenberg (Eds.), *Antisocial behavior in organizations* (pp. 1–17). Thousand Oaks, CA: Sage.

Stewart, S. M., Bing, M. N., Davison, H. K., Woehr, D. J., & McIntyre, M. D. (2009). In the eyes of the beholder: A non-self-report measure of workplace deviance. *Journal of Applied Psychology, 94,* 207–215.

Storms, P. L., & Spector, P. E. (1987). Relationships of organizational frustration with reported behavioral reactions: The moderating effect of locus of control. *Journal of Occupational Psychology, 60,* 227–234.

Stucke, T. S., & Sporer, S. L. (2002). When a grandiose self-image is threatened: Narcissism and self-concept clarity as predictors of negative emotions and aggression following ego-threat. *Journal of Personality, 70,* 509–532.

Taylor, L., & Walton, P. (1971). Industrial sabotage: Motives and meanings. In S. Cohen (Ed.), *Images of Deviance* (pp. 219–245). Harmondsworth: Penguin Books.

Tepper, B. J., Carr, J. C., Breaux, D. M., Geider, S., Hu, C., & Hua, W. (2009). Abusive supervision, intentions to quit, and employees' workplace deviance: A power/dependence analysis. *Organizational Behavior and Human Decision Processes, 109,* 156–167.

Tepper, B. J., Henle, C. A., Lambert, L. S., Giacalone, R. A., & Duffy, M. K. (2008). Abusive supervision and subordinates' organization deviance. *Journal of Applied Psychology, 93,* 721–732.

Trevino, L. K. (1986). Ethical decision making in organizations: A person-situation interactionist model. *Academy of Management Review, 11,* 601–617.

Warren, D. E. (2003) Constructive and destructive deviance in organizations. *Academy of Management Review, 28,* 622–632.

Watson, D., & Clark, L. (1984). Negative affectivity: The disposition to experience aversive emotional states. *Psychological Bulletin, 96,* 465–490.

Wayne, S. J., Shore, L. M., & Liden, R. C. (1997). Perceived organizational support and leader-member exchange: A social exchange perspective. *Academy of Management Journal, 40,* 82–111.

Wellman, D. (1998). The culture of counterproductivity. *Supermarket Business, 53,* 29–34.

Wink, P. (1991). Two faces of narcissism. *Journal of Personality and Social Psychology, 61,* 590–597.

10

Workplace Violence

Prevention and Aftermath

ALLEN K. HESS AND CLARA E. HESS

> *Workplace killings typically take just minutes, but workers and their compa-*
> *nies have been left profoundly traumatized. In the months that follow, some*
> *companies have lost business and seen employees quit. Survivors have been*
> *too devastated to return to work. And family members often face lengthy*
> *criminal trials and questions that will never be answered.*
>
> *"No one is ever the same, no organization is ever completely the same*
> *after a tragedy like this," says Mary Tyler, a psychologist at the Office of Per-*
> *sonnel Management in Washington who specializes in workplace violence.*
> *"It's a new normal."*
>
> *—USA Today, 2004*

Violence has become all too common in our workplaces. These tragic outbursts of mayhem have disparate causes and involve innumerable types of disputes. However, all events of workplace violence share two distressing features: they cause tremendous pain and anguish to the workplace involved and they contribute to a broader environment of fear in the workplace. Who can say his or her office is immune? Indeed, a violent attack can occur in nearly any work environment: a school or university, a factory or store front, a community theater or shopping mall, a hospital or taxi cab. Attacks can be carried out by employees, customers, clients, spouses, or strangers. And despite the sensationalized media focus on violence done unto a coworker, these attacks account for only 4–15% of total workplace homicides (Braverman, 1999; Sygnatur & Toscano, 2000). The remainder demands attention.

Between 2004 and 2008, U.S. workplaces averaged 564 work-related homicides annually (Bureau of Labor Statistics, 2010). From 1993 through 1999, an annual average of 1.7 million people were victims of violent crime while at work in the United States (Bureau of Justice Statistics, 2001). The vast majority of these incidents were either simple assaults (75%) or aggravated assaults (19%; Bureau of Justice Statistics, 2001). While these statistics are staggering, it is widely believed that workplace violence is underreported. Most violent or threatening behavior—including threats, verbal abuse, hostility, and stalking—may not be reported until it reaches physical assault or more disruptive behavior.

Even though violent incidents at work are underreported, media accounts of the most sensational attacks are often over reported, creating the false perception that certain types of violent events occur more often than they do. The archetypal news account of a disgruntled worker exacting revenge on his bosses or colleagues via mass shooting is actually quite rare. Only four percent of people murdered at work are killed by another employee (Toscano & Webber, 1995). Rather, fatalities overwhelmingly result from assaults by nonemployee criminals, such as armed robbers. Moreover, most women murdered at work are killed by their partner or a stalker, not a coworker (Swanberg, Logan & Macke, 2005).

It is clear that workplace violence presents a variety of challenges— humane, economic, legal, and reputational (Barling, Rogers & Kelloway, 2001; O'Leary- Kelly, Griffin & Glew, 1996; Schat & Kelloway, 2000). All organizations must address these challenges to ensure a productive workplace. This chapter explores violence in the workplace and provides suggestions for both preventing violent incidents and preparing for their aftermath. The first section of this chapter defines workplace violence, discusses highrisk occupations, explores the causes of and conditions for violence, and presents some of the costs of workplace violence. Next, we offer suggestions for preventing workplace violence. Finally, we address the aftermath of a violent event, including how to ameliorate harmful repercussions, address legal authorities and the media, and resume operations.

Defining Workplace Violence

Workplace violence is behavior carried out with the intent, or apparent intent, to cause physical pain or injury to another person in the workplace (Greenberg & Barling, 1999; Schat & Kelloway, 2005). Violent behaviors include hitting, kicking, pushing, biting, scratching, sexual attacks, and other similar acts (Hewitt & Levin, 1997). While this includes physical assaults and threats of violence, it does not include other forms of workplace aggression, such as bullying or certain antisocial behaviors. Our treatment of the workplace violence descriptor should not be confused with such issues as workplace incivility (Andersson & Pearson, 1999), antisocial work behavior (Giacalone & Greenberg, 1997; O'Leary-Kelly, Paetzold & Griffin, 2000), bullying (Einarsen, 1999; Hoel, Rayner & Cooper, 1999; Rayner & Cooper, 2006; Zapf, Einarsen, Hoel & Vartia, 2003), and workplace harassment (Rospenda, 2002; Rospenda & Richman, 2005). Our contention is that these actions should be considered under the broader term workplace aggression, which encompasses all activities meant to harm another at work (Neuman & Baron, 1998).

In contrast, we treat workplace violence as a more discrete term reserved for inherently violent behavior. Several factors distinguish workplace violence from aggression, especially the intent of the perpetrators and the severity of their behavior (Anderson & Bushman, 2002; Greenberg & Barling, 1999; Kraus, Blander & McArthur, 1995; Neuman & Baron, 1998). The discussion and analysis presented in this chapter are limited to workplace violence.

After a series of violent attacks by postal employees in the mid 1990s inspired heightened academic interest in this issue, the California Occupational Safety and Health Administration (Cal/OSHA) developed a model that delineated three forms of workplace violence, based on the perpetrator's relationship to either the victim or the workplace (Cal/OSHA, 1995; Howard, 1996). This typology was later modified to separate the third category into two, creating the current four-category system recognized by Barling, Dupre, and Kelloway (2009) and the U.S. Department of Justice (2004). We will briefly review the four broad categories, referred to as Types I—IV, before providing a more detailed analysis of each.

Type I workplace violence occurs when the offender has no legitimate relationship with the victimized employees or organization and enters the workplace to commit a criminal act such as armed robbery, terrorism/protest violence, and random violence. Type II is violence caused by the workplace's customers while being served; perpetrators generally include customers, clients, inmates, students, or patients and their families while victims include clerks, nurses, social workers, teachers, and guards. Type III occurs when the perpetrator is a current or former employee who targets other past or present employees. For example, sexual harassment at work falls into this category. Type IV violence arises from a non-work relationship between the perpetrator (such as a current or former spouse, relative, friend, or acquaintance) and an employee.

We will now examine these four types of violence in greater detail, including their prevalence, common causes, event characteristics, the motivations of offenders, and the types of people who become perpetrators.

Type I—Criminal Intent

Type I violence occurs when a perpetrator who has no legitimate relationship to the workplace enters the affected workplace to commit a robbery or other criminal act. Noteworthy is that more than 65% of workplace homicides occur during a robbery (Sygnatur & Toscano, 2000).

Four factors best predict the risk of external violence: (1) a large amount of cash or valuables on site, (2) few employees on site at one time, (3) extensive evening hours, and (4) face-to-face contact between customers and staff (Mayhew, 2002). While the perpetrator may assume the role of a customer to gain entry, he or she has no legitimate commercial purpose and instead is generally seeking cash or valuables. During the commission of the crime, employees or bystanders are injured or killed. Retail robberies resulting in workplace assaults usually occur between 11 PM and 6 AM and are most often armed.

Because of the cash on site, banks, post offices, casinos, liquor stores, armored vehicles, and service stations are likely targets of external violence (McCarthy & Mayhew, 2004). Retail stores, bars, restaurants, convenience stores, and gas stations are at increased risk because of their late hours, short shifts, and cash transactions (Casteel & Peek-Asa, 2000; LeBlanc & Kelloway, 2002). Beyond cashiers, many victims of late night retail violence are supervisors or proprietors attacked while locking their establishment for the night or assaulted while cleaning the establishment after-hours. Assaults on taxicab drivers involve a similar pattern: an assailant pretending to be a passenger, late into the night, hails the taxicab only to rob the driver. Likewise, security guards risk assault while protecting valuable property that attracts the perpetrators of armed robberies.

Type II—Customer and Client Violence

Unlike the Type I perpetrator who lacks any legitimate commercial purpose for entering the workplace, the next type of violence involves the people whom employees serve—clients, customers, and the public.

A Type II workplace violence event involves an assault by the recipient of a service provided by the affected workplace or the victim. Even though Type I violence represents the most common type of fatal event, fatal Type II events involving victims who provide services to the public are increasing. In 1993, fatal Type II events accounted for 3% of workplace homicides (CAL/OSHA, 1995). Unlike Type I events which often represent irregular occurrences in the life of at-risk establishments, Type II events occur on a daily basis in many service establishments, and therefore represent a more persistent risk for many service providers.

Type II events involve fatal or nonfatal injuries to individuals who provide professional, public safety, or administrative services to the public. The assailant is a current or former client, patient, customer, criminal suspect, or prisoner. Occasionally Type II violence occurs when a family member of clients or patients acts aggressively towards an employee. Type II events involve assaults on

1. Law enforcement and correctional personnel;
2. Medical care providers in hospitals, long-term care facilities, outpatient clinics, and home health services;
3. Mental health and psychiatric care providers in inpatient facilities, outpatient clinics, and residential sites;
4. Alcohol and drug treatment providers;
5. Social welfare service providers in unemployment offices, welfare eligibility offices, homeless shelters, probation offices, and child welfare agencies and;
6. Teaching, administrative, and support staff in schools where students have a history of violent behavior.

Law enforcement officers experience the fourth highest annual rate of nonfatal violent victimizations in the workplace (126 per 1,000 officers; Duhart, 2001). Law enforcement personnel are at risk of assault from public safety violators (suspicious persons, detainees, or arrestees) when making arrests, conducting raids, responding to calls involving robberies or domestic disputes, serving warrants and eviction notices, and investigating suspicious vehicles. Similarly, correctional personnel are at risk of assault while guarding or transporting jail or prison inmates.

In health care settings, nurses face the highest rates of nonfatal workplace assault (Duhart, 2001; Lanza, Zeiss & Rierdan, 2006; Winstanley & Whittington, 2004). Duhart reports 21.9 victimizations per 1,000 nurses per year between 1993 and 1999—twice the rate reported by other medical professionals (2001). And in a 2001 survey of 4,826 nurses conducted by the American Nurses Association, 17% reported that they had been physically assaulted within the past year (Gilmore-Hall & Worthington, 2001). Furthermore, fewer than 20% of the nurses surveyed reported that they felt safe in their current work environments.

The patient–health care provider relationship is fraught with violence issues. The majority of aggressive incidents are committed by patients and to a lesser extent, visitors. (NIOSH, 2002). Incidents are most likely to occur in psychiatric wards, emergency departments, waiting rooms, and geriatric units (Dalphond, Gessner, Giblin, Hijazzi & Love, 2000; Erickson & Williams-Evans, 2000; NIOSH, 2002; Taylor, 2000). Patients can develop aggressive and violent behavior, often as a consequence of illness and the stress of being sick and needing care. The feelings of helplessness, deterioration of physical status, depression, and mental illness exacerbated by physical illness, loss of social support, and financial losses, are all factors that can contribute to aggressive behavior. Health care workers who treat individuals experiencing a life threatening or life-altering crisis are at risk for assault and other types of violence. Patients and family members may become aggressive when frustrated with long waits or limits on their behavior such as the being asked not to smoke or talk on a cell phone. Patients who are involuntarily admitted are more likely to behave aggressively (LeBlanc, Dupre & Barling, 2006).

Teachers also have a high annual rate of nonfatal violent victimizations in the workplace (23 per 1,000; Duhart, 2001). The most at-risk teachers include special education and junior high teachers, followed by high school teachers (Duhart, 2001). Other teachers at risk for violence and assault are men who teach in urban junior high and high schools (National Center for Education Statistics, 2000) and teachers perceived as particularly strict (Hoffman, 1996). Several factors influence attacks on teachers. Verbal or physical maltreatment (such as sarcasm, ridicule, and name calling) of students by school staff, including teachers, principals, and support staff, may influence children to become violent (Hyman, 1998). Student involvement in gangs is also associated with school violence (Hoffman, 1996; Verlinden, Hersen & Thomas, 2000), as is student use of drugs or alcohol (Hoffman, 1996). A chronic preoccupation with weapons (Pastor, 1995) and the presence of impulsive behavior (Pastor, 1995; Verlinden, Hersen & Thomas, 2000) are also indicators of possible student violence.

Overall, risk factors for Type II violence include working alone or in high crime areas, having drugs or alcohol on site, the workplace having a social or legal regulatory role, and situations where there are conflicting expectations regarding the service being provided.

Type III—Employee-on-Employee Violence

Type III workplace violence consists of an assault on one or more employees by an individual currently or previous employed by the organization. This type of workplace violence can capture a significant amount of media attention and is often mischaracterized as representing "the" workplace violence problem. In fact, it is the media visibility which makes this type of violence appear more common than it actually is. Recent data shows that more employees experience Type I or II violence—aggression at the hands of organizational outsiders (customers or strangers)—than at the hands of subordinates, peers, and supervisors (Barling, Dupre & Kelloway, 2009). While estimates of insider violence range from 4%–15% of total workplace homicides (Braverman, 1999; Sygnatur &Toscano, 2000), insider aggression still deserves attention.

Generally, a Type III event involves a physical act of violence resulting in a fatal or nonfatal injury to an employee of the affected workplace by a current or former employee. At first glance, a Type III assailant's actions may defy reasonable explanation. Often, though, his or her actions are motivated by perceived difficulties in his or her relationship with the victim (such as abusive supervision), or with the affected workplace (perceived injustice), and by psychosocial factors which are specific to the assailant (attitudes toward revenge, self-control; Inness, Barling & Turner, 2005). Type III violence usually occurs after a layoff, a disciplinary hearing, an argument with coworkers, or failure to secure a raise or promotion.

Type IV—Intimate Partner Violence

Unlike Type I and Type II violence, which are prevalent in high-risk workplaces such as the retail and transportation industries (Type I), and the public health and safety industries (Type II), there is little evidence to suggest that there are differences between occupations in terms of their likelihood of Type III coworker violence. In this way, it is similar to Type IV, or Interpersonal Relationship Violence, which typically occurs across all industry sectors. While strangers, clients, or coworkers act as the aggressor in the first three types of workplace violence, Type IV violence involves an assault on an employee at his or her workplace by someone he or she knows well. This person is often a family member and usually a current or former spouse or lover.

Intimate partner violence (IPV), also called domestic violence or spouse abuse, is violence committed by a spouse, ex-spouse, or current or former boyfriend or girlfriend (National Center for Injury Prevention and Control, 2003). IPV can occur among married or unmarried couples, it can involve opposite-sex couples or same-sex couples, and victims of IPV can be male or female. In some cases IPV might be categorized as Type III violence (for instance when both intimate partners work for the same employer), however, most IPV falls into the Type IV category. Lifetime prevalence rates of partner violence have been estimated at 25% for women and 8% for men (Tjaden & Thoennes, 2000), and between 1% and 3% of all incidents of workplace violence are perpetrated by intimate acquaintances of the victim (Duhart, 2001). Approximately 20% of all fatal work-related injuries to female employees are committed by an intimate partner (Swanberg, Logan & Macke, 2005).

IPV shifts from a purely domestic conflict to a workplace concern when the aggressive altercations occur at the workplace. For many individuals, partners or family members know where an individual works and his or her schedule. The workplace may be the easiest location to find individuals since they often maintain their employment after they separate from their partner. IPV is exhibited in at least three ways in the workplace: work disruption, stalking, and on-the-job harassment (Swanberg, Macke & Logan, 2006). Work disruption consists of activities that interfere with attendance or promptness at work. Stalking includes unwanted and repeated threatening behaviors such as following someone, vandalizing property, or leaving unwanted messages. On-the-job harassment typically involves the perpetrator appearing at the workplace and directly interfering with the victim's work (Barling, Dupre & Kelloway, 2009). While many of these behaviors are not considered physical forms of assault, the history of violence in the relationship or the threat of harm may increase the fear of Type IV violence for an individual.

Although all forms of workplace violence are challenging for employers, IPV has some unique characteristics that make it particularly challenging to manage. First, employers may be uncertain about their responsibilities since IPV originates outside of the workplace. The absence of clear employment laws or guidelines further exacerbates the problem. Second, compared to other victims of workplace violence, IPV victims are more likely to be reluctant to report experienced violence to their supervisors due to embarrassment or job insecurity (Shepard & Pence, 1988). Lastly, as we will discuss, prevention efforts are likely to be different than those used for other types of workplace violence.

Nonetheless, intimate partner violence is similar to other forms of violence in several significant ways. First, it has negative effects on both the targeted employees and on the employing organization. Second, it can have detrimental effects on coworkers who witness or hear about the violence. Third, through the general duty clause of OSHA, employers are responsible for keeping employees safe from known hazards and risks, regardless of the source of violence (O'Leary-Kelly, Bowes-Sperry, Bates & Lean, 2009).

The Impact of Workplace Violence

Regardless of the type of workplace violence, any incident can cause significant monetary and non-monetary costs. While the exact cost of WPV is difficult to calculate because one must take into account several factors, including easily measurable as well as less concrete costs, a violent incident at the workplace can lead to a variety of financial repercussions. One measurable cost is the likelihood of an increase in claims for workers' compensation.

These claims will affect both injured employees and any other employees who witnessed or were traumatized by the violent incident. A second financial cost emerges when we consider that medical claims for stress-related illnesses as well as psychological counseling for employees could increase after the violent incident. A third cost, the replacement of damaged equipment and facilities may be unavoidable. A fourth cost, lost sales or drop in stock price, can occur if a company must close its site for a period of time after a violent incident. Additionally, customers may cancel orders or postpone purchases in the wake of bad publicity or a business closing. Lastly, litigation costs may increase financial losses significantly.

Organizations may incur additional losses that are more difficult to calculate. First, managers may spend more time dealing with the aftermath of the event rather than handling their normal responsibilities. They may be responding to media requests, planning the organization's reaction, and meeting to help the organization return to normalcy. Second, lost time and absenteeism following a violent incident, as well as a decrease in productivity, can increase the cost incurred after an incident. Third, negative publicity, though hard to quantify, can have a residual effect on the company's financial recovery. Lastly, when in a reactive mode in the wake of a violent incident, an organization may spend excessively to prevent a recurrence of workplace violence by incurring costs for consultants, training programs, enhanced security, and improved safety procedures (Schneid, 1999).

There are also non-monetary damages such as attitudinal, behavioral, and health outcomes. Violence can also lead to the loss of current workforce as well as the loss of future workforce. For example, Type I violence has been linked to turnover intentions (LeBlanc & Kelloway, 2002). Likewise, outsider initiated violence (Type I) and co-worker violence (Type III) are significantly related to job satisfaction, affective commitment, turnover, general health, emotional exhaustion, depression, and decreases in job performance (Hershcovis & Barling, 2010; LeBlanc & Kelloway, 2002). Regardless of who commits the aggressive act, victims and bystanders experience violent behavior as a stressor (Grandey, Dickter & Sin, 2004; Grandey, Cordeiro & Michael, 2007; Hershcovis & Barling, 2010).

Preventing Workplace Violence

Workplace violence can cause severe harm to employees and the organization, yet over 70% of U.S. workplaces do not have a formal program or policy that addresses workplace violence (Survey of Workplace Violence Prevention, 2005 BLS). One major component of any workplace violence program is prevention. Prevention programs and policies are important for any workplace, regardless of the type of violence. Research indicates that when employees believe the organization will take some form of action against workplace aggression, there is a reduction in the occurrence of workplace aggression (Barling, Dupre & Kelloway, 2009).

Braverman (1999) suggests guidelines to reduce the likelihood of violence in almost any workplace setting:

1. Secure support from the leadership of the organization and from the union if applicable.
2. Form a team to design audit process, craft policy, and oversee program training. The team should be composed of a spectrum of professionals: health and safety, legal, human relations, labor relations, employee assistance, union, and operations personnel. Team appointments should include top leaders.
3. Perform a workplace violence audit risk. Address security, organizational structure and culture, existing policies, employee opinions and concerns, and past experience with conflict.
4. Develop policies and procedures; include a definition of workplace violence for employees. Consider setting a zero-tolerance policy and range of consequences. Specify reporting procedure, ensuring safety from retaliation for reporters.
5. Arrange for easy and non-punitive access to medical and mental health services in the event of a violent incident.
6. Set clear and fair policies and procedures for terminations and layoffs.

In the next section, we further explore some of the strategies for preventing workplace violence. We will first review some strategies that can be employed across many settings, regardless of the type of violence. Then, we will more closely examine suggestions for dealing with each of the four types of violence. Prevention strategies can generally be divided into three categories: environmental; organizational and administrative; and behavioral and interpersonal (Wassell, 2009).

Environmental Strategies

Environmental strategies are physical modifications such as bulletproof glass or extra lighting around entrances designed to deter violence or protect employees from a violent attack. Environmental designs have been shown to deter robbery and violence, accordingly reducing the frequency of injury and homicide at work. Environmental practices can vary and may include the installation of security cameras, employee access badges, alarm and intercom systems, and emergency buttons that silently alert the authorities. The majority of these precautions are designed to guard against "outsiders." However, security impacts the workplace in other ways. For example, if employees feel unsafe at work they may carry weapons for their own protection, which may further contribute to acts of violence (Rai, 2002). A combination of environmental designs, implemented simultaneously, proves to be the best approach for reducing incidence of workplace violence. However, even single interventions such as the use of a limited cash-handling policy, effective lighting, or having a security guard present, have demonstrated effectiveness in reducing workplace violence. Indeed, the failure of smaller businesses to implement preventive environmental designs has limited efforts to reduce injury and homicide rates in the workplace (Peek-Asa et al., 2004).

Organizational and Administrative Strategies

As discussed by Benson, Hanley, and Scroggins in this volume, organizational and/or administrative strategies include developing programs and policies to promote a safe working environment (such as eliminating solitary work at night in convenience stores). There are several areas in which organizational administrations can implement policies and procedures to prevent violence. These include employee selection procedures, employee assistance programs, and employee termination policies.

Employee Selection. As previously mentioned, profiling potential aggressors has significant pitfalls. Perhaps because of the seeming simplicity of being able to exclude violent individuals from organizations, the notion of profiling potentially aggressive employees during the selection process is often touted as a way of limiting workplace aggression. The use of background data as a predictor of on-the-job performance has a long history in employment settings and significant attention has focused on using this data in screening for violence prone employees. In addition to personnel screening, some organizations also use other screening devices, such as pre-employment tests that measure propensity towards physical assault, hostility, thrill seeking, trouble with authority, intentional damage, or hostile customer relations. (Rai, 2002). However, attempts to profile potentially aggressive employees are not supported by empirical evidence. There is no single variable, or combination of variables, that have sufficient predictive power to make this process empirically or ethically sound (Barling, Dupre & Kelloway, 2009).

Employee Assistance Programs. Employee support is an important prevention strategy for dealing with a broad range of factors related to preexisting conditions, intervening processes, and behavioral responses. Employee Assistance Programs (EAPs) represent an effort to address employee problems before they intensify and possibly culminate in violence. With respect to specific employee problems that relate to violence, EAPs may help address problems related to alcohol and substance abuse. EAPs may also be useful in addressing problems related to stress, depression, and domestic violence, which have also been linked to workplace violence (Rai, 2002).

Termination Policies. Terminations are extremely stressful events for those being discharged, those who must carry out the dismissals, and in many cases, those remaining employed. The loss of a job can mean more than just the loss of a salary in that it can lead to personal disorientation, challenges to self-identity, changes in daily schedule, and the end of a social network (Fineman, 1983). It is critical for organizations to consider the magnitude of loss that termination has for employees and be proactive in helping employees through the process.

Layoffs should be conducted with dignity and respect. Employers should behave with as much interactional justice as possible, and with consistency, transparency, and an unbiased layoff policy to increase procedural justice (Hemingway & Conte, 2003). Actions like confiscating keys or having people escorted off site are demeaning and likely to increase hostility. Instead, when possible, employees should be allowed to say farewell to coworkers and remove their belongings.

In the case of planned downsizing and layoffs, an effort to help employees with outplacement, counseling, and other related services are useful. The manager responsible for releasing the employee should provide details about procedures for termination, benefits, unemployment benefits, and outplacement services. Recent evidence suggests that after reductions in force, those remaining look to each other for cues on how to respond. To the extent that this is true, unfair treatment may result in widespread discontent and, potentially, increased levels of aggression (Rai, 2002). Managers or human relations professionals should provide guidance on how to react, rather than leaving terminated and remaining employees at a loss for how to proceed.

Behavioral and Interpersonal Strategies

The third category of strategies focuses on behavioral and interpersonal interventions that involve activities such as training staff to anticipate, recognize, and respond to conflict and violence in the work place. Training is a critical component of any prevention strategy. Training is necessary for employees, supervisors, and staff members in any office that may be involved in responding to an incident of workplace violence. Training may make incidents less likely, help employees identify potentially dangerous situations, and provide guidance for organizational leadership and managers on how to actively prevent violence. Providing appropriate training informs employees that management will take threats seriously, encourages employees to report incidents, and demonstrates management's commitment to deal with reported incidents.

To decrease the likelihood of an incident, formal training can provide individuals with skills that are useful in defusing, managing, and responding to aggression. For example, one major reason why individuals become involved in repeated aggressive encounters is that they are severely lacking in basic social skills. Such persons are often insensitive to the emotions of others and are unable to express their wishes or refuse requests in a way that that does not anger others (Rai, 2002). In addition to social skill training, instruction in conflict management, interpersonal communication, and stress management are effective in reducing interpersonal aggression.

A comprehensive violence prevention program includes instruction on how to identify potentially violent individual situations. As previously mentioned, organizations cannot consistently, correctly predict violence and there is no specific profile of a potentially dangerous individual. However, indicators of increased risk of violent behavior have been identified by the Federal Bureau of Investigation's National Center for the Analysis of Violent Crime, Profiling and Behavioral Assessment Unit (1990). Some of these indicators are

1. direct or veiled threats of harm;
2. behaviors comprised of intimidation, belligerence, harassment, and bullying;
3. unresolved conflicts with supervisors or coworkers;
4. bringing a weapon to the workplace, making inappropriate reference to guns, or exhibiting a fascination with weapons;
5. statements showing unusual interest in incidents of workplace violence;
6. statements indicating approval of the use of violence to resolve a problem or identifying with perpetrators of workplace homicides;
7. drug or alcohol abuse; and
8. extreme changes in behaviors.

Each of these behaviors is a signal that something is wrong. By identifying the problem and dealing with it appropriately, managers may be able to prevent violence from happening (Rai, 2002). Along with training to identify potential issues, managers should receive training that includes basic leadership skills such as setting clear standards, addressing employee problems promptly, using a probationary period, performance counseling, discipline, and other management tools consciously. These interventions can keep difficult situations from turning into major problems.

Many of the aforementioned environmental, administrative, and behavioral strategies will help prevent workplace violence in most situations. There are also strategies specific to the four types of violence.

Strategies for Preventing Type I Violence

There are environmental, administrative, and behavioral strategies that may limit outsider aggression. One environmental tactic is to increase visibility. Cameras and bullet-proof partitions can be installed in taxis and chauffeured cars as well as emergency lights on rooftops (LeBlanc, Dupre & Barling, 2006). Retail locations should keep windows clear of signs and displays as there are fewer robberies when visibility is increased. Such locations should also have ample lighting inside and outside of the store and keep the cash register in a location visible from the outside. Similarly, greeting customers and making eye contact may deter offenders by making them feel conspicuous (Desroches, 1995; Gabor & Normandeau, 1989).

Policies that administrations should put into place to reduce outsider attacks often involve policies around money handling since most Type I attacks involve robbery or attempted robbery. One policy involves reducing rewards by installing cashless payment systems in stores and cars (Mayhew, 2000a). Best practices include keeping minimal amounts of cash on hand, using drop safes to remove cash from circulation, and posting signage that minimal cash is on hand and a safe is in use (Desroches, 1995; Gill, 2000). Another common policy for retail, security, and other occupations at risk of Type I violence is to routinely check on employees who work alone (Mayhew, 2000b). Training that may be of use for reducing Type I violence is safety training. Taxi and truck drivers should be knowledgeable about policies and safety equipment (such as locking doors when in line for passengers). Retail clerks should receive training that informs them to cooperate with robbers; cooperative employees sustain fewer injuries (Faulkner, Landsittel & Hendricks, 2001). Employees should keep their hands in sight, tell the robber what they are doing, move slowly, and activate a silent alarm only when it is safe to do so (Tyler, 1999). Because most Type I violence involves cash exchanges rather than personal motives, most prevention involves changes to security in the physical environment and attention to safety procedures that protect from external threats.

Strategies for Preventing Type II Violence

Environmental tactics for preventing violence in client-care settings like hospitals include installing metal detectors, security cameras, bullet resistant glass around nurses' stations, lighting inside and out, curved mirrors at hall intersections, and card controlled access at restricted areas. Waiting rooms can be designed to limit aggressive behavior. To avoid additional irritation and frustration during long waits, waiting rooms should be painted in soothing colors and contain reading material and toys for children. In addition, waiting rooms should be furnished with lightweight furniture with few sharp corners. Furniture should be arranged so personnel cannot be trapped in a room. Emergency rooms should have at least two exits and panic phones.

Organizational and administrative strategies to consider include developing and posting acceptable behavior policies, taking threats seriously, and flagging the charts of high-risk patients (Kelloway, Barling & Hurrell, 2006). Identification badges should be issued to staff and visitor passes to guests so that employees and security personnel know who belongs in the facility and who does not. The amount of personal information on an identification tag should be limited as a perpetrator may only need a last name or Social Security number to discover where that person lives. Other administrative strategies include promoting pairs of workers in high-risk situations, rather than having an employee work alone, and allowing employees to carry mobile phones when working in a non-secure location.

Behavioral and interpersonal tactics include training employees on conflict management and resolution, recognizing agitation, and responding to aggressive behavior (DelBel, 2003; OSHA, 2004; Wassell, 2009). One way hospital staff can lessen the tension in a waiting room is to provide estimates of wait times and explanations for those times.

Strategies for Preventing Type III Violence

Strategies for preventing Type III violence can be particularly nuanced, as the potential offender is a coworker or former coworker. Profiling potential perpetrators is fraught with problems, including ethical and legal concerns. After a violent episode occurs, it may be easy to reflect on selective details and categorize the assailant into a profile, but most people who match many of the items on a profile will never become violent. There are more productive strategies for preventing Type III violence via environmental, administrative, and behavioral approaches.

Because the perpetrator of Type III violence, by definition, is someone who works or worked at the organization, the environmental strategies that aim to prevent the entrance of a violent individual or to provide barriers that protect the possible victims are somewhat limited. However, action should be taken to prevent the entrance of visibly angry workers in a manner that deescalates the situation. Likewise, after layoffs, it may be advisable to remove building access from laid-off employees during normal working hours. Caution should be taken so that actions taken to prevent violence do not in fact contribute to a situation of tension.

Simple administrative actions can help prevent coworker violence at work. As evident from the earlier discussion, having a written policy in place is a best practice for preventing violence. Address any act of violence or aggression, even minor events, to reinforce your policies and emphasize that aggressive behavior is not tolerated. Clearly stating what workplace violence is, and what acceptable behaviors are, may help employees understand what type of behavior to report, which may prevent violence.

Behavioral interventions can also help prevent Type III violence. Training managers to maintain open relationships with employees can help make sure everyone feels included in the organization. While profiling employees is discouraged, be aware of employees who

- mention they are being treated unfairly;
- begin to isolate themselves when they were previously social;
- have recently been disciplined;
- have an increase in drug or alcohol use;
- have an unexplained increase in absenteeism;
- overreact to a change in policies;
- make comments about righting past abuses;
- show empathy with violent individuals;
- reveal previous violent incidents or allude to future violent action; and
- mention that they are being forced to wait for action from management, such as a promotion or raise. (Braverman, 1999)

While most employee grievances do not escalate to violence, violent incidents often follow a trigger that pushes an at-risk employee to extreme behavior.

Problems with Profiling. A troubling result of the singular focus of the media on sensationalized shootings has been the creation not only of a stereotypical event but also a stereotypical perpetrator: the loner, a white, middle-aged male struggling through divorce or separation and often enchanted with firearms. First, the handful of events that underpin this profile are too few to create a legitimately predictable pattern. Second, this type of event is such a rare manifestation of workplace violence that this profile crowds out potentially useful behavioral patterns that offer greater insight into more common types of workplace violence.

More broadly, however, the ultimate flaw with profiling is not the misleading profile that predominates. Rather, the problem is that employers cannot use profiling effectively to select their employees; they cannot use this information to weed out people likely to cause or inspire violence. Employers can, and do, request information regarding an applicant's criminal history. But this can be an overly broad measure that would unfairly penalize reformed former criminals. It can also be unduly narrow, as it would be limited to recidivists and could never hope to detect a future criminal.

Third, obtaining information from potential employees about their history in relation to violent behavior is a difficult process. Even if the selection process is rigorous, a candidate is unlikely to admit to these often socially undesirable characteristics. In addition, possession of these characteristics does not indicate that candidates will inevitably become violent. Further, if an organization were to screen candidates based on these characteristics, they would be likely to exclude good employees based on improbable outcomes. Privacy rights and legal concerns make it difficult for employers to discover whether potential employees possess violent tendencies. Fear of lawsuits can make past employers reluctant to provide negative references (Howard, 2001; Sovereign, 1994). Moreover, little action can be taken with this information that does not open a host of legal, ethical, and practical problems.

The literature on predicting Type III violence focuses on the complex contextual and individual causes of a violent incident. These causes include precipitating situations, personality, stressors, availability of weapons, and more. While violence of this type is often mentioned in the media, it is the least prevalent of the four types (Braverman, 1999; Sygnatur & Toscano, 2000).

Strategies for Preventing Type IV Violence

Because of the degree of difference in origin and root causes of IPV, prevention efforts compared to those for other forms of workplace violence are different and more removed from the organization's typical purview. For example, employers who want to prevent Type III violence often focus on job and work environment factors such as fair treatment in termination and additional lighting (Litzky, Eddelston & Kidder, 2006). Such efforts, however, will be ineffective in regard to IPV, given its distinct source and causes.

Employee assistance programs (EAP) are one of the most useful resources for IPV (Pollack, Austin & Grisso, 2010). An EAP provides employees and their family members with help to resolve personal or work-related problems. EAP services include free, voluntary, short-term counseling and referral services for various issues affecting employee mental and emotional well-being (including alcohol and other substance abuse, stress, grief, family problems, and psychological disorders). In addition, workplace managers and supervisors are likely to refer women affected by IPV to the EAP for assistance. The potential of EAPs to assist employees during crises and their capacity to develop educational programs and policies to address IPV suggest that EAPs are well positioned to address IPV.

EAPs are in a unique position to work with employers to create strategies to increase employee awareness of both the nature and problem of IPV and services for IPV victims. EAPs could develop campaigns to educate managers and workers about the warning signs that an employee is being battered and abused. They could also work with workplace security programs to enhance the visibility of IPV victim services and assistance. In addition, EAPs can ensure that workers are aware of their services. Estimates are that on average 6%–10% of employees use EAP services (Pollack, Austin & Grisso, 2010).

In addition to helping the victim of IPV via the EAP, organizations can prevent domestic violence from spilling into the workplace by encouraging open communication, ensuring manager involvement early on, taking team action by confidentially involving supervisors—the HR director or head of security—and by being familiar with the law (Braverman, 1999). Further, organizations can educate and raise awareness of IPV, improve screening for IPV, and address perpetrators with a no tolerance policy.

Post-Incident Management

Even the best prevention tactics will not be able to prevent every violent incident in the workplace. During an incident, fear and confusion may run high. Employee and manager responses may be automatic—ensuring their own, coworker, and bystander safety, and alerting the authorities. The location must be secured so that no additional employees and customers are injured. The authorities may need information so they can subdue the aggressor. Likewise, medical personnel will need to provide care to injured individuals.

After an incident, there are several steps an organization can take to ameliorate further harm to employees and the organization, address legal authorities and the media, and resume operations. We will now review suggestions for post-incident management.

Preparing a Response

Developing a post-incident response before an incident occurs is essential. The scene immediately following a violent episode is chaotic—news reporters are swarming, law enforcement agents are investigating, and employees and their families are scared. Having a post-incident plan in place with detailed instructions readily accessible to employees allows for quick decisions and action. During a period of high stress it can be difficult to make rational decisions, and at a time like this, numerous decisions must be made. Having a post-incident response plan in place can protect human, financial, and infrastructure assets; provide direction for management, public relations representatives, and employees; and ease communication with law enforcement and the media.

A plan should include arrangements for alternative headquarters or meeting sites so that management can respond to the event and so essential work can continue. Pre-established agreements with vendors such as hazardous waste removal services, counseling or employee assistance programs, and legal counsel should be arranged and included in the plan (Heskett, 1996). Recovery plans should include contact information for all employees, names and numbers of family members, and vendor names and numbers. All personnel tasked with carrying out the plan should have an accessible copy and additional copies should be stored offsite.

Responding after an Incident

Organizational representatives should be prepared to respond promptly to law enforcement as well as legal inquiries. Organizations can prepare by knowing requirements and limitations and having these outlined in the post-incident plan. (Kelley & Mullen, 2006). For example, the Occupational Safety and Health Administration may require notification of injuries or fatalities. Having the reporting procedures outlined in the plan can expedite this process and facilitate compliance with regulations regarding when and how to report incidents. Internal or external legal assistance should be consulted before submitting documents and making public statements. Further, in the event of litigation, legal assistance may be required to review personnel records and document the scene of the incident (Schneid, 1999). Organizations may also want to communicate with stockholders to reassure them after the incident.

Responding to Media Coverage

Given the current 24-hour media cycle, it is likely that violent incidents at the workplace will be reported on the news. This type of coverage can have an impact on the organization as it creates impressions in the eyes of shareholders, competitors, future employees, those in the legal community, and the general public. Reporters may appear before emergency response professionals arrive. Newspapers and television stations usually have an employee designated to monitor police and fire radio channels; further, communications technology is so ubiquitous today that employees and bystanders may broadcast their experiences and rumors via mobile technology, or even upload videos to the internet.

Contrary to some beliefs, the media can be of tremendous assistance following a crisis. Nevertheless, having a detailed media coverage plan will help coordination with the press. Information in the first hours will be, at best, scarce and incomplete. Preparing to address the media after an incident could include preparing sound bites about your organization, identifying a media center on location and requiring that media remain in this area, and selecting a spokesperson. This person, and a back-up person, should be designated in the response plan so there is no question of to whom the media should speak. This person should be skilled in public relations and speaking. He or she should provide only facts, not opinions. Care must be taken not to provide assumptions or provide details that could later be used in litigation. If the suspect is an employee or former employee, do not discuss particulars about his or her history, especially performance related issues (Heskett, 1996). Rarely is "no comment" in the best interests of the company. Reporters are there to get the story, and if the story does not come from the organization's representative, reporters will look elsewhere for information.

Other employees should be instructed not to speak with the media. Most employees do not have experience dealing with the media, and though well intentioned, may not be fully informed, leading to the dissemination of statements that could cause unnecessary harm to coworkers, their families and the company. Employees should be told in advance not to respond to media inquiries (Heskett, 1996; Schneid, 1999).

Helping Employees Manage Stress Responses

Employees impacted by violent events at the workplace, either by witnessing an attack, or by loosing friends and acquaintances, will need time to recover. Support groups and counseling should be made available. People respond differently to traumatic events and recovery times may vary widely for individuals.

Experiencing a violent event can have long-lasting and devastating psychological effects. Symptoms associated with stress range from mild to disabling depending on a variety of factors involving both the characteristics of the victim and circumstances of the incident. Common psychological responses to threatening events can include shock, confusion, anxiety, fear, guilt, anger, sadness, and a sense of insecurity. Individuals may find themselves replaying the events in their mind. They may find they take extra precautions when engaging in activities that remind them of the event. Sleep disturbances and irritability may also occur. These responses are normal and may be relatively short lived as the person adjusts to the realities of the violent event and its aftermath. However, in some cases symptoms may persist longer than would normally be expected and may have a significant impact on social, occupational, or other aspects of the individual's life.

The most common debilitating consequences are Posttraumatic Stress Disorder (PTSD) and Acute Stress Disorder (ASD). The Diagnostic and Statistical Manual of Mental Disorders of the American Psychiatric Association defines PTSD as a syndrome consisting of three clusters of symptoms or signs: (a) repeated re-experiencing of the trauma, (b) emotional numbing and avoidance of activities associated with the traumatic event, and (c) heightened arousal in such forms as exaggerated startle response or insomnia (American Psychiatric Association [DSM-IV-TR], 2000). Diagnosis of PTSD requires symptoms be present at least a month after the event and cause significant distress or impairment in functioning. Post-traumatic stress disorder can manifest a variety of symptoms including recurring dreams about the incident, elevated levels of anxiety, fear, loss, guilt, flashbacks, and reoccurrence of the distress felt at the time of the incident.

ASD results from similar types of traumatic stressors, diagnosed if an individual manifests at least three dissociative symptoms, such as a re-experiencing of the traumatic events, marked avoidance, and marked hyperarousal. ASD differs from PTSD in two ways. First, the problem must last at least two days and no more than 4 weeks (after which PTSD diagnosis may be made). Second, ASD criteria emphasize dissociative reactions, including emotional numbing or detachment, reduced awareness of surroundings, derealization, depersonalization, and amnesia for aspects of the traumatic events. PTSD does not require individual display these dissociative symptoms.

Employees who do not experience PTSD or ASD may still have problems returning to "business as usual." They may experience some of the previously named symptoms, or may feel depressed, excited, or distracted. While people differ as to how they best work through or deal with a trauma, many will find that talking it through with friends or a professional will help them regain perspective and a sense of normalcy. Others, however, may find that talking about the event is not helpful. Effort should be made to use care in creating a workplace environment where the wishes of those not wanting to discuss the event are respected. Additionally, talking about the event, or suppressing feelings about the event, can lead to employees expending a great deal of energy—which in turn, can lead to a loss of productivity. To minimize the emotional and economic impact of work place violence, it is important to have measures in place, such as support groups and EAPs, to address employee's emotional responses (Hesket, 1996).

Resuming Operations

At some point in time, the business must resume normal operations. While "normal" after the event may never revert to the "normal" before the event, the company, its employees, its stakeholders, and the community depend on the business resuming operations and fulfilling the needs of the customers. Those affected by violence may be changed by the events. Key people within the organization may have been lost. And management may struggle as it tries to provide leadership to a wounded organization. Expectations may need to be modified to allow for a gradual return to normality (Heskett, 1996). Security may need to be bolstered and facilities may need to be repaired. Employees should not be subjected to physical reminders of the event by seeing bullet holes or blood stains. The well being of employees, their families, community members, and the customers of the business should be taken into consideration.

Conclusion

It is clear that workplace aggression and violence is a growing concern for society. The magnitude of the problem is so high that approximately half a million workers annually lose 1.75 million days of work and more than $55 million in wages (Rai, 2002). The origins of the problem range widely: loss of personal autonomy, increased surveillance, cumulative physical and mental reactions, fatigue in a troubled economy, changing workforce demographics, anger, stress, and environmental conditions at work. Prevention strategies are important in curtailing the growing problem of workplace aggression and violence. A well-rounded prevention plan should include an increase in training, security, environmental modifications, policy revisions, and interpersonal finesse. Plans should also be made for a response in the event violence is not prevented. These strategies will contribute towards healthier work environments and stronger relationships between workers and employers.

REFERENCES

American Psychiatric Association. (2000). Diagnostic and statistical manual of mental disorders (Revised 4th ed.). Washington, DC: American Psychiatric Association.

Anderson, C. A., & Bushman, B. J. (2002). Human aggression. *Annual Review of Psychology, 53,* 27–51.

Andersson, L. M., & Pearson, C. M. (1999). Tit for tat? The spiraling effect of incivility in the workplace. *Academy of Management Review, 24,* 452–471.

Armour, S. (2004, July 14). Life after workplace violence. USA Today. http://www.usatoday.com/money/workplace/2004-07-14-after-violence_x.htm

Barling, J., Dupre, K. E., & Kelloway, E. K. (2009). Predicting workplace aggression and violence. *Annual Review of Psychology, 60,* 671–692.

Barling, J., Rogers, A. G., & Kelloway, E. K. (2001). Behind closed doors: In-home workers' experience of sexual harassment and work-place violence. *Journal of Occupational Health Psychology, 6,* 255–269.

Braverman, M. (1999). *Preventing workplace violence: A guide for employers and practitioners.* London: Sage.

Bureau of Justice Statistics (BJS). (2001). *Violence in the workplace, 1993–1999: Special report from the National Crime Victimization Survey.* Washington, DC: U.S. Department of Justice, Bureau of Justice Statistics

Bureau of Labor Statistics (BLS). (2010). *Fact sheet: Workplace shootings.* Washington, DC: U.S. Department of Labor, Bureau of Labor Statistics.

California Department of Occupational Safety and Health (1995). *Cal/OSHA Guidelines for Workplace Security.* Sacramento: California Division of Industrial Relations.

Casteel, C., & Peek-Asa, C. (2000). Effectiveness of Crime Prevention Through Environmental Design (CPTED) in reducing robberies. *American Journal of Preventative Medicine, 18,* 99–115.

Dalphond, D., Gessner, M., Giblin, E., Hijazzi, K., & Love, C. (2000). Violence against emergency nurses. *Journal of Emergency Nursing, 26,* 105.

DelBel, J. C. (2003). De-escalating workplace aggression. *Nursing Management, 34,* 31–34.

Desroches, F. J. (1995). *Force and fear: Robbery in Canada.* Scarborough, ON: Nelson Canada.

Duhart, D. T. (2001). *Bureau of Justice Statistics special report: National Crime Victimization Survey: Violence in the workplace, 1993–1999.* Washington, DC: U.S. Department of Justice.

Dupré, K. E., & Barling, J. (2006). Predicting and preventing supervisory workplace aggression. *Journal of Occupational Health Psychology, 11,* 13–26.

Einarsen, S. (1999). The nature and causes of bullying at work. *International Journal of Manpower, 20,* 16–27.

Erickson J. & Williams-Evans S. (2000) Attitudes of emergency nurses regarding patient assaults. *Journal of Emergency Nursing, 26,* 210–215.

Faulkner, K., Landsittel, D., & Hendricks, S. (2001). Robbery characteristics and employee injuries in convenience stores. *American Journal of Industrial Medicine, 40,* 703–709.

Fineman, S. (1983). *White collar unemployment: Impact and stress.* Chichester, UK: Wiley.

Gabor, T., & Normandeau, A. (1989). Preventing armed robbery though opportunity reduction: A critical analysis. *Journal of Security Administration, 12,* 3–18.

Giacalone R. A., & Greenberg, J. (1997). *Antisocial behavior in organizations.* Thousand Oaks. CA: Sage.

Gill, M. (2000). *Commercial robbery.* London: Blackstone.

Gilmore-Hall, A., & Worthington, K. (2001). Online health and safety survey. American Nurses Association. Retrieved from NursingWorld.org.

Grandey, A. A., Cordeiro, B. L., & Michael, J. H. (2007). Work-family supportiveness organizational perceptions: important for the well-being of male blue-collar hourly workers. *Journal of Vocational Behavior, 71,* 460–478.

Grandey, A. A., Dickter, D. N., & Sin, H. P. (2004). The customer is not always right: Customer aggression and emotion regulation of service employees. *Journal of Organizational Behavior, 25,* 397–418.

Greenberg, L., & Barling, J. (1999). Predicting employee aggression against coworkers, subordinates and supervisors: The roles of person behaviors and perceived work-place factors. *Journal of Organizational Behavior, 20,* 897–913.

Hemingway, M. A., & Conte, J. M. (2003). The perceived fairness of layoff practices. *Journal of Applied Social Psychology, 33,* 1588–1617.

Hershcovis, M. S., & Barling, J. (2010). Towards a multi-foci approach to workplace aggression: A meta-analytic review of outcomes from different perpetrators. *Journal of Organizational Behavior, 31,* 2444.

Heskett, S. (1996). *Workplace violence: Before, during and after.* Boston: Butterworth-Heinemann.

Hewitt, J. B., & Levin, P. F. (1997). Violence in the workplace: An integrative review. *Annual Review of Nursing Research, 15,* 81–99.

Hoel, H., Rayner, C., & Cooper, C. L. (1999). Workplace bullying. *International Review of Industrial and Organizational Psychology, 14,* 195–230.

Hoffman, A. (1996). *Schools, violence, and society.* Westport, CT: Greenwood.

Howard, J. (1996). State and local regulatory approaches to preventing WPV. *Occupational Medical State of the Art Reviews, 11,* 293–302.

Howard, J. L. (2001). Workplace violence in organizations: An exploratory study of organizational prevention techniques. *Employee Responsibilities and Rights Journal, 13,* 920–922.

Hyman, C. T. (1998). Violence among youth: A major epidemic in America. *International Journal of Adolescent Medicine and Health, 10,* 243–259.

Inness, M., Barling, J., & Turner, N. (2005). Understanding supervisor–targeted aggression: A within–person, between–jobs design. *Journal of Applied Psychology, 90,* 731–739.

Kelley, E., & Mullen, J. (2006). Organizational response to workplace violence. In E. K. Kelloway, J. Barling, & J. J. Hurrell, Jr. (Eds.), *Handbook of workplace violence* (pp. 493–516). Thousand Oaks, CA: Sage.

Kelloway, E. K., Barling, J., & Hurrell, J. J. (2006). *Handbook of workplace violence.* Thousand Oaks, CA: Sage.

Kraus, J. F., Blander, B., & McArthur, D. L. (1995). Incidence, risk factors, and prevention strategies for work-related assault injuries: A review of what is known, what needs to be known, and countermeasures for intervention. *Annual Review of Public Health, 16,* 355–379.

Lanza, M. L., Zeiss, R., & Rierdan, J. (2006). Violence against psychiatric nurses: Sensitive research as science and intervention. *Contemporary Nurse, 21,* 71–84.

LeBlanc, M. M., & Kelloway, E. K. (2002). Predictors and outcomes of workplace violence and aggression. *Journal of Applied Psychology, 87,* 444–453.

LeBlanc, M. M., Dupré, K. E., & Barling, J. (2006). Public-initiated violence. In E.K. Kelloway, J. Barling, & J. J., Jr. (Eds.), *Handbook of workplace violence* (pp. 261–280). Thousand Oaks, CA: Sage.

Lipsey, M. W., Wilson, D. B., Cohen, M. A., & Derzon, J. H. (1997). Is there a causal relationship between alcohol use and violence? A synthesis of evidence. *Recent Developments in Alcoholism 13*, 245–282.

Litzky, B. E., Eddelston, K. A., & Kidder, D. L. (2006). The good, the bad, and the misguided: How managers inadvertently encourage deviant behaviors. *Academy of Management Perspectives, 20*, 91–103.

Mayhew, C. (2002). Occupational violence in industrialized countries: types, incidence patterns and "at risk" groups of workers. In M. Gil, B. Fisher, and V. Bowie (Eds.), *Violence at Work: Causes, Patterns and Prevention* (pp. 21–40). Portland, OR: Willan.

Mayhew, C. (2000a). Preventing assaults on taxi drivers in Australia. *Trends and issues in Crime and Criminal Justice, 179*, 1–6.

Mayhew, C. (2000b). Violence in the workplace—preventing armed robbery: A practical handbook (Research and Public Policy Series, No 33.). Canberra, ACT: Australian Institute of Criminology.

McCarthy, P., & Mayhew, C. (2004). *Safeguarding the Organization against violence and bullying: An international perspective*. Hampshire, UK: Palgrave Macmillan

National Center for Education Statistics [NCES]. (2000). *Indicators of school crime and safety*. Washington, DC: U.S. Department of Education Institute of Education Sciences.

National Center for Injury Prevention and Control [NCIPC]. (2003). *Costs of intimate partner violence against women in the United States*. Atlanta: Centers for Disease Control and Prevention.

Neuman, J. H., & Baron, R. A. (1998). Workplace violence and workplace aggression: Evidence concerning specific forms, potential causes, and preferred targets. *Journal of Management, 24*, 391–419.

NIOSH. (2002). *Violence: Occupational hazards in hospitals* (DHHS Publication No. 2002–101). Washington, DC: U.S. Government Printing Office.

O'Leary-Kelly, A. M., Griffin, R. W., & Glew, D. J. (1996). Organization-motivated aggression: A research frame-work. *Academy of Management Review, 21*, 225–253.

O'Leary-Kelly, A. M., Paetzold, R. L., Griffin, R. W. (2000). Sexual harassment as aggressive behavior: An actor-based perspective. *Academy of Management Review, 25*, 372–388.

O'Leary-Kelly, A. M., Bowes-Sperry, L., Bates, C. A., & Lean, E. R. (2009). Sexual harassment at work: A decade (plus) of progress. *Journal of Management, 35*(3), 503–536.

Occupational Safety and Health Administration [OSHA]. (2004). *Guidelines for Preventing Workplace Violence for Health Care & Social Service Workers*. Washington, DC: U.S. Department of Labor Occupational Safety and Health Administration.

Pastor, L. (1995). Initial assessment and intervention strategies to reduce workplace violence. *American Family Physician, 52*, 1169–1174.

Peek-Asa, C., Casteel, C., Mineschian, L., Erickson, R. J., & Kraus, J. F. (2004). Compliance to a workplace violence prevention program in small businesses. *American Journal of Preventive Medicine, 26* (4), 276–283.

Pollack K. M., Austin W., Grisso J. A. (2010). Employee assistance programs: A workplace resource to address intimate partner violence. *Journal of Women's Health, 19*, 729–33.

Rai, S. (2002). Preventing workplace aggression and violence: A role for occupational therapy. *Work, 18*, 15–22.

Rayner, C. & Cooper, C. L. (2006). Workplace bullying. In K. E. Kelloway, J. Barling & J. J. Hurrell (Eds.), *Handbook of workplace violence* (pp. 121–145). Thousand Oaks, CA: Sage.

Rospenda, K. M. (2002). Workplace harassment, services utilization, and drinking outcomes. *Journal of Occupational Health Psychology, 7,* 141–155.

Rospenda, K. M. & Richman, J. A. (2005). Harassment and discrimination. In J. Barling , E. K. Kelloway, and M. R. Frone (Eds.), *Handbook of work stress.* Thousand Oaks, CA: Sage.

Schat, A. C. H., & Kelloway, E. K. (2000). The effects of perceived control on the outcomes of workplace aggression and violence. *Journal of Occupational Health Psychology, 4,* 386–402.

Schat, A. C. H., & Kelloway, E. K. (2005). Workplace aggression. In J. Barling, M. Frone, & E. K. Kelloway (Eds.), *Handbook of work stress* (pp. 189–218). Thousand Oaks, CA: Sage.

Schneid, T. D. (1999). *Occupational Health Guide to Violence in the Workplace.* Boca Raton, FL: CRC.

Shepard, M., & Pence, E. (1988). The effect of battering on the employment status of women. AFFILIA, *Journal of Women and Social Work, 3,* 55–61.

Sovereign, K. L. (1994). *Personnel law* (3rd ed.). Englewood Cliffs, NJ: Prentice Hall.

Swanberg, J. E., Macke, C., & Logan T. K. (2006). Intimate partner violence, women, and work: Coping on the Job. *Violence and Victim, 21,* 561–578.

Swanberg, J. E., Logan, T. K., & Macke, C. (2005). Intimate partner violence, employment, and the workplace: Consequences and Future Directions. *Trauma, Violence and Abuse, 4,* 1–26.

Swanberg, J., & Logan, T. K. (2005). The effects of intimate partner violence on women's labor force attachment: Experiences of women living in rural and urban Kentucky. *Journal of Occupational Health Psychology, 10,* 3–17.

Sygnatur, E. F., & Toscano, G. A. (2000). Work-related homicides: The facts. *Compensation and Working Conditions, 5,* 3–8.

Taylor, D. (2000). Student preparation in managing violence and aggression. *Nursing Standard, 14,* 39–41.

Tjaden, P., & Thoennes, N. (2000). *Full report of the prevalence, incidence, and consequences of violence against women: Findings from the national violence against women survey.* Washington, DC: National Institute of Justice and Centers for Disease Control and Prevention.

Toscano, G. & Webber, W. (1995). *Violence in the Workplace: Patterns of fatal workplace assaults differ from those of non-fatal ones. Compensation and Working Conditions, 47,* Washington, DC: U.S. Department of Labor.

Tyler, K. (1999). Targets behind the counter. *HR Magazine, 44,* 106–111.

U.S. Department of Justice, Federal Bureau of Investigation. (2004). *Introduction: What is violence? Workplace Violence: Issues in Response.* 11–14.

Verlinden, S., Hersen, M., & Thomas, J. (2000). Risk factors in school shootings. *Clinical Psychology Review, 20,* 3–56.

Wassell, J. (2009). Workplace violence intervention effectiveness: A systematic literature review. *Safety Science, 47,* 1049–1055.

Winstanley, S., & Whittington, R. (2002). Anxiety, burnout and coping styles in general hospital staff exposed to workplace aggression: A cyclical model of burnout and vulnerability to aggression. *Work and Stress, 16,* 302–315.

Zapf, D., Einarsen, S., Hoel, H., & Vartia, M. (2003). Empirical findings on bullying. In S. Einarsen, H. Hoel, D. Zapf, & C. L. Cooper (Eds.), *Bullying and emotional abuse in the workplace: International perspectives in research and practice* (pp. 103–126). London: Taylor & Francis.

Neal M. Ashkanasy is Professor in the UQ Business School at the University of Queensland, where he received his PhD in social/organizational psychology. His research is in leadership, organizational culture, ethics, and emotions in organizations. He has published in the *Academy of Management Journal, Academy of Management Review, Journal of Organizational Behavior, Leadership Quarterly,* and *Journal of Management.* He serves on several editorial boards including the *Journal of Applied Psychology* and the *Journal of Management,* and is editor-in-chief of the *Journal of Organizational Behavior,* associate editor of the *Academy of Management Review and Emotion Review,* and series coeditor of Research on Emotion in Organizations. Ashkanasy is a fellow of the Academy for the Social Sciences in Australia (ASSA); the Association for Psychological Science (APS); the Society for Industrial and Organizational Psychology (SIOP); and the Australia and New Zealand Academy of Management (ANZAM), where he also served as president.

Chet E. Barney is a doctoral student in the Department of Management at New Mexico State University. His primary research interests include deviant workplace behavior, job insecurity, and core self-evaluations.

Philip G. Benson is the Bank of America Professor in the management department at New Mexico State University where he teaches primarily in the areas of human resource management and international management. His PhD was awarded by Colorado State University in 1982, in the area of industrial/organizational psychology.

Russell Cropanzano is a professor of organizational behavior at the University of Colorado's Leeds School of Business. Dr. Cropanzano's primary research areas include perceptions of organizational justice, as well as, the experience and impact of workplace emotion. He has edited four books, presented over seventy papers and published over one hundred scholarly articles and chapters. He is coauthor (with Robert Folger) of *Organizational Justice and Human Resources Management,* which won the 1998 Book Award from the International Association of Conflict Management. Dr. Cropanzano was also a winner of the 2000 Outstanding Paper Award from the *Consulting Psychology Journal* and the 2007 Best Paper Award from *Academy of Management Perspectives.* He is a past editor of the *Journal of Management,* a charter member of the American Psychological Society, and a fellow in the Society for Industrial/Organizational Psychology.

Steven M. Elias earned his PhD in applied social psychology in 2001 from Colorado State University and is associate professor and head of the Department of Management at New Mexico State University. He is interested in several areas of organizational behavior, with his primary research revolving around managerial influence, social power, self-efficacy, job attitudes, and deviant workplace behavior. His research has been published in the *Journal of Management, Journal of Management History, Journal of Applied Social Psychology, Journal of General Psychology, International Journal of Organizational Analysis, Social Influence, Journal of College Student Development,* and *Southern Business and Economics Journal.* A past member of the *Journal of Management* editorial board, Steven is currently on the editorial board of the *Journal of Organizational Behavior, Human Resource Management Review, Journal of Applied Social Psychology,* and *PsycCRITIQUES.*

Lindsey A. Gibson is an assistant professor of organizational management at Hawai'i Pacific University. She is a member of the Academy of Management. Her primary research interests include social power and influence in effective organizational change, as well as influence tactics in upward influence attempts.

Sharon L. Grant is a senior lecturer in psychology on the Faculty of Higher Education at Swinburne University of Technology. She has been conducting research on occupational stress for approximately ten years. Her PhD was based on a longitudinal study of personality and occupational stress among two hundred managers in forty department stores across Australia. Currently conducting research on stress in entrepreneurs, Sharon has published in a range of topic areas in organizational and personality psychology, including the role of personality in the occupational stressor-strain relationship; the Big Five, health and well being; entrepreneurship; managerial styles; personality assessment; and shared cognition and teamwork in organizations. Her current research interests involve occupational stress including stress intervention; measuring stress in entrepreneurs; personality and work; and personality, health, and well being.

Ricky W. Griffin is Distinguished Professor of Management in Mays Business School at Texas A&M University and holds the Blocker Chair in Business there. His research on task design and dysfunctional work behavior has appeared in *Academy of Management Journal, Academy of Management Review, Administrative Science Quarterly, Journal of Management* and other outlets, and he served as editor of the *Journal of Management.* Ricky has been program chair and division chair of the Organizational Behavior Division and program chair of the Research Methods Division of the of the Southwest Academy of Management, and program chair and president of the academy, and a member of the board of the Southern Management Association. He is a fellow of both the Academy of Management and the Southern Management Association. He is the author of several widely used textbooks and his current research interests include workplace culture, managerial skills development, and decision making during times of crisis.

Michael A. Gross is an associate professor in the Department of Management at Colorado State University. He earned his PhD at Arizona State University. His current research interests focus on conflict with managing experience design, trust and trust repair, conflict and verbal aggression, and personality and abusive supervision. He has published in a variety of journals including *Decision Sciences, Journal of Organizational Behavior, Journal of Management Inquiry, International Journal of Conflict Management, Management Communication Quarterly, Journal of Applied Communication Research,* and *Journal of Management Education.* He teaches negotiation and conflict management at the undergraduate level and in the graduate and executive programs as well as courses in organizational behavior and human resource management.

Brandon Hill Haines is a partner at CliftonLarsonAllen LLP (CLA) in Albuquerque, NM. Upon completion of his degree in accounting with a minor in economics, he began his career in public accounting in the audit department of Peat, Marwick, Mitchell & Company (now KPMG). His professional career has included serving as vice president in charge of the internal audit function for a multibank holding company as well as serving as chairman of the audit committee of a financial institution for more than fifteen years. He is a licensed Certified Public Accountant in the state of New Mexico and also a Certified Fraud Examiner. He currently serves on the Business Advisory Council for New Mexico State University as well as the Accounting Advisory

Board for the University of New Mexico. In 1992 he founded the Non-Profit Financial Managers' Association and in 2009 he founded the CFO Academy. Brandon was an adjunct professor at the University of New Mexico, teaching at the graduate level from 2002 to 2010.

Glennis M. Hanley is a senior lecturer in the Department of Management at Monash University, Melbourne, Australia. Her teaching disciplines are general management; human resource management and development; employee relations; and small firms management. Her PhD was awarded by Deakin University (Australia) in 1998, in the area of industrial relations.

Christine (Chris) A. Henle is an assistant professor in the Department of Management at Colorado State University, where she received her PhD in industrial/organizational psychology. Her research interests include counterproductive work behaviors such as abusive supervision, resume fraud, and cyberloafing as well as the legality of various human resource practices. Her work has been published in the *Journal of Applied Psychology*, *Personnel Psychology*, *Journal of Organizational Behavior*, and *Journal of Business Ethics*. She teaches courses in human resource management and organizational behavior at the undergraduate and graduate levels.

Allen K. Hess (1945–2010) worked in several areas of intersecting research, including psychological assessment, personality and psychopathology, psychotherapy supervision, and forensic and correctional psychology. He had extensive experience with angry, hostile, and violent people. He worked with the Public Health Service assessing, treating, and conducting research on drug addicts in residential care, lived in a delinquency treatment facility in Baton Rouge, and consulted for the Georgia Department of Corrections, among his varied experiences. He edited three editions of *The Handbook of Forensic Psychology* and wrote the chapter "Psychotherapy Supervision and Angry, Hostile, and Violent Patients" in *Psychotherapy Supervision: Theory, Research, and Practice*, which contained an analysis of the people and environments that lead to violence and a guide for teaching student-psychotherapists how to deal with such patients. Until Allen's untimely death in 2010, he was the series editor for the New York University Press Psychology and Crime series.

Clara E. Hess has conducted research on workplace factors that contribute to teacher burnout and turnover, leadership in university-based cooperative research centers, and perceptions of work-family conflict for homosexual employees. She coedited the graduate student column in *The Industrial-Organizational Psychologist* (published by SIOP Division 14 of the American Psychological Association and organizational affiliate of the Association for Psychological Science) and has contributed articles to that publication concerning job search strategies, student stressors, and graduate school ethics. She coauthored the chapter "Interpersonal Approaches to Psychotherapy Supervision: A Vigotskyian Perspective" with Allen Hess and Joel H. Hess in *Psychotherapy Supervision: Theory, Research, and Practice*, and has presented at various conferences on topics ranging from the Validation of a Learning Styles Instrument to Hybrid Professional Development to Support Teachers in 1:1 Computer Learning Environments.

Randy Hodson is a professor of sociology at Ohio State University. His research interests include bureaucracy and management, employee, and coworker relations. He is also engaged in research on economic transformations in Eastern Europe and China. His recent books include *Dignity at Work* and *Worlds of Work: Building an International Sociology of Work* (coauthored with Daniel B. Cornfield) and *Social Theory at Work* (coauthored with Marek Korczynski and Paul Edwards). He is also coauthor with Teresa A. Sullivan of *The Social Organization of Work*, 4th edition, and is currently editor of the *American Sociological Review*. He is the author of over eighty articles appearing in sociology, human relations, and organizational journals.

Gary F. Jensen is a professor of sociology and religious studies at Vanderbilt University. He held prior appointments at the University of North Carolina, Chapel Hill and the University of Arizona. He has authored or coauthored books and articles on a wide range of topics in criminology and was initiated a fellow of the American Society of Criminology in 2001. He has been Joe B. Wyatt Distinguished University Professor at Vanderbilt and has been appointed an associate or deputy editor of the *American Sociological Review* four times in his career. He is currently serving as editor of *Homicide Studies*. His recent work includes a National Science Foundation funded study, *The Path of the Devil: Early Modern Witch Hunts*, and *Delinquency and Youth Crime*, 4th edition, co-authored with Dean G. Rojek.

Yvette P. Lopez received her PhD in management from Mays Business School at Texas A&M University. She is an assistant professor in the Department of Management, College of Commerce and the Charles H. Kellstadt Graduate School of Business at DePaul University. Her research interests include psychological contracts, business ethics, and workplace violence. Her work appears in *Journal of Management, Journal of Business Ethics*, and *Journal of Workplace Rights*.

Rebecca Michalak has been employed in senior management, consulting, and human resources roles in the private, tertiary education, not-for-profit, and public sectors. Her employment history includes strategic and operational human resources, industrial/employee relations, OSH (including risk management), change /project management, and quality assurance. She possesses more than a decade of experience in learning and development, and is a TAA certified trainer and assessor. Her qualifications include a masters in business administration, a masters in management research, and bachelor of arts in psychology (Hons). She is a certified professional member of the Australian Human Resources Institute (CAHRI), a member of the Australian Institute of Company Directors (MAICD), a member of both the Australian New Zealand Academy of Management (ANZAM) and the Academy of Management (AOM) and a member of the International Association of Applied Psychology. Rebecca is undertaking doctoral studies at the Business School, University of Queensland, where she also lectures postgraduate business students in managing organizational behavior.

Carolina Moliner is an associate professor at the University of Valencia and a researcher at the Research Institute of Psychology of Human Resources, Organizational Development and Quality of Working Life (IDOCAL). Professor Moliner is a frequent reviewer for the Academy of Management Annual Meeting, *Journal of Organizational Behavior, European Journal of Work and Organizational Psychology, Work and Stress*, and *International Journal of Stress Management*. Moliner is also a past member of the *Journal of Management* editorial board. Her research has been published in the *Journal of Applied Social Psychology, European Journal of Organizational Psychology, International Journal of Stress Management, Psychological Reports*, and *Psicothema*. Her current research is focused on organizational justice, service quality, and quality of life, well-being, and emotions in the workplace.

Wesley A. Scroggins is an associate professor of management at Missouri State University. His primary teaching areas are human resource management and organizational behavior. He received his PhD from New Mexico State University in 2003 in the area of management/business administration.

Cindy L. Seipel is a professor and director of the Master of Accountancy Program in the Department of Accounting and Information Systems at New

Mexico State University. She began her career as an auditor with Coopers and Lybrand (now PwC). In 1990, she earned a PhD from Oklahoma State University. She has been a licensed CPA for over twenty years and became licensed as a Certified Fraud Examiner in 2007. Her areas of research include education, auditing, and taxation. She has published in the *Journal of Accountancy*; *CPA Journal*; *Oil, Gas & Energy Quarterly*; and *Journal of International Accounting, Auditing, and Taxation*.

William L. Smith is currently an assistant professor in the Department of Accounting and Information Systems at New Mexico State University. He started his career with Peat, Marwick, Mitchell & Company, now KPMG. He holds both an undergraduate and graduate degree in accounting, has been a licensed CPA for over twenty years, and is a Chartered Global Management Accountant. In 2004 he earned his PhD in business administration from New Mexico State University. His current areas of research include analysis of financial disclosures, critical theory, and behavior analysis. His publications have appeared in *Journal of Accounting and Finance*, *Organizational Research Methods*, *Business Education Forum*, *Behaviour & Information Technology*, and *Qualitative Research in Accounting & Management*. He recently coauthored accounting chapters in the textbooks *Critical Theory for Business and Public Administration Ethics* and *Storytelling and the Future of Organizations*.

INDEX